# SHOW ME THE MONEY

## Other Books by the Authors

*Proving the Value of Meetings and Events: How and Why to Measure ROI (with Monica Myhill and James B. McDonough)*

*How to Build a Successful Consulting Practice*

*Investing in Your Human Capital*

*Return on Investment Basics*

*Proving the Value of HR: How and Why to Measure ROI*

*ROI at Work*

*Make Training Evaluation Work*

*The Leadership Scorecard (with Lynn Schmidt)*

*Return on Investment in Training and Performance Improvement Programs, 2nd Edition*

# SHOW ME THE
# MONEY

## How to Determine ROI in People, Projects, and Programs

### Jack J. Phillips PhD
### Patricia Pulliam Phillips PhD

BERRETT-KOEHLER PUBLISHERS, INC.
San Francisco

**Berrett-Koehler Publishers, Inc.**
235 Montgomery Street, Suite 650
San Francisco, CA 94104-2916
Tel: (415) 288-0260  Fax: (415) 362-2512
www.bkconnection.com

**Ordering Information**
**Quantity sales.** Special discounts are available on quantity purchases by corporations, associations, and others. For details, contact the "Special Sales Department" at the Berrett-Koehler address above.

**Individual sales.** Berrett-Koehler publications are available through most bookstores. They can also be ordered directly from Berrett-Koehler: Tel: (800) 929-2929; Fax: (802) 864-7626; www.bkconnection.com

**Orders for college textbook/course adoption use.** Please contact Berrett-Koehler: Tel: (800) 929-2929; Fax: (802) 864-7626.

**Orders by U.S. trade bookstores and wholesalers.** Please contact Publishers Group West, 1700 Fourth Street, Berkeley, CA 94710. Tel: (510) 528-1444; Fax (510) 528-3444.

Berrett-Koehler and the BK logo are registered trademarks of Berrett-Koehler Publishers, Inc.

Printed in the United States of America

Book Producer: Publication Services, Inc.
Book Designer: Foti Kutil
Copyeditor: Dave Mason and Jennifer Putman

Production Manager: Susan Yates
Production Coordinator: Megan Timian
Indexer: Nancy Gerth

Berrett-Koehler books are printed on long-lasting acid-free paper. When it is available, we choose paper that has been manufactured by environmentally responsible processes. These may include using trees grown in sustainable forests, incorporating recycled paper, minimizing chlorine in bleaching, or recycling the energy produced at the paper mill.

**Library of Congress Cataloging-in-Publication Data**
Phillips, Jack J., 1945-
   Show me the money : how to determine ROI in people, projects, and programs/Jack J. Phillips, Patricia Pulliam Phillips.
     p. cm.
   Includes bibliographical references.
   ISBN 978-1-57675-399-6 (hardcover)
  1. Project management. 2. Project management—Evaluation. 3. Rate of return. 4. Human capital. I. Phillips, Patricia Pulliam. II. Title. III. Title: How to determine ROI in people, projects, and programs. IV. Title: How to determine return on investment in people, projects, and programs.
HD69.P75P493 2007
658.15'54—dc22
2006034577
First Edition
12  11  10  09  08  07                10  9  8  7  6  5  4  3  2  1

*To:*
*Sarah Ryan, Jessica Ferry, Amanda Ryan,*
*Ashley Crowder, Brandon Crowder*
*The next generation—*
*May you enjoy your life's work as much as we do.*

# CONTENTS

# PREFACE

## The Need

In recent years, we have witnessed change in organizational accountability, especially toward investment in people, programs, projects, and processes. Project sponsors and those who have responsibility for project success have always been concerned about the value of their initiatives. Today this concern translates into financial impact—the actual monetary contribution from a project or program. Although monetary value is becoming a critical concern, it is the comparison of this value with the project costs that captures stakeholders' attention—and translates into ROI.

"Show me the money" is the familiar response from individuals asked to invest (or continue to invest) in organizational efforts. At times, this response is appropriate. At other times, it may be misguided; measures not subject to monetary conversion are also important, if not critical, to most projects. However, excluding the monetary component from a success profile is unacceptable in this age of the "show me" generation. The monetary value is often required before a project is approved. Sometimes, it is needed as the project is being designed and developed. Other times, it is needed after project implementation.

This issue is compounded by concern that most projects today fail to live up to expectations. A systematic process is needed that can identify barriers to and enablers of success and can drive organizational improvements.

The challenge lies in doing it—developing the measures of value, including monetary value, when they are needed and presenting them in a way so that stakeholders can use them

- Before the project is initiated
- During design and development, to plan for maximum value
- During implementation, so that maximum value can be attained
- During post-analysis, to assess the delivered value against the anticipated value

*Show Me the Money* is a guide that addresses all four scenarios.

## A Guide to Showing the Money

*Show Me the Money* is a basic guide for anyone involved in implementing major projects—human capital programs, technology implementations, systems integration, new processes, Six Sigma, product design, new policies, and procedures, or any other type of project where significant expenditures of time and money are at stake. Strategies to assist in forecasting the value of the project in advance and in collecting data during and after project implementation are presented. This book uses a results-based approach to project implementation, focusing on a variety of measures that are categorized into six data types:

1. Reaction and Perceived Value
2. Learning and Confidence
3. Application and Implementation
4. Impact and Consequences
5. Return on Investment
6. Intangibles

*Show Me the Money* is a step-by-step guide to identifying, collecting, analyzing, and reporting all six types of data in a consistent manner that leads to credible results.

### Credibility Is Key

*Show Me the Money* focuses on building a credible process—one that will generate a balanced set of data that are believable, realistic, and accurate, particularly from the viewpoint of sponsors and key stakeholders. More specifically, the methodology presented in this book approaches credibility head-on through the use of

- Balanced categories of data
- A logical, systematic process
- Guiding principles, a conservative set of standards
- A proven methodology based on thousands of applications
- An emphasis on implementing the methodology within an organization to ensure that the process is sustained
- A procedure accepted by sponsors, clients, and others who fund projects

The book explores the challenges of measuring the hard to measure and placing monetary values on the hard to value. It is a reference that clarifies much of the mystery surrounding the allocation of monetary values. Building on a tremendous amount of experience, application, practice, and research, the book draws on the work of many individuals and organizations, particularly those who have attained the ultimate levels of accountability using the ROI methodology. Developed in an easy-to-read format and fortified with examples and tips, this is an indispensable guide for audiences who seek to understand more about bottom-line accountability.

## Audience

The primary audience for this book are managers and executives concerned with the valuation of projects, programs, processes, and people. Executives generally are strongly committed to their projects; however, they need to see value in terms they can appreciate and understand—money.

This book is also intended for professionals, analysts, and practitioners who are responsible for evaluating the success of a project. It shows how the various types of data are collected, processed, analyzed, and reported.

Another audience includes consultants, researchers, and professors who are dedicated to unraveling the value mystery, trying to understand more about the difficult and demanding challenges of developing measures and values for a variety of target areas.

## Target Areas

*Show Me the Money* is geared toward a variety of functional areas in organizations. These areas include (but are not limited to)

- Human resources, human capital
- Learning and development, performance improvement
- Technology, IT systems

- Meetings and events
- Sales, marketing
- Public relations, community affairs, government relations
- Project management solutions
- Quality, Six Sigma
- Operations, methods, engineering
- Research and development, innovation
- Finance, compliance
- Logistics, distribution, supply chain
- Public policy initiatives
- Social programs
- Charitable projects

## The Difference

While other books attempt to address accountability in these and other functional areas, *Show Me the Money* presents a methodical approach that can be replicated throughout an organization, enabling comparisons of results. The process described in this book is the most documented method in the world, and its implementation has been phenomenal, with over three thousand organizations currently using it in one function or another. While many books tackle accountability in a certain function or process, this book shows a method that works across all types of processes, ranging from leadership development to the implementation of new technology and from educational programs to public policy initiatives.

## Flow of the Book

*Show Me the Money* presents a methodology for determining the monetary value associated with a project, referred to as the ROI methodology. After identifying and exploring the factors that have created interest in this level of accountability, the book focuses on the process, showing how the actual money is developed, step by step, with each chapter devoted to one major element. In addition, two other chapters highlight matters that are critical to the overall process. One discusses the up-front analysis necessary to define the specific need for the project or program, and the other focuses on forecasting the value before the project is developed and implemented. The remainder of the book details the strategies and actions needed to sustain the methodology.

## Terminology: Programs, Projects, Solutions . . .

In *Show Me the Money*, the terms *program* and *project* are used to describe a variety of processes that can be evaluated using the ROI methodology. This is an important issue because readers may vary widely in their perspective. Individuals involved in technology applications may use the terms *system* and *technology* rather than *program*. In public policy, on the other hand, the word *program* is prominent. For a professional meetings and events planner, the word *program* may not be very pertinent, but in human resources, *program* fits quite well. Finding one term that fits all these situations would be difficult. Consequently, the terms *program* and *project* are used interchangeably. Table 1 lists these and other terms that may be used depending on the context.

**Table 1  Terms and Applications**

| Term | Example |
| --- | --- |
| Program | Leadership development skills enhancement for senior executives |
| Project | A reengineering scheme for the plastics division |
| System | A fully interconnected network for all branches |
| Initiative | A faith-based effort to reduce recidivism |
| Policy | A new preschool plan for disadvantaged citizens |
| Procedure | A new scheduling arrangement for truck drivers |
| Event | A golf outing for customers |
| Meeting | U.S. Coast Guard innovations conference |
| Process | Quality sampling |
| People | Staff additions in the customer care center |
| Tool | A new means of selection for the hotel staff |

# ACKNOWLEDGMENTS

No book is the work of the authors alone. Many individuals, groups, and organizations shaped the development of this book. We owe particular thanks to the hundreds of clients we have had the pleasure to work with in the past two decades. They have helped to develop, mold, and refine this methodology. Their contributions are evident.

We are particularly indebted to Steve Piersanti, Berrett-Koehler's president, whom we also had the pleasure to work with in the past—almost two decades ago. Steve and the Berrett-Koehler staff are without exception the best publishing group in the world, and we are honored to be part of this publishing family. Thanks to the marketing, production, and editorial staff for making this book attractive, understandable, and affordable.

Many thanks go to Jaime, Crystal, and Kat, who invariably come through when we need them most. Special thanks go to Lori Ditoro, who approached this project with a vengeance.

We would also like to thank our families. In spite of our "absence," you continued to cheer us on. We love you for that and much more!

*From Jack:*

I owe much of my success in this effort to my lovely spouse, Patti, who served as my partner, friend, and colleague in this endeavor. She is an excellent consultant, an outstanding facilitator, a tenacious researcher, and an outstanding writer. Her contribution to this book is immeasurable.

*From Patti:*

As always, much love and thanks go to Jack. You invest in others much more than you get in return. What a contribution you make! Thank you for your inspiration and the fun you bring to my life.

Jack and Patti Phillips
Birmingham, Alabama
February, 2007

# Chapter 1

# THE VALUE EVOLUTION

"Show me the money." There's nothing new about the statement, especially in business. Organizations of all types want value for their investments. What's new is the method that organizations can use to get there. While "showing the money" is the ultimate report of value, organization leaders recognize that value lies in the eye of the beholder; therefore, the method used to show the money must also show the value as perceived by all stakeholders. Just as important, organizations need a methodology that provides data to help improve investment decisions. This book presents an approach that does both: it evaluates the value that organizations receive for investing in programs and projects, and it develops data to improve those programs.

This chapter presents the evolution of value—moving from activity-focused value to the ultimate value, return on investment (ROI). This chapter also describes issues and challenges faced by those seeking a technique to show the money.

## Value Redefined

### The Value Shift

"Show me the money" represents the newest value statement. In the past, program, project, or process success was measured by activity: number of people involved, money spent, days to complete. Little consideration was given to the benefits derived from these activities. Today the value definition has shifted: value is defined by results versus activity. More frequently, value is defined as monetary benefits compared with costs. The following organizations illustrate this paradigm shift:

- The U.S. Air Force developed the ROI for data security to prevent intrusion into its databases.
- Apple Computer calculated the ROI for investing in process improvement teams.
- Sprint/NEXTEL developed the ROI on its diversity program.
- The Australian Capital Territory Community Care agency forecast the ROI for the implementation of a client relationship management (CRM) system.
- Accenture calculated the ROI on a new sales platform for its consultants.
- Wachovia developed the forecast and actual ROI for its negotiations program.
- A major hotel chain calculated the financial value and ROI of its coaching program.
- The cities of New York, San Francisco, and Phoenix showed the monetary value of investing in projects to reduce the number of homeless citizens on the streets.
- Cisco Systems is measuring the ROI for its key meetings and events.
- A major U.S. Defense Department agency developed the ROI for a master's degree program offered by a major university.

From Motorola's Six Sigma quality improvement process to project management, to learning and development, to meetings and events, to public policy, organizations are showing value by using the comprehensive evaluation process described in this book.

Although this methodology to "show the money" had its beginnings in the 1970s, it has expanded in recent years to become the most comprehensive and broad-reaching approach to demonstrating the value of project investment.

## Types of Values

Value is determined by stakeholders' perspectives, which may include organizational, spiritual, personal, and social values. Value is defined by consumers, taxpayers, and shareholders. Capitalism defines value as the economic contribution to shareholders. The global reporting initiative (GRI), established in 1997, defines value from three perspectives: environmental, economic, and societal.

Even as projects, processes, and programs are implemented to improve the social, environmental, and economic climates, however, the monetary value is often sought to ensure that resources are allocated appropriately and that investments reap a return. No longer is it enough to report the number of programs offered, the number of participants or volunteers trained, or the dollars generated through a fundraising effort. Stakeholders at all levels—including executives, shareholders, managers and supervisors, taxpayers, project designers, and participants—are looking for outcomes, and in many cases, the monetary values of those outcomes.

## The Importance of Monetary Values

Many people are concerned that too much focus is placed on economic value. But it is economics, or money, that allows organizations and individuals to contribute to the greater good. Monetary resources are limited, and they can be put to best use—or underused or overused. Organizations and individuals have choices about where they invest these resources. To ensure that monetary resources are put to best use, they must be allocated to programs, processes, and projects that yield the greatest return.

For example, if a process improvement initiative is begun to improve efficiencies, and it does improve efficiencies, one might assume that the initiative was successful. But if the initiative cost more than the efficiency gains are worth, has value been added to the organization? Could a less expensive process have yielded similar or even better results, possibly reaping a positive ROI? Questions like these are, or should be, asked on a routine basis. No longer will activity suffice as a measure of results. A new generation of decision makers is defining value in a new way.

## The "Show Me" Generation

Figure 1-1 illustrates the requirements of the new "show me" generation. "Show me" implies that stakeholders want to see actual data (i.e., numbers and measures). This accounted for the initial attempt to see value in programs. This evolved into "show me the money," a direct call for financial results. But this alone does not provide the needed evidence to ensure that projects add value. Often, a connection between projects and value is assumed, but that assumption soon must give way to the need to show an actual connection. Hence, "show me the real money" was an attempt at establishing credibility. This phase, though critical, still left stakeholders with

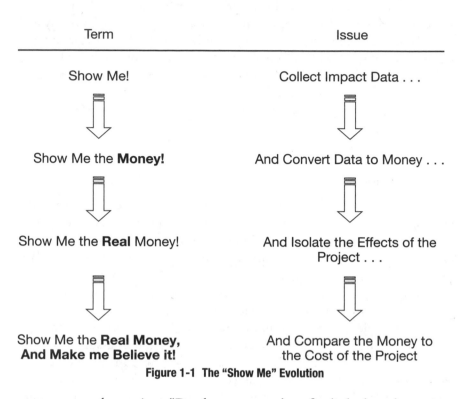

Figure 1-1  The "Show Me" Evolution

an unanswered question: "Do the monetary benefits linked to the project outweigh the costs?" This question is the mantra for the new "show me" generation: "Show me the real money, and make me believe it." But this new generation of project sponsors also recognize that value is more than just a single number: value is what makes the entire organization system tick— hence the need to report value based on people's various definitions.

## The New Definition of Value

The changing perspectives on value and the shifts that are occurring in organizations have all led to a new definition of value. Value is not defined as a single number. Rather, its definition is composed of a variety of data points. Value must be balanced with quantitative and qualitative data, as well as financial and nonfinancial perspectives. The data sometimes reflect tactical issues, such as activity, as well as strategic issues, such as ROI. Value must be derived using different time frames and not necessarily represent a single point in time. It must reflect the value systems that are important to stakeholders. The data composing value must be collected from credible sources, using cost-effective methods; and value must be action oriented, compelling individuals to make adjustments and changes.

The processes used to calculate value must be consistent from one project to another. Standards must be in place so that results can be compared. These standards must support conservative outcomes, leaving assumptions to decision makers. The ROI methodology presented in this book meets all these criteria. It captures six types of data that reflect the issues contained in the new definition of value: reaction and perceived value, learning and confidence, application and implementation, impact and consequences, return on investment, and intangible benefits.

## Why Now?

In the past decade, a variety of forces have driven additional focus on measuring the impact of programs, including the financial contribution and ROI. These forces have challenged old ways of defining program success.

### Project Failures

Almost every organization encounters unsuccessful projects—projects that go astray, costing far too much and failing to deliver on promises. Project disasters occur in business organizations as well as in government and nonprofit organizations. Some project disasters are legendary. Some are swept into closets and covered up, but they are there, and the numbers are far too large to tolerate.[1] The endless string of failures has generated increased concerns about measuring project and program success—before, during, and after implementation. Many critics of these projects suggest that the failure could be avoided if: (1) the project is based on a legitimate need from the beginning; (2) adequate planning is in place at the outset; (3) data are collected throughout the project to confirm that the implementation is on track; and (4) an impact study is conducted to detail the project's contribution. Unfortunately, these steps are sometimes unintentionally omitted, not fully understood, or purposely ignored; hence, greater emphasis is being placed on the processes of accountability. This book attempts to show how these four elements come together to create value-adding projects and programs.

## Project Costs

The costs of projects and programs continue to grow. As costs rise, the budgets for these projects become targets for others who would like to have the money for their own projects. What was once considered a mere cost of doing business is now considered an investment, and one to be wisely allocated. For example, consider the field of learning and development in the United States. Learning and development is, of course, necessary, particularly to introduce new skills and technology to employees, but 20 years ago it was regarded by some company executives as a frivolous expense. These days, the annual direct cost of organizational learning and development is estimated to be over $100 billion in the United States. A few large organizations spend as much as $1 billion every year on corporate learning and development. With numbers like these, learning and development is no longer considered a frivolous expense; rather, it is regarded as an investment, and many executives expect a return.

The same is true for information technology (IT). Years ago, it seemed a necessary but minor part of most organizational structures. Not so today. Consider, for example, Federal Express. Casual observers may not regard FedEx as a high-tech company. It apparently consists of trucks and airplanes moving packages. Yet FedEx handles and keeps track of more than 6 million packages per day, coordinating the work of two hundred thousand employees, and operating 677 airplanes and more than ninety thousand vehicles in 220 countries. Seconds and minutes count with FedEx. A technology glitch could amount to a public relations disaster.[2] Because of the importance of IT, the company gives it an annual budget of $1 billion, a significant amount that attracts the attention of many executives.

## Accountability Trend

A consistent and persistent trend in accountability is evident in organizations across the globe: almost every function, process, project, or initiative is judged based on higher standards than in the past. Various functions in organizations are attempting to show their worth by capturing and demonstrating the value they add to the organization. They compete for funds; therefore, they have to show value. For example, the research and development function must show its value in monetary terms to compete with mainstream processes, such as sales and production, which for more than a century have shown their value in direct monetary terms.

## Process Improvement Mandate

The use of ROI and the need to show monetary value have increased because of the organizational improvement processes that have dominated many organizations, particularly in North America, Europe, and Asia. These process improvement efforts have elevated the need to show value in two important ways. First, these processes themselves often create or enhance a measurement culture within organizations. Second, the quest to show the value of these change processes has created the need for tools to show their actual monetary impact, up to and including ROI.

## Support Managers' New Business Focus

In the past, managers of many support functions in government, non-profit, and private organizations had no business experience. Today, things have changed. Many of these managers have a business background, a formal business education, or a business focus. These new, enlightened managers are more aware of bottom-line issues in the organization and are more knowledgeable of operational and financial concerns. They often take a business approach to their processes, with ROI being a part of that strategy. Because of their background, ROI is a familiar term. They have studied the use of ROI in their academic preparation, where the ROI methodology was used to evaluate purchasing equipment, building new facilities, or buying a new company. Consequently, they understand and appreciate ROI and are eager to apply it in other areas.

## The Growth of Project Management

Few processes in organizations have grown as much as project management. Just two decades ago it was considered a lone process attempting to bring organizational and management structure to projects. Today, the Project Management Institute, which offers three levels of certification for professional project managers, has more than two hundred thousand members in 125 countries. Jobs are being restructured and designed to focus on projects. With the growing use of project management solutions, tools, and processes, a corresponding need to show the accountability for investing so heavily in this process has developed.

## Evidence-Based or Fact-Based Management

Recently there has been an important trend to move to fact-based or evidence-based management. Although many key decisions have been made using instinctive input and gut feelings, more managers are now using sophisticated and detailed processes to show value. Quality decisions must be based on more than gut feelings or the blink of an eye. With a comprehensive set of measures, including financial ROI, better organizational decisions regarding people, products, projects, and processes are possible. When taken seriously, evidence-based management can change how every manager thinks and acts. It is a way of seeing the world and thinking about the craft of management. Evidence-based management proceeds from the premise that using better, deeper logic and facts to the extent possible helps leaders do their jobs better. It is based on the belief that facing the hard facts about what works and what doesn't work, and understanding and rejecting the total nonsense that often passes for sound advice, will help organizations perform better.[3] This move to fact-based management makes expanding measurement to include ROI easier.

## Overhead Reduction

Support functions are often regarded as overhead, a burden on the organization, and an unnecessary expense. The approach of many managers is to outsource, automate, or eliminate the overhead. Great strides have been made in all three approaches. These days, staff support departments must show value to exist as viable support functions or administrative processes.

## Benchmarking Limitations

Many managers have been obsessed with benchmarking. They have used benchmarking to compare every type of process, function, and activity. Unfortunately, benchmarking has its limitations. First, the concept of best practices is sometimes an elusive issue. Not all participants in a benchmarking project or report necessarily represent the best practices. In fact, they may represent just the opposite: many benchmarking studies are developed by organizations willing to pay to participate. Also, what is needed by one organization is not always needed by another. A specific benchmarked measure or process may be limited in its actual use. Finally, the benchmarking data are often devoid of financial aspects, reflecting few if any measures of the actual financial contributions with ROI values. Therefore, managers have asked for more specific internal processes that can show these important measures.

## The Executive Appetite for Monetary Value

Providing monetary contribution and ROI is receiving increased interest in the executive suite. Top managers who watch budgets continue to grow without appropriate accountability measures are frustrated, and they are responding to the situation by turning to ROI. Top executives now demand ROI calculations and monetary contributions from departments and functions where they were not previously required. For years, function managers and department heads convinced executives that their processes could not be measured and that the value of their activities should be taken on faith. Executives no longer buy that argument; they demand the same accountability from these functions as they do from the sales and production areas of the organization. These major forces are requiring organizations to shift their measurement processes to include the financial impact and ROI.

# Challenges along the Way

The journey to increased accountability and the quest to show monetary value, including ROI, are not going unchallenged. This movement represents a tremendous cultural shift for individuals, a systemic change in processes, and often a complete rethinking of the initiation, delivery, and maintenance of processes in organizations.

## The Commitment Dilemma

Commitment is key to successful implementation of the ROI methodology. Many hope to obtain an immediate ROI using the ROI methodology, but, as previously mentioned, there is more to it than a simple calculation. To achieve success, commitment to making changes when the data reveal that the change needed is imperative, as is commitment to using the information the process provides.

## Preparation and Skills

Although interest in showing the value and measuring ROI is now heightened and much progress has been made, these are still issues that challenge even the most sophisticated and progressive functions. The problem often lies in the lack of preparation and skills that are needed to conduct these types of analyses. The preparation for most jobs in these areas often lacks the required skill building. Rarely do the curricula in degree programs or the courses in a professional development program include processes and techniques to show accountability at this level. Consequently, these skills must be developed by the organization, using a variety of resources, so that they are in place for successful implementation.

## Fear of ROI

Few business topics stir up emotions to the degree that ROI does. For some executives, the conclusion behind the ROI value is simple: if it is negative, they kill the program; if it is extremely positive, they do not believe it. The potential for this response from executives causes some professionals to avoid the issue altogether. A familiar reaction emerges: "If my project or program is not delivering value, the last thing I want to do is publish a report for my principal sponsor." Unfortunately, if the project is not delivering value, the sponsor probably already knows it, or at least someone in the organization does. The best thing to do is to show the value using a systematic, credible process.

Then there is the fear of abuse of the data. Will the data be used to punish people, reward individuals, or improve processes? Ideally, results should be used to improve processes. The challenge is to ensure that data are not misused or abused. The fear of ROI can be minimized when the individuals involved understand the process, how it is designed and delivered, and the value that it can bring from a positive perspective.

## Time to Respond

Thorough analysis takes time. Many practitioners and some sponsors are restless and do not want to take the time to do the appropriate analyses. In a fast-paced work environment where decisions are often made quickly and with little input or data, some executives question the time and the effort involved in this type of analysis. What must be shown, however, is that this effort is necessary and appropriate, and will ultimately payoff. Once the process is implemented, the individuals involved usually see that the value of the increased effort and activity far outweighs the cost of the time.

## Power and Politics

Having appropriate data represents power to many individuals. How that power is used is important. If used for constructive purposes or to improve processes, data are perceived as valuable. If data are used for destructive or political purposes, they may be seen as less valuable. The important issue is that if the information is based on credible facts, then it generates power. If it is based on opinions or gut feelings, then the person who provides those opinions is more influential than the opinions themselves. Essentially, facts create a level playing field for decision making. As one executive from a high-technology company said, "If a decision is based on facts, then anyone's facts are equal as long as they are relevant; however, if it must be based on opinions, then my opinion counts a lot more." This underscores the power of having credible data for making decisions.[4]

## Misleading Hype

Claims abound about success and the use of data to support an idea, project, or program. When the facts are examined, however, they often reveal something completely different. Tremendous claims, ads, and success stories are presented to promote a concept or idea. Exaggerated statements in marketing campaigns add to the confusion. For example, SAP ran a series of ads claiming that companies that use their software are more profitable than those that do not. An independent research unit found the opposite to be true. SAP then refused to show how they arrived at the conclusion. Projects and programs are evaluated in a variety of ways, and few accepted standards, rules, and processes exist with which to validate those assumptions and claims. A systematic process with conservative, accepted standards can create a credible story of program success.

## Sustainability

The final challenge is sustaining such a radical shift in accountability. The implementation of the ROI methodology must consist of more than just conducting one or two studies to show the value of the project or program. It must represent a complete change in processes so that future projects and programs focus on results. This change will require building capability, developing consistent and compelling communication, involving stakeholders, building the process into projects, creating expectations, and using data for process improvements. This is the only way to sustain any change for the long-term; otherwise, it becomes a one-shot or short-term project opportunity.

## Final Thoughts

So what? What does all this mean? This chapter makes the case for having a more comprehensive, credible process to show the value of projects. Many stakeholders, particularly important stakeholders, are demanding, requiring, or suggesting more accountability up to and including value. "Show me the money" has become a common request—and is being made now more than ever. A variety of forces have created this current focus on results, leaving project planners with only one recourse: to step up to the accountability challenge, create a process that can make a difference, develop data that please a variety of important stakeholders, and use a process that makes projects and programs better in the future. That is the intent of the process described in this book. The next chapter introduces this methodology.

# Chapter 2

# THE ROI METHODOLOGY
## A BRIEF OVERVIEW

## The Process

The process for showing monetary value, including ROI, is a comprehensive, systematic methodology that includes defining the types of data, conducting an initial analysis, developing objectives, forecasting value (including ROI), using the ROI process model, and implementing and sustaining the process. This chapter briefly describes the approach necessary to achieve the level of accountability demanded in today's business climate.

## Types of Data

The richness of the ROI methodology is inherent in the types of data monitored during the implementation of a particular project. These data are categorized by levels. Figure 2-1 shows the levels of data and describes their measurement focus. Subsequent chapters provide more detail on each level.

Level 0 represents the input to a project and details the numbers of people and hours, the focus, and the cost of the project. These data represent the activity around a project versus the contribution of the project. Level 0 data represent the scope of the effort, the degree of commitment, and the support for a particular program. For some, this equates to value. However, commitment as defined by expenditures is not evidence that the organization is reaping value.

Reaction and Perceived Value (Level 1) marks the beginning of the project's value stream. Reaction data capture the degree to which the participants involved in the project, including the stakeholders, react favorably or

| Level | Measurement Focus | Typical Measures |
|---|---|---|
| 0-Inputs and Indicators | Inputs into the project including indicators representing the scope of the project | Types of projects<br>Number of projects<br>Number of people<br>Hours of involvement<br>Cost of projects |
| 1-Reaction and Perceived Value | Reaction to the project including the perceived value of the project | Relevance<br>Importance<br>Usefulness<br>Appropriateness<br>Fairness<br>Motivational |
| 2-Learning and Confidence | Learning how to use the project, content, materials, system including the confidence to use what was learned | Skills<br>Knowledge<br>Capacity<br>Competencies<br>Confidences<br>Contacts |
| 3-Application and Implementation | Use of project content, materials, and system in the work environment including progress with implementation | Extent of use<br>Task completion<br>Frequency of use<br>Actions completed<br>Success with use<br>Barriers to use<br>Enablers to use |
| 4-Impact and Consequences | The consequences of the use of the project content, materials, and system expressed as business impact measures | Productivity<br>Revenue<br>Quality<br>Time<br>Efficiency<br>Customer Satisfaction<br>Employee Engagement |
| 5-ROI | Comparison of monetary benefits from project to project costs | Benefit Cost Ratio (BCR)<br>ROI (%)<br>Payback period |

**Figure 2-1 Types and Levels of Data**

unfavorably. The key is to capture the measures that reflect the content of the project, focusing on issues such as usefulness, relevance, importance, and appropriateness. Data at this level provide the first sign that project success may be achievable. These data also present project leaders with information they need to make adjustments to project implementation to help ensure positive results.

The next level is Learning and Confidence (Level 2). For every process, program, or project there is a learning component. For some—such as projects for new technology, new systems, new competencies, and new processes—this component is substantial. For others, such as a new policy or new procedure, learning may be a small part of the process but is still necessary to ensure successful execution. In either case, measurement of learning is essential to success. Measures at this level focus on skills, knowledge, capacity, competencies, confidence, and networking contacts.

Application and Implementation (Level 3) measures the extent to which the project or program is properly applied and implemented. Effective implementation is a must if bottom-line value is the goal. This is one of the most important data categories, and most implementation breakdowns occur at this level. Research has consistently shown that in almost half of all projects, participants and users are not doing what they should to make it successful. At this level, data collection involves measures, such as the extent of use of information, task completion, frequency of use of skills, success with use, and actions completed. Data collection also requires the examination of barriers and enablers to successful application. This level provides a picture of how well the system supports the successful transfer of knowledge, skills, and attitude changes.

Impact and Consequences (Level 4) is important for understanding the business consequences of the project. Here, data are collected that attract the attention of the sponsor and other executives. This level shows the output, productivity, revenue, quality, time, cost, efficiencies, and level of customer satisfaction connected with the project. For some, this level reflects the ultimate reason the project exists: to show the impact within the organization on various groups and systems. Without this level of data, they assert, there is no success. Once this level of measurement is achieved, it is necessary to isolate the effects of the program on the specific measures. Without this extra step, the link between the project and business measures is not evident.

The ROI (Level 5) is calculated next. This shows the monetary benefits of the impact measures compared with the cost of the project. This value is typically stated in terms of either a benefits/costs ratio, the ROI as a percentage, or the payback period. This level of measurement requires two important steps: first, the impact data (Level 4) must be converted to monetary values; second, the cost of the project must be captured.

Along with the five levels of results and the initial level of activity (Level 0), there is a sixth type of data—not a sixth level—developed through this methodology. This sixth type of data is the intangible benefits—those benefits that are purposefully not converted to money but nonetheless constitute important measures of success.

## The Initial Analysis

Our research suggests that the number 1 reason for projects failing is lack of alignment with the business. The first opportunity to obtain business alignment is in the initial analysis. Several steps are taken to make sure that the project or program is absolutely necessary. As shown in Figure 2-2, this is the beginning of the complete, sequential model representing the ROI methodology. The first step in this analysis examines the potential payoff of solving a problem or taking advantage of an opportunity. Is this a problem worth solving, or is the project worthy of implementation? For some situations the answer is obvious: yes, the project is worthy because of its critical nature, its relevance to the issue at hand, or its effectiveness in tackling a major problem affecting the organization. A serious customer service problem, for example, is one worth pursuing.

The next step is to ensure that the project is connected to one or more business measures. The measures that must improve as a reflection of the overall success of the project are defined. Sometimes the measure is obvious; at other times it is not.

Next, the job performance needs are examined with the question "What must change on the job to influence the business measures previously defined?" This step aligns the project with the business and may involve a series of analytical tools to solve the problem, analyze the cause of the problem, and ensure that the project is connected with business improvement in some way. This appears to be quite complex, but it is a simple approach. A series of questions helps: What is keeping the business measure from being where it needs to be? If it is a problem, what is its cause? If it is an opportunity, what is hindering it from moving in the right direction? This step is critical because it provides the link to the project solution.

After job performance needs have been determined, the learning needs are examined by asking: What specific skills, knowledge, or perceptions must change or improve so that job performance can change? Every solution

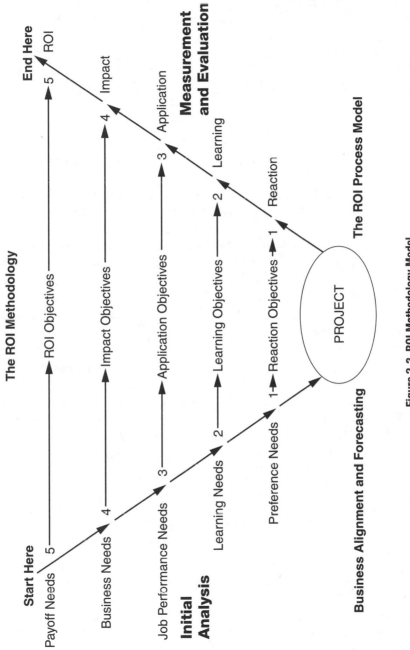

**Figure 2-2 ROI Methodology Model**

involves a learning component, and this step defines what the participants or users must know to make the project successful. The needed knowledge may be as simple as understanding a policy, or be as complicated as learning many new competencies.

The final step is identifying the structure of the solution. How best can the information be presented to ensure that needed knowledge will be acquired and job performance will change to solve the business problem? This level of analysis involves issues surrounding the scope, timing, structure, method, and budget for project implementation and delivery.

Collectively, these steps clearly define the issues that led to initiation of the project. When these preliminary steps are completed, the project can be positioned to achieve its intended results.

Understanding the need for a project is critical to positioning that project for success. Positioning a program or project requires the development of clear, specific objectives that are communicated to all stakeholders. Objectives should be developed for each level of need and should define success, answering the question "How will we know the need has been met?" If the criteria of success are not communicated early and often, process participants will go through the motions, with little change resulting. Developing detailed objectives with clear measures of success will position the project to achieve its ultimate objective.

Before a project is launched, forecasting the outcomes may be important to ensure that adjustments can be made or alternative solutions can be investigated. This forecast can be simple, relying on the individuals closest to the situation, or it can be a more detailed analysis of the situation and expected outcome. Recently, forecasting has become a critical tool for project sponsors who need evidence that the project will be successful before they are willing to plunge into a funding stream for it. Because of its importance, forecasting is the focus of Chapter 12.

## The ROI Process Model

The next challenge for many project leaders is to collect a variety of data along a chain of impact that shows the project's value. Figure 2-3 displays the sequential steps that lead to data categorized by the five levels of results.[1] This figure shows the ROI methodology, a step-by-step process beginning with the objectives and concluding with reporting of data. The model assumes that proper analysis is conducted to define need before the steps are taken.

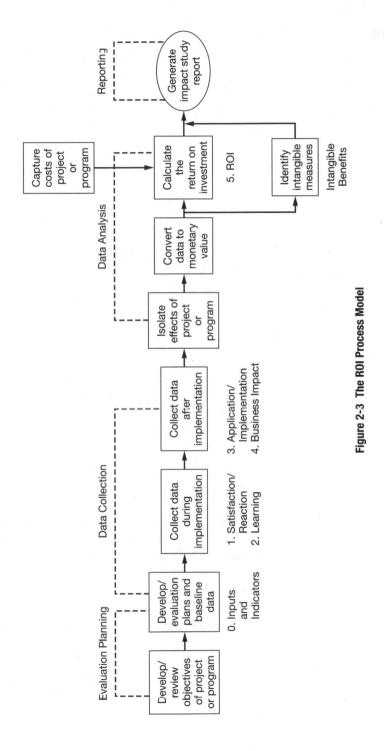

**Figure 2-3  The ROI Process Model**

## Planning the Evaluation

The first phase of the ROI methodology is evaluation planning. This phase involves several procedures, including understanding the purpose of the evaluation, determining the feasibility of the planned approach, planning data collection and analysis, and outlining the details of the project.

### Evaluation Purpose

Evaluations are conducted for a variety of reasons:

- To improve the quality of projects and outcomes
- To determine whether a project has accomplished its objectives
- To identify strengths and weaknesses in the process
- To enable the cost-benefit analysis
- To assist in the development of marketing projects or programs in the future
- To determine whether the project was the appropriate solution
- To establish priorities for project funding

The purposes of the evaluation should be considered prior to developing the evaluation plan because the purposes will often determine the scope of the evaluation, the types of instruments used, and the type of data collected. As with any project, understanding the purpose of the evaluation will give it focus, and will help gain support from others.

### Feasibility

An important consideration in planning the ROI impact study is the determination of the levels at which the program will be evaluated. Some evaluations will stop at Level 3, where analysis will determine the extent to which participants are using what they have learned. Others will be evaluated at Level 4, where the consequences of on-the-job applications are monitored and measures directly linked to the project are examined. If the ROI calculation is needed, the evaluation will proceed to Level 5. To reach this level of measurement, two additional steps are required: the Level 4 impact data must be converted to monetary values, and the costs of the program must be captured so that the ROI can be developed. Evaluation at Level 5 is intended for projects that are expensive, are high-profile, and have a direct link to business needs.

The initial analysis, which defines the needs along the five levels, also defines the objectives at these levels. Projects and programs need very clear direction, and the objectives provide this clarity. Objectives, when defined precisely, provide the participants and other stakeholders with the direction they need to make the project successful. The objectives are defined along the same five levels as the needs assessment:

- Reaction objectives (1)
- Learning objectives (2)
- Application and implementation objectives (3)
- Impact objectives (4)
- ROI objectives (5)

These specific objectives take the mystery out of what this project should achieve.

On occasion, the initial analysis may stop with Level 2 objectives, excluding the application and impact objectives that are needed to direct the higher levels of evaluation. If application and impact objectives are not available, they must be developed using input from such groups as job incumbents, analysts, project developers, subject matter experts, facilitators, and on-the-job team leaders.

Three simple planning documents are developed next: the data collection plan, the ROI analysis plan, and the project plan. These documents should be completed during evaluation planning and before the evaluation project is implemented—ideally, before the program is designed or developed. Appropriate up-front attention will save time later, when data are actually collected.

### Data Collection Plan

Figure 2-4 shows a completed data collection plan for a project undertaken to reduce bus drivers' absenteeism in a major city.

This document provides a place for the major elements and issues regarding data collection. Broad objectives are appropriate for planning. Specific, detailed objectives are developed later, before the program is designed. Entries in the Measures column define the specific measure for each objective; entries in the Method/Instruments column describe the technique used to collect the data; in the Sources column, the source of the data is identified; the Timing column indicates when the data are collected; and the Responsibilities column identifies who will collect the data.

## Data Collection Plan - Metro Transit Authority

**Program:** Absenteeism Reduction   **Responsibility:** Patti Phillips   **Date:** January 15

| Level | Broad Program Objective(s) | Measures | Data Collection Method/Instruments | Data Sources | Timing | Responsibilities |
|---|---|---|---|---|---|---|
| 1 | REACTION & SATISFACTION • Positive Employee Reaction to the No Fault Policy | • Positive reaction from employees | • Feedback Questionnaire | • Employees | • At the end of employee meetings | • Supervisors |
| 2 | LEARNING • Employee understanding of the policy | • Score on post test, at least 70 | • True/False test | • Employees | • At the end of employee meetings | • Supervisors |
| 3 | APPLICATION/ IMPLEMENTATION 1. Effective and consistent implementation and enforcement of the programs 2. Little or no adverse reaction from current employees regarding No Fault policy 3. Use the new screening process | 1. Supervisors' response on program's influence 2. Employee complaints and union cooperation | 1. & 2. Follow-up questionnaire to supervisors (2 sample groups) 3. Sample review of interview and selection records | 1. Supervisors 2. Company records | 1. Following emp. meetings, sample 1 group at 3 months and another group at 6 months 2. Three mos and six mos after imp | • HR Program Coordinator |
| 4 | BUSINESS IMPACT 1. Reduce driver absenteeism at least 2% during first year 2. Maintain present level of job satisfaction as new policy is implemented 3. Improved customer service and satisfaction with reduction in schedule delays | 1. Absenteeism 2. Employee Satisfaction 3. Delays impact on customer service | 1. Monitor absenteeism 2. Follow-up questionnaire to supervisors 3. Monitor bus schedule delays | 1. Company records 2. Supervisors 3. Dispatch records | 1. Monitor monthly analyze 1 year pre and 1 year post imp 2. Three months and six months after employee meetings 3. Monthly | • HR Program Coordinator |
| 5 | ROI Target ROI ➤ 25% | Comments: _____ | | | | |

**Figure 2-4 Data Collection Plan**

### ROI Analysis Plan

Figure 2-5 shows a completed ROI analysis plan for the absenteeism reduction project. This planning document captures information on key items that are necessary to develop the actual ROI calculation. In the first column, significant data items are listed. Although these are usually Level 4 impact data, in some cases this column includes Level 3 items. These items will be used in the ROI analysis.

The method employed to isolate the project's effects is listed next to each data item in the second column. The method of converting data to monetary values is included in the third column for those items that will be converted to money. The cost categories that will be captured for the project are outlined in the next column. Normally, the cost categories will be consistent from one project to another. The intangible benefits expected from the program are outlined in the fifth column. This list is generated from discussions about the program with sponsors and subject-matter experts. Communication targets are outlined in the sixth column. Finally, other issues or events that might influence program implementation and its outputs are highlighted in the last column. Typical items include the capability of participants, the degree of access to data sources, and unique data analysis issues.

The ROI analysis plan, when combined with the data collection plan, provides detailed information for calculating the ROI, illustrating how the evaluation will develop from beginning to end.

### Project Plan

The final plan developed for the evaluation planning phase is a project plan, as shown in Figure 2-6. A project plan consists of a description of the project and brief details, such as duration, target audience, and number of participants. It also shows the timeline of the project, from the planning of the study through the final communication of the results. This plan becomes an operational tool to keep the project on track.

Collectively, the three planning documents provide the direction necessary for the ROI impact study. Most of the decisions regarding the process are made as these planning tools are developed. The remainder of the project becomes a methodical, systematic process of implementing the plan. This is a crucial step in the ROI methodology, in which valuable time allocated to planning will save precious time later.

## ROI Analysis Plan - Metro Transit Authority

**Program:** Absenteeism Reduction  **Responsibility:** Patti Phillips  **Date:** January 15

| Data Items (Usually Level 4) | Methods for Isolating the Effects of the Program/Process | Methods of Converting Data to Monetary Values | Cost Categories | Intangible Benefits | Communication Targets for Final Report | Other Influences/ Issues During Application | Comments |
|---|---|---|---|---|---|---|---|
| 1. Absenteeism | 1. Trend line analysis and Supervisor Estimates | 1. Wages & benefits and standard values | Screening Process • Development • Interviewer preparation | • Sustain employee satisfaction • Improve employee morale • Improve customer satisfaction • Fewer disruptive bottlenecks in transportation grid • Ease of implementation by supervisors | • Senior management • Managers and supervisors • Union representatives • HR staff | • Concern about supervisors consistent administration • Partner with Union reps on how to communicate results of study to employees | |
| 2. Employee Job Satisfaction | 2. Supervisor estimates | N/A | • Administration • Materials No Fault Policy | | | | |
| 3. Bus Schedule Delays (Influence on Customer Satisfaction) | 3. Management estimates | N/A | • Development • Implementation • Materials | | | | |

**Figure 2-5  ROI Analysis Plan**

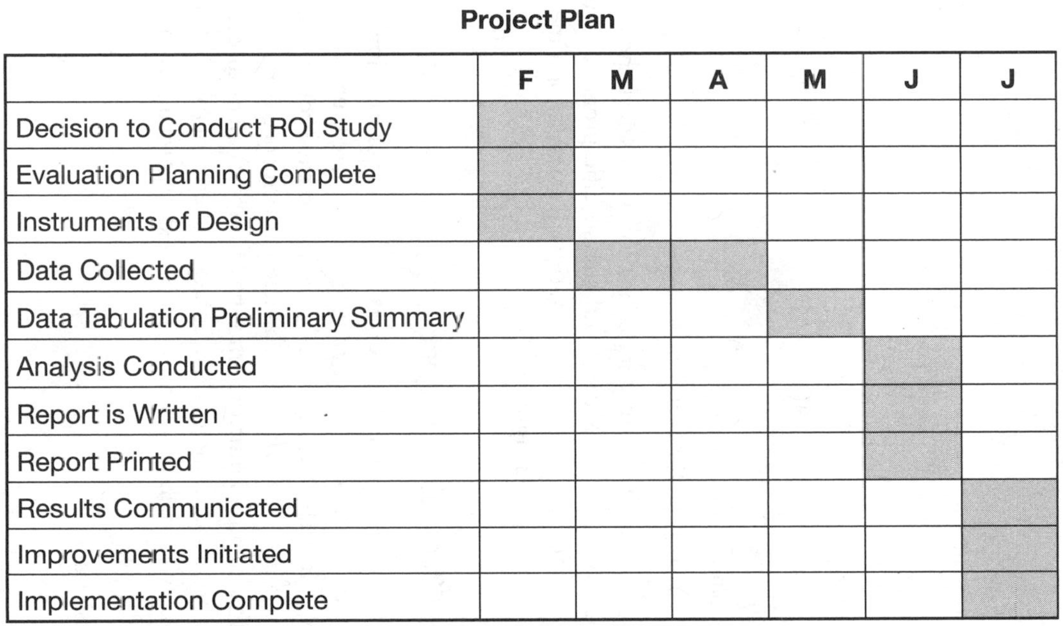

Project Plan

| | F | M | A | M | J | J |
|---|---|---|---|---|---|---|
| Decision to Conduct ROI Study | ▓ | | | | | |
| Evaluation Planning Complete | ▓ | | | | | |
| Instruments of Design | ▓ | | | | | |
| Data Collected | | ▓ | | | | |
| Data Tabulation Preliminary Summary | | | | ▓ | | |
| Analysis Conducted | | | | | ▓ | |
| Report is Written | | | | | ▓ | |
| Report Printed | | | | | ▓ | |
| Results Communicated | | | | | | ▓ |
| Improvements Initiated | | | | | | ▓ |
| Implementation Complete | | | | | | ▓ |

**Figure 2-6  Project Plan**

25

## Collecting Data

Data collection is central to the ROI methodology. Both hard data (representing output, quality, cost, and time) and soft data (including job satisfaction and customer satisfaction) are collected. Data are collected using a variety of methods, including

- Surveys
- Questionnaires
- Tests
- Observations
- Interviews
- Focus groups
- Action plans
- Performance contracts
- Business performance monitoring

The important challenge in data collection is to select the method or methods appropriate for the setting and the specific program, within the time and budget constraints of the organization. Data collection methods are covered in more detail in Chapters 4–7.

## Isolating the Effects of the Project

An often overlooked issue in evaluation is the process of isolating the effects of the project. In this step, specific strategies are explored that determine the amount of output performance directly related to the project. This step is essential because many factors will influence performance data. The specific strategies of this step pinpoint the amount of improvement directly related to the project, resulting in increased accuracy and credibility of ROI calculations. The following techniques have been used by organizations to tackle this important issue:

- Control groups
- Trend line analysis
- Forecasting models
- Participant estimates
- Managers' estimates
- Senior management estimates

- Experts' input
- Customer input

Collectively, these techniques provide a comprehensive set of tools to handle the important and critical issue of isolating the effects of projects. Chapter 8 is devoted to this important step in the ROI methodology.

## Converting Data to Monetary Values

To calculate the return on investment, Level 4 impact data are converted to monetary values and compared with project costs. This requires that a value be placed on each unit of data connected with the project. Many techniques are available to convert data to monetary values. The specific technique selected depends on the type of data and the situation. The techniques include

- Use of output data, as standard values
- Cost of quality, usually as a standard value
- Time savings converted to participants' wage and employee benefits
- An analysis of historical costs
- Use of internal and external experts
- Search of external databases
- Use of participant estimates
- Use of manager estimates
- Soft measures mathematically linked to other measures

This step in the ROI model is important and absolutely necessary in determining the monetary benefits of a project. The process is challenging, particularly with soft data, but can be methodically accomplished using one or more of these strategies. Because of its importance, this step in the ROI methodology is described in detail in Chapter 9.

## Identifying Intangible Benefits

In addition to tangible, monetary benefits, intangible benefits, those not converted to money, are identified for most projects. Intangible benefits include items such as

- Increased employee engagement
- Increased brand awareness

- Improved networking
- Improved customer service
- Fewer complaints
- Reduced conflict

During data analysis, every attempt is made to convert all data to monetary values. All hard data—such as output, quality, and time—are converted to monetary values. The conversion of soft data is attempted for each data item. However, if the process used for conversion is too subjective or inaccurate, and the resulting values lose credibility in the process, then the data are listed as an intangible benefit with the appropriate explanation. For some projects, intangible, nonmonetary benefits are extremely valuable, and often carry as much influence as the hard data items. Chapter 10 is devoted to the nonmonetary, intangible benefits.

## Tabulating Project Costs

An important part of the ROI equation is the calculation of project costs. Tabulating the costs involves monitoring or developing all the related costs of the project targeted for the ROI calculation. Among the cost components to be included are

- Initial analysis costs
- Cost to design and develop the project
- Cost of all project materials
- Costs for the project team
- Cost of the facilities for the project
- Travel, lodging, and meal costs for the participants and team members
- Participants' salaries (including employee benefits)
- Administrative and overhead costs, allocated in some convenient way
- Evaluation costs

The conservative approach is to include all these costs so that the total is fully loaded. Chapter 11 includes this step in the ROI methodology.

## Calculating the Return on Investment

The return on investment is calculated using the program benefits and costs. The benefits/costs ratio (BCR) is calculated as the project benefits divided by the project costs. In formula form,

$$BCR = \frac{\text{Project benefits}}{\text{Project costs}}$$

The return on investment is based on the net benefits divided by project costs. The net benefits are calculated as the project benefits minus the project costs. In formula form, the ROI becomes

$$ROI(\%) = \frac{\text{Net project benefits}}{\text{Project costs}} \times 100$$

This is the same basic formula used in evaluating other investments, in which the ROI is traditionally reported as earnings divided by investment. Chapter 11 provides more detail.

## Reporting

The final step in the ROI process model is reporting, a critical step that is often deficient in the degree of attention and planning required to ensure its success. The reporting step involves developing appropriate information in impact studies and other brief reports. At the heart of this step are the different techniques used to communicate to a wide variety of target audiences. In most ROI studies, several audiences are interested in and need the information. Careful planning to match the communication method with the audience is essential to ensure that the message is understood and that appropriate actions follow. Chapter 13 is devoted to this critical step in the ROI process.

## Operating Standards and Philosophy

To ensure consistency and replication of impact studies, operating standards must be developed and applied as the process model is used to develop ROI studies. The results of the study must stand alone and must not vary with the individual who is conducting the study. The operating standards detail how each step and issue of the process will be handled. Table 2-1 shows the 12 guiding principles that form the basis for the operating standards.

The guiding principles serve not only to consistently address each step, but also to provide a much needed conservative approach to the analysis. A conservative approach may lower the actual ROI calculation, but it will also build credibility with the target audience.

**Table 2-1 Twelve Guiding Principles of ROI**

1. When conducting a higher-level evaluation, collect data at lower levels.
2. When planning a higher-level evaluation, the previous level of evaluation is not required to be comprehensive.
3. When collecting and analyzing data, use only the most credible sources.
4. When analyzing data, select the most conservative alternative for calculations.
5. Use at least one method to isolate the effects of a project.
6. If no improvement data are available for a population or from a specific source, assume that little or no improvement has occurred.
7. Adjust estimates of improvement for potential errors of estimation.
8. Avoid use of extreme data items  and unsupported claims when calculating ROI.
9. Use only the first year of annual benefits in ROI analysis of short-term solutions.
10. Fully load all costs of a solution, project, or program when analyzing ROI.
11. Intangible measures are defined as measures that are purposely not converted to monetary values.
12. Communicate the results of ROI methodology to all key stakeholders.

## Implementing and Sustaining the Process

A variety of environmental issues and events will influence the successful implementation of the ROI process. These issues must be addressed early to ensure its success. Specific topics or actions include

- A policy statement concerning results-based projects
- Procedures and guidelines for different elements and techniques of the evaluation process
- Formal meetings to develop staff skills with the ROI process
- Strategies to improve management commitment to and support for the ROI process
- Mechanisms to provide technical support for questionnaire design, data analysis, and evaluation strategy
- Specific techniques to place more attention on results

The ROI process can fail or succeed based on these implementation issues. Chapter 14 is devoted to this important topic.

In addition to implementing and sustaining ROI use, the process must undergo periodic review. An annual review is recommended to determine the extent to which the process is adding value. This final element involves checking satisfaction with the process, and determining how well it is under stood and applied. Essentially, this review follows the process described in this book to determine the ROI on ROI.

# Benefits of This Approach

The methodology presented in this book has been used consistently and routinely by thousands of organizations in the past decade. In some fields and industries, it has been more prominent than in others. Much has been learned about the success of this methodology and what it can bring to the organizations using it.

## Aligning with Business

The ROI methodology ensures alignment with the business, enforced in three steps. First, even before the project is initiated, the methodology ensures that alignment is achieved up front, at the time the project is validated as the appropriate solution. Second, by requiring specific, clearly defined objectives at the impact level, the project focuses on the ultimate outcomes, in essence driving the business measure by its design, delivery, and implementation. Third, in the follow-up data, when the business measures may have changed or improved, a method is used to isolate the effects of the project on that data, consequently proving the connection to that business measure (i.e., showing the amount of improvement directly connected to the project and ensuring there is business alignment).

## Validating the Value Proposition

In reality, most projects are undertaken to deliver value. As described in this chapter, the definition of value may on occasion be unclear, or may not be what a project's various sponsors, organizers, and stakeholders desire. Consequently, there are often value shifts. Once the values are finally determined, the value proposition is detailed. The ROI methodology will forecast the value in advance, and if the value has been delivered, it verifies the value proposition agreed to by the appropriate parties.

## Improving Processes

This is a process improvement tool by design and by practice. It collects data to evaluate how things are—or are not—working. When things are not where they should be—as when projects are not proceeding as effectively as expected—data are available to indicate what must be changed to make the project more effective. When things are working well, data are available to show what else could be done to make them better. Thus, this is a process improvement system designed to provide feedback to make changes. As a project is conducted, the results are collected and feedback is provided to the various stakeholders for specific actions for improvement. These changes drive the project to better results, which are then measured while the process continues. This continuous feedback cycle is critical to process improvement and is inherent in the ROI methodology approach.

## Enhancing the Image; Building Respect

Many functions, and even entire professions, are criticized for being unable to deliver what is expected. For this, their public image suffers. The ROI methodology is one way to help build the respect a function or profession needs.

The ROI methodology can make a difference in any function—not just those under fire. Many human resources (HR) executives have used ROI to show their projects' and programs' value, perhaps changing the perception of a project from one based on activity to one that credibly adds value. This methodology shows a connection to the bottom line and shows the value delivered to stakeholders. It removes issues about value and a supposed lack of contribution to the organization. Consequently, this methodology is an important part of the process of changing the image within the function of the organization and building needed respect.

## Improving Support

Securing support for projects is critical, particularly at the middle manager level. Many projects enjoy the support of the top-level managers who allocated the resources to make the projects viable. Unfortunately, some middle-level managers may not support certain projects because they do not see the value the projects deliver in terms the managers appreciate and understand. Having a methodology that shows how a project or program is connected to the manager's business goals and objectives can change this support level. When middle managers understand that a project is helping them meet specific performance indicators or departmental goals, they will usually support the process, or will at least resist it less. In this way, the ROI methodology may actually improve manager support.

## Justifying or Enhancing Budgets

Some organizations have used the ROI methodology to support proposed budgets. Because the methodology shows the monetary value expected or achieved with specific projects, the data can often be leveraged into budget requests. When a particular function is budgeted, the amount budgeted is often in direct proportion to the value that the function adds. If little or no credible data support the contribution, the budgets are often trimmed—or at least not enhanced. Such organizations as Black & Decker and Progressive Insurance have reported significant budget increases for an entire function based on ROI projects pursued during the previous year. Bringing accountability to this level is one of the best ways to secure future funding.

## Building a Partnership with Key Executives

Almost every function attempts to partner with operating executives and key managers in the organization. Unfortunately, some managers may not want to be partners. They may not want to waste time and effort on a relationship that does not help them succeed. They want to partner only with groups and individuals who can add value and help them in meaningful ways. Showing the projects' results will enhance the likelihood of building these partnerships, with the results providing the initial impetus for making the partnerships work.

## Earning a Seat at the Table

Many functions are attempting to earn a seat at the table, however defined. Typically, "earning a seat at the table" means being at the strategy- or decision-making table, and in high-level discussions at the top of the organization. Department and program leaders hope to be involved in strategic decision making, particularly in areas that will affect their functions, and the projects and processes in their functions. Showing the actual contribution and getting others to understand how the function adds value can help earn the coveted seat at the table. Most executives want to include those who are genuinely helping the business, and will seek input that is valuable and constructive. The use of the ROI methodology may be the single most important action that can be taken to earn the seat at the table.

## Final Thoughts

This chapter presents the overall approach to *Show Me the Money*. It presents the different elements and steps in the ROI methodology, the standards, and the different concepts necessary to understand how ROI works, but without a great deal of detail. This chapter brings the methodology into focus. Before one can accept the approach, the steps and the detail have to be shown. This detail will be presented in the rest of the book.

# Chapter 3

# PROJECT NEEDS AND OBJECTIVES
## ENSURING BUSINESS ALIGNMENT

Chapter 2 provided an overview of the ROI methodology. This chapter presents the first step of the process: defining the initial need and corresponding objectives for a project. This step positions the program or project for success by aligning its intended outcome with the needs of the business. This business alignment is essential if the investment in a project is to reap a return.

## Creating Business Alignment

### The Purpose of Alignment

Based on approximately two thousand published and unpublished case studies, the number 1 cause of project failure is moving forward without a clearly defined need. The second most common cause of failure is misalignment between the project objectives and business needs.

Projects must begin with a clear focus on the desired outcome. The end must be specified in terms of business needs and business measures so that the outcome—the actual improvement in the measures—and the corresponding ROI are clear. This establishes the expectations throughout the analysis and project design, development, delivery, and implementation stages.

Beginning with the end in mind requires pinning down all the details to ensure that the project is properly planned and executed according to schedule. But conducting this up-front analysis is not as simple as one might think—it requires a disciplined approach.

## Disciplined Analysis

Proper analysis requires discipline and determination to adhere to a structured, systematic process supported by standards. This standardized approach adds credibility and allows for consistent application so that the analysis can be replicated. A disciplined approach maintains process efficiency as various tools and templates are developed and used. This initial phase of project development calls for focus and thoroughness, with little allowance for major shortcuts.

Not every project should be subjected to the type of comprehensive analysis described in this chapter. Some needs are obvious and require little analysis other than that necessary to develop the project. Additional analysis may be needed to confirm that the project addresses the perceived need and perhaps to fine-tune the project for future application. The amount of analysis required often depends on the expected opportunity to be gained if the project is appropriate or the negative consequences anticipated if the project is inappropriate.

When analysis is proposed, individuals may react with concern or resistance. Some are concerned about the potential for "paralysis by analysis," where requests and directives lead only to additional analyses. Such reactions can pose a problem for an organization because analysis is necessary to ensure that the project is appropriate. Unfortunately, analysis is often misunderstood— conjuring up images of complex problems, confusing models, and a deluge of data along with complicated statistical techniques to ensure that all bases are covered. In reality, analysis need not be so complicated. Simple techniques can uncover the cause of a problem or the need for a particular project.

Organizations often avoid analysis because

1. *The specific need appears to point to a particular solution.* Sometimes the information gained from asking individuals what they need appears to point to a legitimate solution, but in fact the solution is inadequate or inappropriate. For example, when employees are asked what they need to improve work unit performance in terms of efficiency, quality, and productivity, they may identify specific tools, templates, software, or equipment. In reality, the solution may be as simple as learning to fully use existing tools. Implementing a solution in response to an individual request can prove shortsighted and costly.

2. *The solution appears to be obvious.* In the process of examining a problem or identifying a potential opportunity, some solutions will arise that seem obvious. For example, if employees take too long to complete a particular task, the immediate conclusion may be that a new technology is needed that will reduce task completion time. Although this solution

appears obvious, deeper analysis may reveal that other solutions—such as increasing motivation, minimizing resistance, removing obstacles, and eliminating bottlenecks—are more appropriate.

3. *Everyone has an opinion about the cause of a problem.* The person requesting a particular project may think that he or she has the best solution. Choosing the solution championed by the highest-ranking or most senior executive is often tempting. Unfortunately, this person may not be close enough to the situation to offer a solution that will have a lasting effect on the problem.

4. *Analysis takes too much time.* Yes, analysis takes time and consumes resources. However, the consequences of a lack of analysis can be more expensive. If the implemented solutions do not appropriately address the needs, time and money may be wasted and the problem left unsolved. The consequences of ill-advised solutions implemented without an analysis can be devastating. When designed properly and conducted professionally, an analysis can be completed within the budgetary and time constraints of most organizations. The secret is to focus on the right tools for the situation.

5. *Analysis sounds confusing.* Determining a problem's causes may seem complex and puzzling. However, analyses can be simple and straight-forward and achieve excellent results. The challenge is to select the level of analysis that will yield the best solution with minimal effort and the simplest techniques.

In the face of these misconceptions, the difficulty of promoting additional analysis is apparent. But this step is critical and should not be omitted, or else the process will be flawed from the outset.

The remainder of the chapter delves into the components of analysis that are necessary for a solid alignment between a project and the business. First, however, reviewing the model introduced in the previous chapter may be helpful. It is presented here as Figure 3-1.

## Determining the Potential Payoff

The first step in up-front analysis is to determine the potential payoff of solving a problem or seizing an opportunity. This step begins with answers to a few crucial questions: Is this project worth doing? Is it feasible? What is the likelihood of a positive ROI?

For projects addressing significant problems or opportunities with high potential rewards, the answers are obvious. The questions may take longer to

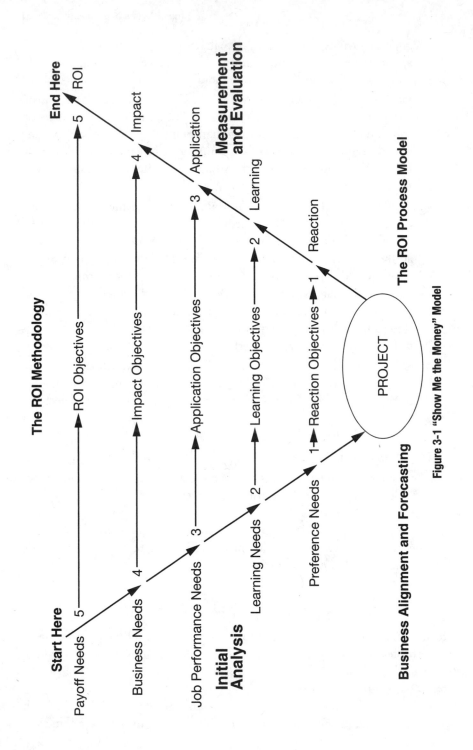

The ROI Methodology

Start Here

Payoff Needs 5 ——→ 5 ROI Objectives ——→ 5 ROI — End Here

Business Needs 4 ——→ 4 Impact Objectives ——→ 4 Impact

Job Performance Needs 3 ——→ 3 Application Objectives ——→ 3 Application

Initial Analysis

Learning Needs 2 ——→ 2 Learning Objectives ——→ 2 Learning

Preference Needs 1 ——→ 1 Reaction Objectives ——→ 1 Reaction

PROJECT

Measurement and Evaluation

Business Alignment and Forecasting

The ROI Process Model

Figure 3-1 "Show Me the Money" Model

answer for lower-profile projects or those for which the expected payoff is less apparent. In any case, these are legitimate questions, and the analysis can be as simple or as comprehensive as required.

Essentially, a project will pay off in profit increases or in cost savings. Profit increases are generated by projects that drive revenue (e.g., that improve sales, drive market share, introduce new products, open new markets, enhance customer service, or increase customer loyalty). Other revenue-generating measures include increasing membership, increasing donations, obtaining grants, and generating tuition from new and returning students—all of which, after subtracting the cost of doing business, should leave a significant profit.

However, most projects drive cost savings. Cost savings can come through cost reduction or cost avoidance. Improved quality, reduced cycle time, lowered downtime, reduced complaints, reduced employee turnover, and minimized delays are all examples of cost savings.

Cost avoidance projects are implemented to reduce risks, avoid problems, or prevent unwanted events. Some finance and accounting professionals may view cost avoidance as an inappropriate measure to use to determine monetary benefits and calculate ROI. However, if the assumptions prove correct, an avoided cost (e.g., compliance fines) can be more rewarding than reducing an actual cost. Preventing a problem is more cost-effective than waiting for the problem to occur and then having to focus on solving it.

Determining the potential payoff is the first step in the needs analysis process. This step is closely related to the next one, determining the business need, since the potential payoff is often based on a consideration of the business. The payoff depends on two factors: the monetary value derived from the business measure's improvement and the approximate cost of the project. Identifying these monetary values in detail usually yields a more credible forecast of what can be expected from the chosen solution. However, this step may be omitted in situations where the problem (business need) must be resolved regardless of the cost, or if it becomes obvious that this is a high-payoff activity.

The target level of detail may also hinge on the need to secure project funding. If the potential funding source does not recognize the value of the project compared with the potential costs, more detail may be needed to provide a convincing case for funding.

Knowledge of the actual payoff is not necessary if widespread agreement exists that the payoff from the project will be high, or if the problem in question must be resolved regardless of cost. For example, if the problem involves a safety concern, a regulatory compliance issue, or a competitive matter, a detailed analysis is not needed.

## Obvious versus Not-So-Obvious Payoff

The potential payoff is obvious for some projects and not so obvious for others. Opportunities with obvious payoffs may include

- Operating costs 47 percent higher than industry average
- Customer satisfaction rating of 3.89 on a 10-point scale
- A cost to the city of $75,000 annually for each homeless person
- Noncompliance fines totaling $1.2 million, up 82 percent from last year
- Turnover of critical talent 35 percent above benchmark figure

Each item appears to reflect a serious problem that needs to be addressed by executives, administrators, or politicians.

For other projects, the issues are sometimes unclear and may arise from political motives or bias. These potential opportunities are associated with payoffs that may not be so obvious. Such opportunities may include

- Become a technology leader
- Become a "green" company
- Improve leadership competencies for all managers
- Improve branding for all products
- Create a great place to work

With each of these opportunities, there is a need for more specific detail regarding the measure. For example, if the opportunity is to become a "green" company, one might ask: What is a green company? What are the advantages of becoming a green company? How is green defined? Projects with not-so-obvious payoffs require greater analysis than those with clearly defined outcomes.

The potential payoff establishes the fundamental reason for pursuing new or enhanced projects. But the payoff—whether obvious or not—is not the only reason for moving forward with a project. The cost of a problem is another factor. If the cost is excessive, it should be addressed. If not, then a decision must be made as to whether the problem is worth solving.

## The Cost of a Problem

Problems are expensive and their solution can result in high returns, especially when the solution is inexpensive. To determine the cost of the problem, its potential consequences must be examined and converted to monetary values. Problems may encompass time, quality, productivity, and team or customer issues. All of these factors must be converted to monetary values if the cost of the problem is to be determined. Inventory shortages are often directly associated with the cost of the inventory as well as with the cost of carrying the inventory. Time can easily be translated into money by calculating the fully loaded cost of an individual's time spent on unproductive tasks. Calculating the time for completing a project, task, or cycle involves measures that can be converted to money. Errors, mistakes, waste, delays, and bottlenecks can often be converted to money because of their consequences. Productivity problems and inefficiencies, equipment damage, and equipment under use are other items whose conversion to monetary value is straightforward.

In examining costs, considering *all* the costs and their implications is crucial. For example, the full cost of an accident includes not only the cost of lost workdays and medical expenses, but their effects on insurance premiums, the time required for investigations, damage to equipment, and the time spent by all involved employees addressing the accident. The cost of a customer complaint includes not only the cost of the time spent resolving the complaint, but also the value of the item or service that has to be adjusted because of the complaint. The costliest consequence of a customer complaint is the price to the company of lost future business and goodwill from the complaining customer and from potential customers who learn of the complaint.

Placing a monetary value on a problem helps in determining if the problem's resolutions is economically feasible. The same applies to opportunities.

## The Value of an Opportunity

Just as the cost of a problem can be easily tabulated in most situations, the value of an opportunity can also be calculated. Examples of opportunities include implementing a new process, exploring new technology, increasing research and development efforts, and upgrading the workforce to create a more competitive environment. In these situations a problem may not exist, but an opportunity to get ahead of the competition or to prevent a problem's occurrence by taking immediate action does. Assigning a proper value to this opportunity requires considering what may happen if the project is not pursued or acknowledging the windfall that might be realized if the opportunity is seized. The value is determined by following the different possible scenarios to convert specific business impact measures to money. The difficulty in this process is conducting a credible analysis. Forecasting the value of an opportunity entails many assumptions compared with calculating the value of a known outcome.

## To Forecast or Not to Forecast?

The need to seek and assign value to opportunities leads to an important decision: to forecast or not to forecast ROI. If the stakes are high and support for the project is not in place, a detailed forecast may be the only way to gain the needed support and funding for the project or to inform the choice between multiple potential projects. In developing the forecast, the rigor of the analysis is an issue. In some cases, an informal forecast is sufficient, given certain assumptions about alternative outcome scenarios. In other cases, a detailed forecast is needed that uses data collected from a variety of experts, previous studies from another project, or perhaps more sophisticated analysis. Chapter 12 provides techniques useful for developing forecasts.

Once the potential payoff, including its financial value, has been determined, the next step is to clarify the business needs.

# Determining Business Needs

Determining the business needs requires the identification of specific measures so that the business situation can be clearly assessed. The concept of business needs refers to gains in productivity, quality, efficiency, time, and cost. This is true for the private sector as well as in government, nonprofit, and academic organizations.

## The Opportunity

A business need is represented by a business measure. Any process, item, or perception can be measured, and such measurement is critical to this level of analysis. If the project focuses on solving a problem, preventing a problem, or seizing an opportunity, the measures are usually identifiable. The important point is that the measures are present in the system, ready to be captured for this level of analysis. The challenge is to define the measures and to find them economically and swiftly.

## Hard Data Measures

To focus on the desired measures, distinguishing between hard data and soft data may be helpful. Hard data are primary measures of improvement presented in the form of rational, undisputed facts that are usually gathered within functional areas throughout an organization. These are the most desirable type of data because they are easy to quantify and are easily converted to monetary values. The fundamental criteria for gauging the effectiveness of an organization are hard data items such as revenue, productivity, and profitability, as well as measures that quantify such processes as cost control and quality assurance.

Hard data are objective and credible measures of an organization's performance. Hard data can usually be grouped in four categories, as shown in Table 3-1. These categories—output, quality, costs, and time—are typical performance measures in any organization.

**Table 3-1 Examples of Hard Data**

| Output | Quality | Costs | Time |
|---|---|---|---|
| Units produced | Failure rates | Shelter costs | Cycle time |
| Tons manufactured | Dropout rates | Treatment costs | Equipment downtime |
| Items assembled | Scrap | Budget variances | Overtime |
| Money collected | Waste | Unit costs | On-time shipments |
| Items sold | Rejects | Cost by account | Time to project completion |
| New accounts generated | Error rates | Variable costs | Processing time |
| Forms processed | Rework | Fixed costs | Supervisory time |
| Loans approved | Shortages | Overhead cost | Time to proficiency |
| Inventory turnover | Product defects | Operating costs | Learning time |
| Patients visited | Deviation from standard | Project cost savings | Adherence to schedules |
| Applications processed | Product failures | Accident costs | Repair time |
| Students graduated | Inventory adjustments | Program costs | Efficiency |
| Tasks completed | Time card corrections | Sales expense | Work stoppages |
| Output per hour | Incidents | | Order response |
| Productivity | Compliance discrepancies | | Late reporting |
| Work backlog | Agency fines | | Lost-time days |
| Incentive bonus | | | |
| Shipments | | | |
| Completion rate | | | |

Hard data from a particular project or program involve improvements in the output of the work unit, section, department, division, or entire organization. Every organization, regardless of the type, must have basic measures of output, such as number of patients treated, students graduated, tons produced, or packages shipped. Since these values are monitored, changes can easily be measured by comparing "before" and "after" outputs.

Quality is a very important hard data category. If quality is a major priority for the organization, processes are likely in place to measure and monitor quality. The rising prominence of quality improvement processes (such as Total Quality Management, Continuous Quality Improvement, and Six Sigma) has contributed to the tremendous recent successes in pinpointing the proper quality measures—and assigning monetary values to them.

Cost is another important hard data category. Many projects and programs are designed to lower, control, or eliminate the cost of a specific process or activity. Achieving cost targets has an immediate effect on the bottom line. Some organizations focus narrowly on cost reduction. For example, consider Wal-Mart, whose tagline is "Always low prices. Always." All levels of the organization are dedicated to lowering costs on processes and products and passing the savings along to customers.

Time is a critical measure in any organization. Some organizations gauge their performance almost exclusively in relation to time. When asked what business FedEx is in, company executives say, "We engineer time."

## Soft Data Measures

Soft data are probably the most familiar measures of an organization's effectiveness, yet their collection can present a challenge. Values representing attitude, motivation, and satisfaction are examples of soft data. Soft data are more difficult to gather and analyze, and therefore, they are used when hard data are not available or to supplement hard data. Soft data are also more difficult to convert to monetary values, a process requiring subjective methods. They are less objective as performance measurements and are usually behavior related, yet organizations place great emphasis on them. Improvements in these measures represent important business needs, but many organizations omit them from the ROI equation because they are soft values. However, they can contribute to economic value to the same extent as hard data measures. Table 3-2 shows common examples of soft data by category. The key is not to focus too much on the hard versus soft data distinction. A better approach is to consider data as tangible or intangible.

**Table 3-2 Examples of Soft Data**

| | |
|---|---|
| **Work Habits** | **Customer Service** |
| Excessive breaks | Customer complaints |
| Tardiness | Customer satisfaction |
| Visits to the dispensary | Customer dissatisfaction |
| Violations of safety rules | Customer impressions |
| Communication breakdowns | Customer loyalty |
| | Customer retention |
| **Work Climate/Satisfaction** | Lost customers |
| Grievances | |
| Discrimination charges | **Employee Development/Advancement** |
| Employee complaints | Promotions |
| Job satisfaction | Capability |
| Organization commitment | Intellectual capital |
| Employee engagement | Requests for transfer |
| Employee loyalty | Performance appraisal ratings |
| Intent to leave | Readiness |
| Stress | Networking |
| | |
| **Initiative/Innovation** | **Image** |
| Creativity | Brand awareness |
| Innovation | Reputation |
| New ideas | Leadership |
| Suggestions | Social responsibility |
| New products and services | Environmental friendliness |
| Trademarks | Social consciousness |
| Copyrights and patents | Diversity |
| Process improvements | External awards |
| Partnerships/alliances | |

# Tangible versus Intangible Benefits: A Better Approach

A challenge with regard to soft versus hard data is converting soft measures to monetary values. The key to this problem is to remember that, ultimately, all roads lead to hard data. Although creativity may be categorized as a form of soft data, a creative workplace can develop new products or new patents, which leads to greater revenue—clearly a hard data measure. Although it is possible to convert the measures listed in Table 3-2 to monetary amounts, it is often more realistic and practical to leave them in nonmonetary form. This decision is based on considerations of credibility and the cost of the conversion. According to the standards of the ROI methodology, an intangible measure is defined as a measure that is intentionally not converted to money. If a soft data measure can be converted to a monetary amount credibly using minimal resources, it is considered tangible, reported as a monetary value, and incorporated in the ROI calculation. If a data item cannot be converted to money credibly with minimal resources, it is listed as an intangible measure. Therefore, in defining business needs, the key difference between measures is not whether they represent hard or soft data, but whether they are tangible or intangible. In either case, they are important contributions toward the desired payoff and important business impact data.

## Impact Data Sources

The sources of impact data, whether tangible or intangible, are diverse. The data come from routine reporting systems in the organization. In many situations, these items have led to the need for the project or program. A vast array of documents, systems, databases, and reports can be used to select the specific measure or measures to be monitored throughout the project. Impact data sources include quality reports, service records, suggestion systems, and employee engagement data.

Some project planners and project team members assume that corporate data sources are scarce because the data are not readily available to them. However, data can usually be located by investing a small amount of time. Rarely do new data collection systems or processes need to be developed in order to identify data representing the business needs of an organization.

In searching for the proper measures to connect to the project and to identify business needs, it is helpful to consider all possible measures that could be influenced. Sometimes, collateral measures move in harmony with the project. For example, efforts to improve safety may also improve productivity and increase job satisfaction. Weighing adverse impacts on certain measures may also help. For example, when cycle times are reduced, quality may suffer; or when sales increase, customer satisfaction may deteriorate. Finally, project team members must anticipate unintended consequences and capture them as other data items that might be connected to or influenced by the project.

In the process if settling on the precise business measures for the project, it is useful to examine various "what if" scenarios. If the organization does nothing, the potential consequences of inaction should be made clear. The following questions may help in understanding the consequences of inaction:

- Will the situation deteriorate?
- Will operational problems surface?
- Will budgets be affected?
- Will we lose influence or support?

Answers to these questions can help the organization settle on a precise set of measures and can provide a hint of the extent to which the measures may change as a result of the project.

## Determining Job Performance Needs

The next step in the needs analysis is to understand what led to the business need. If the proposed project addresses a problem, this step focuses on the cause of the problem. If the project makes use of an opportunity, this step focuses on what is inhibiting the organization from taking advantage of that opportunity.

### Analysis Techniques

Uncovering the causes of the problem or the inhibitors to success requires a variety of analytical techniques. These techniques—such as problem analysis, nominal group technique, force field analysis, and just plain brainstorming—are used to clarify job performance needs. The technique that is used will depend on the organizational setting, the apparent depth of the problem, and the budget allocated to such analysis. Multiple techniques can be used since job performance may be lacking for a number of reasons. Detailed approaches of techniques can be found in many sources.[1]

### A Sensible Approach

Analysis takes time and adds to a project's cost. Examining records, researching databases, and observing individuals can provide important data, but a more cost-effective approach might include employing internal and/or external experts to help analyze the problem. Job performance needs can vary considerably and may include ineffective behavior, a dysfunctional work climate, inadequate systems, a disconnected process flow, improper procedures, a nonsupportive culture, outdated technology, and a non-accommodating environment, to name a few. When needs vary and with many techniques to choose from, the opportunity exists for overanalysis and excessive costs. Consequently, a sensible approach is needed.

## Determining Learning Needs

The solution to job performance needs uncovered in the previous step often requires a learning component—such as participants and team members learning how to perform a task differently, or learning how to use a process, system, or technology. In some cases learning is the principal solution, as in competency or capability development, major technology change, and system installations. For other projects, learning is a minor aspect of the solution and may involve simply understanding the process, procedure, or policy. For example, in the implementation of a new ethics policy for an organization, the learning component requires understanding how the policy works as well as the participant's role in the policy. In short, a learning solution is not always needed, but all solutions have a learning component.

A variety of approaches are available for measuring specific learning needs. Often, multiple tasks and jobs are involved in a project and should be addressed separately. Sometimes the least effective way to identify the skills and knowledge that are needed is to ask the participants involved in implementing the project. They may not be clear on what is needed and may not know enough to provide adequate input. One of the most useful ways to determine learning needs is to ask the individuals who understand the process. They can best determine what skills and knowledge are necessary to address the job performance issues that have been identified. This may be the appropriate time to find out the extent to which the knowledge and skills already exist.

Job and task analyses are effective when a new job is created or when an existing job description changes significantly. As jobs are redesigned and the new tasks must be identified, this type of analysis offers a systematic way of detailing the job and task. Essentially, a job analysis is the collection and evaluation of work-related information. A task analysis identifies the specific knowledge, skills, tools, and conditions necessary to the performance of a particular job.

Observation of current practices and procedures in an organization may be necessary as the project is implemented. This can often indicate the level of capability and help to identify the correct procedures. Observations can be used to examine work flow and interpersonal interactions, including those between management and team members. Observers may be previous employees, third-party participant observers, or mystery shoppers.

Sometimes, the demonstration of knowledge surrounding a certain task, process, or procedure provides evidence of what capabilities exist and what is lacking. Such demonstration can be as simple as a skill practice or role play, or as complex as an extensive mechanical or electronic simulation. The point is to use this as a way of determining if employees know how to perform a particular process. Through demonstration, specific learning needs can evolve.

Testing as a learning needs assessment process is not used as frequently as other methods, but it can be very useful. Employees are tested to reveal what they know about a particular situation. This information helps to guide learning issues.

In implementing projects in organizations where there is an existing manager or team leader, input from the management team may be used to assess the current situation and to indicate the knowledge and skills required by the new situation. This input can be elicited through surveys, interviews, or focus groups. It can be a rich source of information about what the users of the project, if it is implemented, will need to know to make it successful.

Where learning is a minor component, learning needs are simple. Determining learning needs can be time-consuming for major projects where new procedures, technologies, and processes must be developed. As in developing job performance needs, it is important not to spend excessive time analyzing learning needs but rather to collect as much data as possible with minimal resources.

## Determining Preference Needs

The final level of needs analysis determines the preferences that drive the project requirements. Essentially, individuals prefer certain processes, schedules, or activities for the structure of the project. These preferences define how the particular project will be implemented. If the project is a solution to a problem, this step defines how the solution will be installed. If the project makes use of an opportunity, this step outlines how the opportunity will be addressed, taking into consideration the preferences of those involved in the project.

Preference needs typically define the parameters of the project in terms of scope, timing, budget, staffing, location, technology, deliverables, and the degree of disruption allowed. Preference needs are developed from the input of several stakeholders rather than from one individual. For example, participants in the project (those who must make it work) may have a particular preference, but the preference could exhaust resources, time, and budgets. The immediate manager's input may help minimize the amount of disruption and maximize resources. The funds that can be allocated are also a constraining resource.

The urgency of project implementation may introduce a constraint in the preferences. Those who support or own the project often impose preferences on the project in terms of timing, budget, and the use of technology. Because preferences correspond to a Level 1 need, the project structure and solution will relate directly to the reaction objectives and to the initial reaction to the project.

In determining the preference needs, there can never be too much detail. Projects often go astray and fail to reach their full potential because of misunderstandings and differences in expectations surrounding the project. Preference needs should be addressed before the project begins. Pertinent issues are often outlined in the project proposal or planning documentation.

## Case Study: Southeast Corridor Bank

### Payoff Needs

At this point, following a case study through the different levels of needs may be helpful. The following discussion explores the analysis at Level 5, determining payoff needs. Southeast Corridor Bank (SCB) operated branches in four states. (SCB has since been acquired by Regions Bank, one of the nation's top 10 banks.) Like many other fast-growing organizations, SCB faced merger and integration problems, including excessive employee turnover.

SCB's annual employee turnover was 57 percent, compared with an industry average of 26 percent. The first step in addressing the problem was answering these questions:

- Is this a problem worth solving?
- Is there a potential payoff to solving the problem?

To the senior vice president of human resources, the answers were clear. After reviewing several published studies about the cost of turnover—including one from a financial institution—he concluded that the cost of employee turnover ranged between 110 percent and 225 percent of annual pay. At the current rate, employee turnover was costing the bank more than $6 million per year. Lowering the rate to the industry average would save the bank at least $3 million annually. Although the structure and cost of the solution had not been determined at this point, it became clear that this problem was worth solving. Unless the solution appeared to be very expensive, solving the problem would have a tremendous impact. This was the only analysis that was needed at this level.

## Business Needs

The specific measure in question was voluntary turnover: the number of employees leaving voluntarily divided by the average number of employees, expressed as a percentage. Clearly defining the measure was important. Still, with improvement in any one measure, other measures should also improve, depending on the specific solution. For example, staffing levels, job satisfaction, customer service, sales revenue, and other measures could change. These considerations are detailed in the context of determining the solution.

## Job Performance Needs

To identify the job performance needs, the cause of the problem had to be determined. Once the cause was known, a solution could be developed.

The nominal group technique was selected as the analysis method because it allowed unbiased input to be collected efficiently and accurately across the organization. Focus groups were planned consisting of 12 employees from each region, for a total of six groups representing all the regions. In addition, two focus groups were planned for the clerical staff in the corporate headquarters. This approach provided approximately a 10 percent sample, which was considered sufficient to pinpoint the problem.

The focus group participants who represented areas in which turnover was highest described why their colleagues were leaving, not why they themselves would leave. Data were collected from individuals using a carefully structured format—during two-hour meetings at each location, with third-party facilitators—and were integrated and weighted so that the most important reasons were clearly identified. This process had the advantages of low cost and high reliability, as well as a low degree of bias. Only two days of external facilitator time were needed to collect and summarize the data for review.

Following are the 10 major reasons given for turnover in the bank branches:

1. Lack of opportunity for advancement
2. Lack of opportunity to learn new skills and gain new product knowledge

3. Pay level not adequate

4. Not enough responsibility and empowerment

5. Lack of recognition and appreciation of work

6. Lack of teamwork

7. Lack of preparation for customer service problems

8. Unfair and nonsupportive supervisor

9. Too much stress at peak times

10. Not enough flexibility in work schedules

A similar list was developed for the clerical staff. However, the remainder of this case study will focus on the efforts to reduce turnover in the branch network. Branch turnover was the most critical issue, because of its high rate and the large number of employees involved, and the focus group results provided a clear pattern of specific needs. Recognizing that not all causes of the turnover could be addressed immediately, the bank's management concentrated on the top five reasons and considered a variety of options.

## The Solution

Management determined that a skill-based pay system would address the top five reasons for employee turnover. The program was designed to expand the scope of the jobs, with increases in pay awarded for the acquisition of skills and a clear path provided for advancement and improvement. Jobs were redesigned from narrowly focused duties to an expanded role with a new title: every teller became a banking representative I, II, or III.

A branch employee would be designated a banking representative I if he or she could perform one or two simple tasks, such as processing deposits and cashing checks. As an employee at this level took on additional responsibilities and learned to perform different functions, he or she would be eligible for a promotion to banking representative II. A representative who could perform all the basic functions of the branch, including processing consumer loan applications, would be promoted to banking representative III.

Training opportunities were available to help employees develop the needed skills, and structured on-the-job training was provided by the branch managers, assistant managers, and supervisors. Self-study information was also available. The performance of multiple tasks was introduced to broaden responsibilities and enable employees to provide excellent customer service. Pay increases were used to recognize skill acquisition, demonstrated accomplishment, and increased responsibility.

Although the skill-based system had obvious advantages from the employee's perspective, the bank also benefited. Not only was turnover expected to decline, but required staffing levels were expected to decrease in the larger branches. In theory, if all employees in a branch could perform all the necessary duties, fewer employees would be needed. Previously, certain critical jobs required minimum staffing levels, and employees in those positions were not always available for other duties.

In addition, the bank anticipated improved customer service. The new approach would prevent customers from having to wait in long lines for specialized services. For example, in the typical bank branch, long lines for special functions—such as opening a checking account, closing out a certificate of deposit, or accepting a consumer loan application—were not unusual under the old setup, whereas routine activities such as paying bills and receiving deposits often required little or no waiting. With each employee now performing all the tasks, shorter waiting lines could be expected.

To support this new arrangement, the marketing department featured the concept in its publicity about products and services. Included with checking account statements was a promotional piece stating, "In our branches, there are no tellers." This document described the new process and announced that every employee could now perform all branch functions and consequently provide faster service.

## Learning Needs

At Level 2, learning needs fell into two categories. First, for each learning program, both skill acquisition and knowledge development needs were identified. Learning measurements included self-assessment, testing, and demonstrations, among others, and were connected to each specific program.

Second, it was necessary for employees to learn how the new program worked. As the program was introduced in meetings with employees, a simple measurement of learning was necessary to capture employee understanding of the following issues:

- How the program is being pursued
- What employees must do to succeed in the program
- How promotion decisions are made
- The timing of various stages of the program

These major learning needs were identified and connected specifically with the solution being implemented.

## Preference Needs

As the project was rolled out and the solution was developed, the preference needs were defined. The project had to be rolled out as soon as possible so that its effects could be translated into lower employee turnover. All the training programs must be in place and available to employees. The amount of time employees must spend away from their jobs for training was an issue, as was the managers' control over the timing of promotions. This process must move swiftly, or it would result in disappointment to employees who were eager to be trained and promoted. At the same time, the staffing and workload concerns had to be balanced so that the appropriate amount of time was devoted to training and skill building. More specifically, with the program's announcement, the desired employee reaction was defined. Project leaders wanted employees to view the program as challenging, motivational, rewarding, and fair and as a solid investment in their futures. These needs were easily translated into the solution design.

# Developing Objectives for Projects and Programs

Projects and programs are driven by objectives. These objectives will position the project or program for success if they represent the needs of the business and include clearly defined measures of achievement. A project may be aimed at implementing a solution that addresses a particular dilemma, problem, or opportunity. In other situations, the initial project is designed to develop a range of feasible solutions, with one specific solution selected prior to implementation. Regardless of the project or program, multiple levels of objectives are necessary. These levels follow the five-level data categorization scheme and define precisely what will occur as a project is implemented. They correspond to the levels of evaluation and the levels of needs presented in Figure 3-1.

## Reaction Objectives

For a project to be successful, the stakeholders immediately involved in the process must react favorably—or at least not negatively—to the project. Ideally, those directly involved should be satisfied with the project and see the value in it. This feedback must be obtained routinely during the project in order to make adjustments, keep the project on track, and redesign certain aspects as necessary. Unfortunately, for many projects, specific objectives at this level are not developed, nor are data collection mechanisms put in place to allow channels for feedback.

Developing reaction objectives should be straightforward and relatively easy. The objectives reflect the degree of immediate as well as long-term satisfaction and explore issues important to the success of the program. They also form the basis for evaluating the chain of impact, and they emphasize planned action, when this is feasible and needed. Typical issues addressed in the development of reaction objectives are relevance, usefulness, importance, appropriateness, rewards, and motivation.

## Learning Objectives

Every project or program involves at least one learning objective, and most involve more. With projects entailing major change, the learning component is quite important. In situations narrower in scope, such as the implementation of a new policy, the learning component is minor but still necessary. To ensure that the various stakeholders have learned what they need to know to make the project successful, learning objectives are developed. The following are examples of learning objectives:

- Identify the six features of the new ethics policy.
- Demonstrate the use of each software routine within the standard time.
- Score 75 or better on the new-product quiz.
- Explain the value of diversity in a work group.
- Successfully complete the leadership simulation.
- Know how to apply for housing assistance.

Objectives are critical to the measurement of learning because they communicate the expected outcomes from the learning component and define the competency or level of performance necessary to make project implementation successful. They provide a focus to allow participants to clearly identify what it is they must learn and do—sometimes with precision.

## Application and Implementation Objectives

The application and implementation objectives clearly define what is expected of the project or program and often the target level of performance. Application objectives are similar to learning objectives but relate to actual performance.

They provide specific milestones indicating when one part or all of the process has been implemented. Typical application objectives are as follows:

**When the project or program is implemented. . .**

- At least 99.1 percent of software users will be following the correct sequences after three weeks of use.
- Within one year, 10 percent of employees will submit documented suggestions for cutting costs.
- Ninety-five percent of high-potential employees will complete individual development plans within two years.
- Forty percent of the city's homeless population will apply for special housing within one year of program launch.
- Eighty percent of employees will use one or more of the three cost containment features of the health care plan.
- Fifty percent of conference attendees follow up with at least one contact from the conference.

Application objectives are critical because they describe the expected outcomes in the intermediate area—between the learning of new tasks and procedures and the delivery of the impact of this learning. Application and implementation objectives describe how things should be or the desired state of the workplace once the project solution has been implemented. They provide a basis for evaluating on-the-job changes and performance.

## Impact Objectives

Impact objectives indicate key business measures that should improve as the application and implementation objectives are achieved. The following are typical impact objectives:

- Grievances should be reduced from three per month to no more than two per month at the Golden Eagle tire plant.
- Tardiness at the Newbury foundry should decrease by 20 percent within the next calendar year.
- The average number of product defects should decrease from 214 to 153 per month at all Amalgamated Rubber extruding plants in the Midwest region.
- The company-wide job satisfaction index should rise by 2 percent during the next calendar year.

- There should be a 10 percent increase in Pharmaceuticals Inc. brand awareness among physicians during the next two years.
- The dropout rate for high school students in the Barett County system should decrease by 5 percent within three years.

Impact objectives are critical to measuring business performance because they define the ultimate expected outcome from the project. They describe the business unit performance that should result from the project. Above all, impact objectives emphasize achievement of the bottom-line results that key client groups expect and demand.

## ROI Objectives

The fifth level of objectives for projects or programs represents the acceptable return on investment (ROI), the monetary impact. Objectives at this level define the expected payoff from investing in the project. An ROI objective is typically expressed as an acceptable ROI percentage, which is expressed as annual monetary benefits minus cost, divided by the actual cost, and multiplied by one hundred. A 0 percent ROI indicates a break-even project. A 50 percent ROI indicates recapture of the project cost and an additional 50 percent "earnings" (50 cents for every dollar invested).

For some projects, such as the purchase of a new company, a new building, or major equipment, the ROI objective is large relative to the ROI of other expenditures. However, the calculation is the same for both. For many organizations, the ROI objective for a project or program is set slightly higher than the ROI expected from other "routine investments" because of the relative newness of applying the ROI concept to the types of projects or programs described in this book. For example, if the expected ROI from the purchase of a new company is 20 percent, the ROI from a new advertising project might be around 25 percent. The important point is that the ROI objective should be established up front and in discussions with the project sponsor. Excluding the ROI objective leaves stakeholders questioning the economic success of a project. If a project reaps a 25 percent ROI, is that successful? Not if the objective was a 50 percent ROI.

## Final Thoughts

This chapter outlines the beginning point in the ROI methodology, showing how a project can be structured from the outset, with detailed needs identified, ultimately leading to project objectives at five levels. This kind of detail ensures that the project is aligned with business needs and remains results focused throughout the process. Without this analysis, the project runs the risk of failing to deliver the value that it should, or of not being in alignment with one or more business objectives. The outputs of the analysis are objectives, which provide a focus for project designers, developers, and implementers, as well as participants and users who must make the project successful. Issues surrounding data collection are discussed in the next four chapters. Collecting reaction and perceived value data will be covered first.

# Chapter 4

# REACTION AND PERCEIVED VALUE

Once the initial analysis is completed and the project is positioned for success, implementation occurs. During implementation, feedback is gathered from participants involved in the project. Their reactions and value perceptions with regard to the project provide indications of its potential for success.

This chapter focuses on the measurement of reaction and perceived value. Collecting these data at the beginning of the project corresponds to the first operational phase of the ROI methodology. Participant feedback supplies powerful information to use in making adjustments and measuring success. This chapter outlines the most common approaches to collecting data and explores ways to use the information for maximum value.

## Why Measure Reaction and Perceived Value?

It is difficult to imagine a project being conducted without the collection of feedback from those involved in the project, or at least from the sponsor. Collecting reaction and perceived value data serves several purposes. Participant feedback is critical to understanding how well a project serves the customer and the potential of the project to meet the identified business needs.

### Customer Satisfaction

Reaction and perceived value are customer satisfaction measures for the project. Without sustained, favorable reactions, the project may not succeed. The individuals who have a direct role in the project are immediately affected by it and often have to change processes or procedures or make other job adjustments in response to the project's initiation. Participant feedback on preferences is critical to making adjustments and changes in the project as it unfolds.

The feedback of project supporters is also important because this group will be in a position to influence the project's continuation and development.

The sponsors, who approve budgets, allocate resources, and ultimately live with the project's success or failure, must be completely satisfied with the project—and their overall satisfaction must be verified early and often.

## Immediate Adjustments

A project can go astray quickly, and sometimes a project ends up being the wrong solution for the specified problem. A project can also be mismatched to the solution from the beginning, so getting feedback early in the process is necessary to allow for immediate adjustments. This can help prevent misunderstandings, miscommunications, and, more important, misappropriations. Gathering and using reaction data promptly can enable an improperly designed project to be altered before more serious problems arise.

## Predictive Capability

A relatively recent application of reaction data is predicting the success of a project using analytical techniques. The project participants are asked to estimate the effectiveness of the project's application and, in some cases, the resulting value of that application. The reaction data thus become a forecast (forecasting is described in detail in Chapter 12). Figure 4-1 shows the

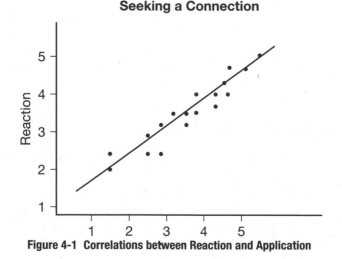

**Figure 4-1 Correlations between Reaction and Application**

correlation between reactive feedback and application data. Studies have been conducted to verify this correlation.

In this analysis, the reaction measures are taken as the project is introduced, and the success of the implementation is later judged using the same scale (e.g., a 1 to 5 rating). When significant positive correlations are present, reaction measures can have predictive capability. Some reaction measures shown to have predictive capability are

- The project is relevant to my job.
- The project is necessary.
- The project is important to my success.
- The project contains information that I intend to implement.
- I intend to implement the project.
- I would recommend that others pursue similar projects.

Measures such as these consistently lead to strong positive correlations and consequently represent more powerful feedback than typical measures of satisfaction with the project. Some organizations collect these or similar reaction measures for every project or program initiated.

## Important but Not Exclusive

Feedback data are critical to a project's success and should be collected for every project. Unfortunately, however, in some organizations, feedback alone has been used to measure project success. For example, in a financial services firm in Israel, the traditional method of measuring the effectiveness of the ethics program was to rely entirely on feedback data from employees, by asking them if the ethics policy was appropriate, fair, and necessary. Positive feedback is obviously critical to the policy's acceptance but is no guarantee the new policy will be successfully executed. As subsequent policy changes were made, executives became interested in the extent to which employees actually understood the policy (learning), the extent to which employees followed the policy in their work (application), and the effectiveness of the policy in reducing ethical violations and infractions (impact). Only when these additional measures were taken could the full scope of success be identified.

# Sources of Data

Possible sources of reaction and perceived value data concerning the success of a project can be grouped into distinct categories.

## Participants

The most widely used data source for project evaluation is the participants, those directly involved in the project. These "users" must take the skills and knowledge they acquired in the project or process and apply them on the job. They also may be asked to explain the potential impact of that application. Participants are a rich source of data for almost every aspect of a project. They are by far the most credible source of reaction and perceived value data.

## Participant Managers

Another key source of data are the individuals who directly supervise or lead the participants. They have a vested interest in the project and are often in a position to observe the participants as they attempt to apply the knowledge and skills acquired in the project. Consequently, they can report on the successes associated with the project as well as the difficulties and problems. Although managerial input is usually most valuable as a source of reaction and perceived value data, it is also useful for other levels of evaluation.

## Other Employees

When entire teams are involved in the implementation of the project, all employees can provide useful information about the perceived changes prompted by the project. Input from this group is pertinent only to issues directly related to their work. Although data from this group can be helpful and instructive, it is sometimes not elicited because of the potential for introducing inaccuracies to the feedback process. Data collection should be restricted to those team members capable of providing meaningful insight into the value of the project.

## Internal or External Customers

The individuals who serve as internal customers of the project are another source of reaction, perceived value, and other types of data. In some situations, internal or external customers provide input on perceived changes linked to the project. This source of data is more appropriate for projects directly affecting the customers. They report on how the project has influenced (or will influence) their work or the service they receive. Although this group may be somewhat limited in their knowledge of the scope of a project, their perceptions can be a source of valuable data that may indicate a direction for change in the project.

## Project Leaders and Team Members

The project leader and project team may also provide input on the success of the project. This input may be based on on-the-job observations during the course of the project and after its completion. Data from this source have limited utility because project leaders often have a vested interest in the outcome of the evaluation, and thus may lack objectivity.

## Sponsors and Senior Managers

One of the most useful data sources is the sponsor or client group, usually a senior management team. The perception of the sponsor, whether an individual or a group, is critical to project success. Sponsors can provide input on all types of issues and are usually available and willing to offer feedback. This is a preferred source for reaction data, since these data usually indicate what is necessary to make adjustments and to measure success.

## Records and Previous Studies

In some cases, reaction data can be compared with other data available within the organization. Frequently, routine data collection systems are available from which feedback data can be obtained systematically. Also, external benchmarking studies may present data from similar projects. When such sources are available and appropriate, they can be very helpful, although their credibility must be established. It must be ensured that the reaction measures from these sources are directly related to the project at hand.

# Areas of Feedback

In capturing reaction and perceived value data, it is important to focus on the content of the project, program, or initiative. Too often, feedback data reflect aesthetic issues that may not be relevant to the substance of the project. Table 4-1 distinguishes content and non-content issues explored in a reaction questionnaire from a marketing event for relationship managers. The traditional way to evaluate activities is to focus on non-content issues or

**Table 4-1  Content versus Non-Content Issues**

| Non-Content Issues | Content Issues |
| --- | --- |
| Demographics | Service |
| Facilities | Relevance of meeting theme |
| Location | Importance of topics |
| Transportation | Timing of meeting |
| Registration | Use of time |
| Logistics | Amount of new information |
| Hotel service | Perceived value |
| Media | Contacts made |
| Food | Planned use of material |
| Breaks and refreshments | Forecast of impact |
| Cocktail reception | Overall satisfaction |
| Gala party | |
| Closing dinner | |
| Opening keynote | |
| Quality of speakers | |
| Future needs | |
| Overall satisfaction | |

inputs. In the table, the column on the left represents areas important to the activity surrounding the marketing event, but contains nothing indicating results achieved from the event. The column on the right reflects a focus on content. This is not to suggest that the nature of the service, the atmosphere of the event, and the quality of the speakers are not important; it is assumed that these issues will be taken care of and addressed appropriately. A more important set of data, focused on results, incorporates detailed information about the perceived value of the meeting, the importance of the content, and the planned use of material or a forecast of the impact—indicators that successful results were achieved.

Many topics are critical targets for feedback. Feedback is needed in connection with almost every major issue, step, or process to make sure things are advancing properly. Stakeholders will provide reaction input as to the appropriateness of the project planning schedule and objectives, and the progress made with the planning tools. If the project is perceived as irrelevant or unnecessary to the participants, more than likely it will not succeed in the workplace. Support for the project—including resources—represents an important area of feedback.

Participants must be assured that the project has the necessary commitment. Issues important to project management and the organization sponsoring the project include project leadership, staffing levels, coordination, and communication. Also, it is important to collect feedback on how well the project team is working to address such issues as motivation, cooperation, and capability.

Finally, the perceived value of the project is often a critical parameter. Major funding decisions are made based on perceived value when stronger evidence of value is unavailable.

## Data Collection Timing

The timing of data collection centers on particular events connected with the project. As discussed previously, feedback during the early stages of implementation is critical. Ideally, this feedback validates the decision to go forward with the project and confirms that alignment with business needs exists. The noting of problems in the initial feedback means that adjustments can be made early in its implementation. In practice, however, many organizations omit this early feedback, waiting until significant parts of the project have been implemented, at which point feedback may be more meaningful.

For longer projects, concerns related to the timing of feedback may require data collection at multiple points in time. Measures can be taken at the beginning of the project and then at routine intervals once the project is under way.

## Data Collection Methods

A variety of methods can be used to collect reaction data. Instruments range from simple surveys to comprehensive interviews. The appropriate instrument depends on the type of data needed (quantitative vs. qualitative), the convenience of the method to potential respondents, the culture of the organization, and the cost of a particular instrument.

### Questionnaires and Surveys

The questionnaire or survey is the most common method of collecting and measuring reaction data. Questionnaires and surveys come in all sizes, ranging from short forms to detailed, multiple-page instruments. They can be used to obtain subjective data about participants' reactions as well as to document responses for future use in a projected ROI analysis. Proper design of questionnaires and surveys is important to ensure versatility.

Several basic types of questions are used. The dichotomous question (yes/no) and the numerical scale (e.g., 1 to 5) are typical reaction measurement formats. Essentially, the individual is indicating the extent of his or her agreement with a particular statement or is giving an opinion of varying conviction on an issue. Surveys are a type of questionnaire but focus on attitudinal elements. Surveys have many applications in the measurement of reaction and satisfaction for projects designed to improve work. Depending on the purpose of the evaluation, the questionnaire or survey may contain one or more question types. The key is to select the question or statement that is most appropriate for the information sought. However, open-ended questions can sometimes be used, particularly in asking about specific problem areas. Checklists, multiple-choice questions, and ranking scales are more appropriate for measuring learning and application, which are described in later chapters.

For most reaction evaluations, questionnaires and surveys are used. When a follow-up evaluation is planned, a wide range of issues will be covered in a detailed questionnaire. Asking for too much detail in either the reaction questionnaire or the follow-up questionnaire can reduce the response rate. The following actions can help maximize response rates:

- Provide advance communication regarding the need for data.
- Identify who will see the data.
- Describe the data integration process.
- Design the instrument for simplicity and ease of response.
- Use local management support, if feasible.
- If applicable, let the participants know they are part of the sample.
- Consider the use of incentives.
- Have an executive sign the introductory letter or memo.
- Issue at least two follow-up reminders.
- Send a copy of the results to the participants.
- Make sure the survey or questionnaire looks professional.
- Introduce the questionnaire or survey in the early stages of the project.
- Collect the data anonymously or confidentially.

## Interviews

Interviews, although not used as frequently as questionnaires to capture reaction data, may be conducted by the project team, the client team, or a third party to secure data that are difficult to obtain through written responses. Interviews can uncover success stories that may help to communicate early achievements of the project. Respondents may be reluctant to describe their experiences using a questionnaire but may volunteer the information to a skillful interviewer using probing techniques. The interview is versatile and is appropriate for soliciting reaction data as well as application and implementation data. A major disadvantage of the interview is that it consumes time, which increases the cost of data collection. It also requires interviewer preparation to ensure that the process is consistent. Careful consideration is necessary before an organization commits to using interviews to collect reaction and perceived value data, especially when a follow-up evaluation is planned.

## Focus Groups

Focus groups are particularly useful when in-depth feedback is needed. The focus group format involves a small-group discussion conducted by an experienced facilitator. It is designed to solicit qualitative judgments on a selected topic or issue. All group members are required to provide input, with individual input building on group input.

Compared with questionnaires, surveys, and interviews, the focus group approach has several advantages. The basic premise behind the use of focus groups is that when quality judgments are subjective, several individual judgments are better than one. The group process, where participants often motivate one another, is an effective method for generating and clarifying ideas and hypotheses. It is inexpensive and can be quickly planned and conducted. Its flexibility allows exploration of a project's unexpected outcomes or applications.

# Data Use

Unfortunately, reaction and perceived value data are often collected and then disregarded. Too many project evaluators use the information to feed their egos and then allow it to quietly disappear into their files, forgetting the original purpose behind its collection. In an effective evaluation, the information collected must be used to make adjustments or verify success; otherwise, the exercise is a waste of time.

Because this input is the principal measure supplied by key stakeholders, it provides an indication of their reaction to, and satisfaction with, the project. More important, these data provide evidence relating to the potential success of the project. Data collected at this level, Level 1, should be used to

- Identify the strengths and weaknesses of the project and make adjustments.
- Evaluate project team members.
- Evaluate the quality and content of planned improvements.
- Develop norms and standards.
- Link with follow-up data.
- Market future projects based on the positive reaction.

## Final Thoughts

This chapter discusses data collection at the first level of evaluation, reaction and perceived value. Measuring reaction and perceived value is a component of every study and is a critical factor in a project's success. The data are collected using a variety of techniques, although surveys and questionnaires are most often used because of their cost-effectiveness and convenience. The data are important in allowing immediate adjustments to be made to the project.

Level 1 data is important, but data's value to executives increases as the evaluation moves up the chain of impact. Data collection at the second level, learning, is discussed in the next chapter.

# Chapter 5

# LEARNING AND CONFIDENCE

Measuring learning is an important part of the evaluation process, especially when a project is intended to change behaviors or processes on the job. Participant knowledge of what to do and how to do it is critical to a project's success. This chapter focuses on simple, commonly used techniques for measuring learning and begins with a look at the reasons for measuring learning.

## Why Measure Learning and Confidence?

Several key principles illustrate the importance of measuring learning during the course of a project. Each of these in itself is sufficient to justify the measurement of learning; collectively, they provide an indication of the full range of benefits that result from measuring the changes in skills, knowledge, and other qualities that occur during a project.

### The Importance of Intellectual Capital

Intellectual capital has become an important concept as organizations have progressed from agricultural to industrial to knowledge-based systems. Intellectual capital is what the organization knows, and it can be classified in a variety of ways for measurement purposes. Figure 5-1 illustrates one categorization of intellectual capital, showing intellectual capital as a combination of human capital, renewable capital, structural capital, and relationship capital.[1] As projects are implemented, they focus on increasing one or more of these major elements of intellectual capital. For some organizations, intellectual capital translates directly into success, in the form of rewards by

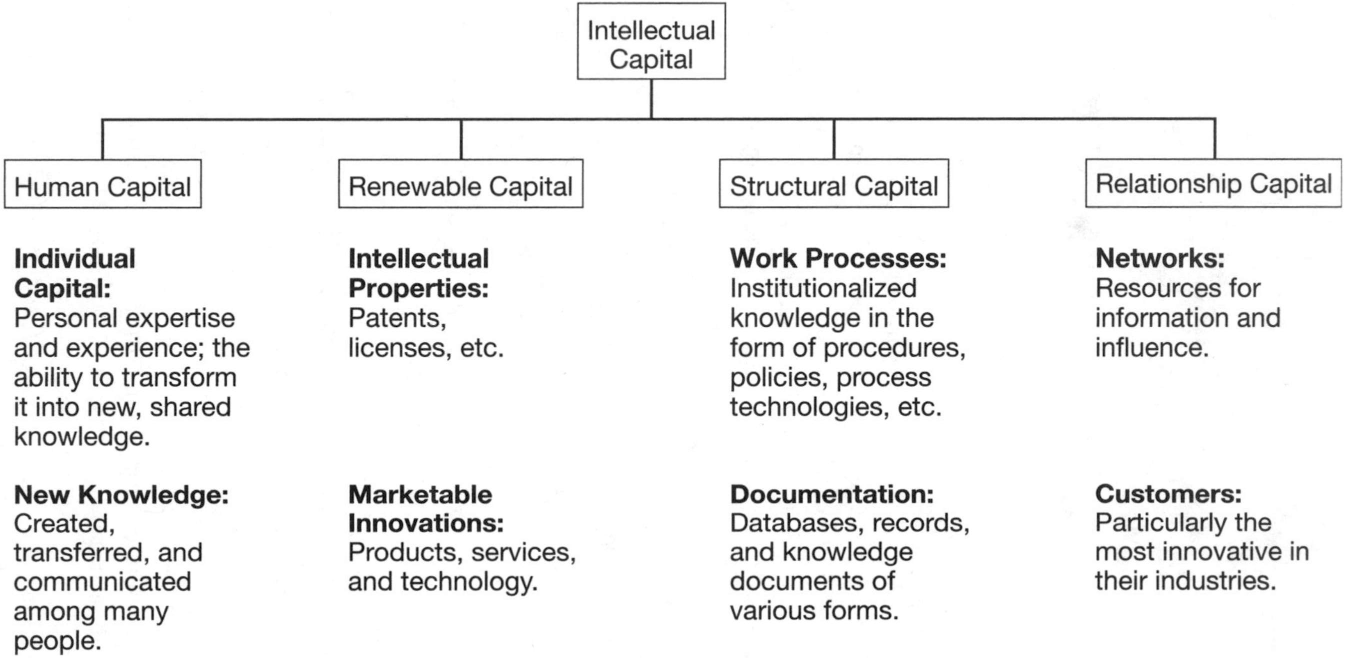

# Intellectual Capital

## Human Capital

**Individual Capital:** Personal expertise and experience; the ability to transform it into new, shared knowledge.

**New Knowledge:** Created, transferred, and communicated among many people.

## Renewable Capital

**Intellectual Properties:** Patents, licenses, etc.

**Marketable Innovations:** Products, services, and technology.

## Structural Capital

**Work Processes:** Institutionalized knowledge in the form of procedures, policies, process technologies, etc.

**Documentation:** Databases, records, and knowledge documents of various forms.

## Relationship Capital

**Networks:** Resources for information and influence.

**Customers:** Particularly the most innovative in their industries.

**Figure 5-1   Categories of Intellectual Capital**

the stock market. Up to 80 percent of the market value of some high-technology firms is attributed to intellectual capital. This demonstrates the value of measuring learning in projects aimed at improving intellectual capital.

## The Learning Organization

In the past two decades, organizations have experienced a rapid transformation of competitive global markets as a result of economic changes. Organizations must learn new ways to serve customers and use innovations and technology to enhance their efficiency, to restructure, to reorganize, and to execute their functions globally. In response to this need for a change in strategy, the concept of the learning organization evolved. This concept requires organizations to use learning proactively in an integrated way and to support growth for individuals, teams, and entire organizations. Peter Senge popularized the learning organization idea, suggesting that an organization capture, share, and use knowledge so that its members can work together to change how the organization responds to challenges.[2] Managers must question the old social constructs and practice new ways of thinking.

Learning must take place within and support the framework of teams and larger groups where individuals can work together to generate new knowledge. The process must be continuous, because a learning organization is a never-ending journey.[3]

With the new focus on creating learning organizations—where countless activities and processes are in place to promote continuous learning—measurement has become an even more important issue. How do we know if an organization has become a learning organization? How is such an organization measured? Can learning actually be measured on a large scale?

## The Compliance Issue

Organizations face an increasing number of regulations with which they must routinely comply. These regulations involve all aspects of business and are considered essential by governing bodies to protect customers, investors, and the environment. Employees must have a certain amount of knowledge about the regulations to maintain compliance. Consequently, an organization must measure the extent of employee learning and understanding with regard to regulations to ensure that compliance is not a problem.

Some projects are compliance driven. For example, one large banking organization had to implement a major project to ensure that its employees were all familiar with money laundering regulations. This project was precipitated by the bank's continuing failure to comply with the regulations. The problem appeared to be a lack of knowledge of the rules. When projects such as this are initiated, learning must be measured.

## The Use and Development of Competencies

The use of competencies and competency models has dramatically increased in recent years. In the struggle for a competitive advantage, many organizations have focused on people as the key to success. Competency models are used to ensure that employees do the right things, clarifying and articulating what is required for effective performance. Competency models help organizations align behavior and skills with the strategic direction of the company. A competency model describes a particular combination of knowledge, skills, and characteristics necessary to perform a role in an organization. Competencies are used as tools for recruiting, selecting, training, reviewing performance, and even removing individuals from the organization.[4] With the increased focus on competencies, measuring learning is a necessity.

## The Role of Learning in Projects

Although some projects involve new equipment, processes, and technology, the human factor remains critical to project success. Whether an organization is restructuring or adding new systems, employees must learn how to work in the new environment, and this requires the development of new knowledge and skills. Simple tasks and procedures do not automatically come with new processes. Instead, complex environments, procedures, and tools must be used in an intelligent way to reap the desired benefits for the organization. Employees must learn in different ways—not just in a formal classroom environment, but through technology-based learning and on-the-job practice. Team leaders and managers serve as coaches or mentors in some projects. In a few cases, learning coaches or on-the-job trainers are used in conjunction with a project to ensure that learning is transferred to the job and is implemented as planned.

Project team members and participants don't always fully understand what they must do. Although the chain of impact can be broken at any level, a common place for such a break is at Level 2, learning and confidence. Employees simply may not know what to do or how to do it properly. When the application and implementation does not go smoothly, project leaders can determine if a learning deficiency is the problem, and if so, they may be able to eliminate it. In other words, learning measurement is necessary to contribute to leaders' understanding of why employees are, or are not, performing the way they should.

## The Challenges and Benefits of Measuring Learning

Measuring learning involves major challenges that may inhibit a comprehensive approach to the process. However, besides being an essential part of the ROI methodology, this measurement provides many other benefits that help ensure a project's success.

### Challenges

The greatest challenge in measuring learning is to maintain objectivity without crossing ethical or legal lines while keeping costs low. A common method of measuring learning is testing, but this approach generates additional challenges.

The first challenge is the "enjoyment" factor. Few people enjoy being tested. Many are offended by it and feel that their professional prowess is being questioned. Some people are intimidated by tests, which bring back memories of their third-grade math teacher, red pen in hand.

Another challenge with tests is the legal and ethical repercussions of basing decisions involving employee status on test scores. Therefore, organizations use other techniques to measure learning, such as surveys, questionnaires, role plays, and simulations. The challenge with these methods, however, is the potential for inaccurate measures and the financial burden they impose. Consequently, there is a constant trade-off between additional resources and the accuracy of the learning measurement process.

### The Benefits of Measuring Learning

The benefits of measuring learning are reflected in the reasons for learning measurement described earlier. First, measurement at this level checks the progress of the project against the objectives. Objectives are critical to a project, and they should be established at each level. Fundamentally, the measurement of learning reveals the extent of knowledge and skill acquisition in relation to the project. This is a critical element, particularly for knowledge-based projects, new technology applications, and projects designed to build competencies.

In addition to assessing improvement in skills or at this level provides feedback to the individuals delivering the skills or knowledge so that adjustments can be made. If project participants are not learning, there may be a problem with the way the learning is being delivered. A learning measure can identify strengths and weaknesses in the method of project presentation or instruction and may point out flaws in the design or delivery. Thus, measuring learning can pinpoint mismatches among various aspects of a project and thereby lead to changes or improvement.

Another important benefit is that, in many cases, learning measures enhance participant performance. Verification and feedback concerning the knowledge and skills acquired can encourage participants to improve in certain areas. When employees excel, feedback motivates them to enhance their performance even further. In short, positive feedback on learning builds confidence and the desire to continue improving. Without such measurement, participants will never know their potential to perform.

Finally, measuring learning helps to maintain accountability. Because projects are aimed at making organizations better—whether a learning organization is being built, competencies are being improved, or systems and processes are being enhanced—learning is an important part of any project and its measurement is vital in confirming that improvement has in fact occurred.

## Measurement Issues

Several items affect the nature and scope of measurement at the learning level. These include project objectives, the measures themselves, and timing.

### Project Objectives

The starting point for any level of measurement is development of the project objectives. The measurement of learning builds on the learning objectives. Learning and development professionals are skilled in generating detailed learning objectives following the process described in Chapter 3. However, for projects where the focus is not necessarily on a learning activity— such as implementing a public policy program, initiating a new procedure, or constructing a new wellness and fitness center—the first step again is to ensure that objectives are in place.

Typically, the objectives of the project are broad and indicate only major skills or general knowledge areas that should be achieved as the project is implemented. These are sometimes called key project learning objectives. They can be broken down into subcomponents that provide more detail. This is necessary when a tremendous number of tasks, procedures, or new skills must be learned to make the project successful. For other projects, this level of detail might not be needed; identifying the major objectives and indicating what must be accomplished to meet each objective is often sufficient.

## Typical Measures

Measuring learning focuses on knowledge, skills, and attitudes as well as the individual's confidence in applying or implementing the project or process as desired. Typical measures collected at this level are

- Skills
- Knowledge
- Awareness
- Understanding
- Contacts
- Attitudes
- Capacity
- Readiness
- Confidence

Obviously, the more detailed the knowledge area, the greater the number of objectives. The concept of knowledge is quite general and often includes the assimilation of facts, figures, and ideas. Instead of knowledge, terms such as *awareness*, *understanding*, and *information* may be used to denote specific categories. Sometimes, perceptions or attitudes are changed based on what a participant has learned. For example, participants' perceptions about a diverse work group are often changed with the implementation of a major diversity program. In some cases, the issue is developing a reservoir of knowledge and related skills toward improving capability, capacity, or readiness. Networking is often part of a project, and developing contacts who may be valuable later is important. This may occur within or external to an organization. For example, within the organization, a project may include different functional parts of the organization, and an expected outcome from a learning perspective is knowing who to contact at particular times in the future. For projects that involve different organizations, such as a marketing event, new contacts that result from the event can be important and ultimately pay off in terms of efficiency and/or revenue growth.

## Timing

The timing of learning measurement can vary. In some situations, a preliminary measure is taken, generating a pretest to determine the extent to which the participants understand the specific objectives in the program. A pretest can be important for assessing the current skills and knowledge so that the learning of additional skills and knowledge can be planned more efficiently. This may prevent participants from being taught information they already know. In these situations, the use of a posttest to compare with the pretest is common. The posttest can be collected early in the project or as soon as the learning portion is completed. The pre- and posttesting should be conducted under the same or similar conditions using questions or other test items that are identical or very similar.

Assuming that no pretest is administered, the measurement of learning can occur at various times. If formal learning sessions connected with the project are offered, the measure is taken at the end of those sessions to ensure that participants are ready to apply their newly acquired knowledge. If a project has no formal learning sessions, measuring may occur at different intervals. For long-term projects, as skills and knowledge grow, routine assessment may be necessary to measure both the acquisition of additional skills and knowledge and retention of the previously acquired skills. The timing of measurement is balanced with the need to know the new information; this is offset by the cost of obtaining, analyzing, and responding to the data. In an ideal situation, the timing of measurement is part of the data collection plan, as presented in Chapter 2.

# Data Collection Methods

One of the most important considerations with regard to measuring learning is the specific way in which data are collected. Learning data can be collected using many different methods. The following list of instruments are just some of the data collection methods used:

- Questionnaires
- Performance tests
- Technology and task simulations
- Case studies
- Role-playing/skill practice
- Informal assessments

## Questionnaires and Surveys

Questionnaires and surveys were introduced in Chapter 4, with the focus on measuring reaction. Questionnaires are also used to collect data at Level 2. These questionnaires include two-way or true/false questions, where participants are provided with statements and must either agree or disagree. Rating scales are common in surveys gathering learning data. Multiple-choice is probably the most common question type, where participants are asked to choose one or more items from a series of alternative answers. This has the advantage of ease of scoring and is relatively objective. Matching exercises are also useful, where participants match particular items on a choice basis. Short-answer questions can be easy to develop but difficult to score. Essay questions are less likely to be used because they are difficult to score and rely, to some degree, on the subjective opinion of the scorer rather than the participant. Developing questions in an attempt to measure learning can be fairly simple. The key is to ensure that the questions asked are relevant to the knowledge, skills, or information presented.

## Performance Tests

Performance testing allows participants and users to exhibit the skills (and occasionally knowledge or attitudes) that have been learned in a project. A skill can be manual, verbal, or analytical, or a combination of the three. Performance testing is used frequently in task-related projects; here the participants are allowed to demonstrate what they have learned and to show how they would use the skill on the job. In other situations, performance testing may involve skill practice or role-playing (e.g., participants are asked to demonstrate discussion or problem-solving skills that they have acquired).

In one situation, computer systems engineers were participating in a system reengineering project. As part of the project, participants were given the assignment of designing and testing a basic system. A project team manager observed participants as they checked out the system; then the manager carefully completed the same design and compared his results with those of the participants. These comparisons and the performance of the designs provided an evaluation of the project and represented an adequate reflection of the skills learned in the project.

## Technology and Task Simulations

Another technique for measuring learning is simulation. This method involves the construction and application of a procedure or task that simulates or models the work involved in the project or program. The simulation is designed to represent, as closely as possible, the actual job situation. Participants try out the simulated activity and their performance is evaluated based on how well they accomplish the task. Simulations offer several advantages. They permit a job or part of a job to be reproduced in a manner almost identical to the real setting. Through careful planning and design, the simulation can have all the central characteristics of the real situation. Even complex jobs, such as that of the manager, can be simulated adequately.

Although the initial development can be expensive, simulations can be cost-effective in the long run, particularly for large projects or situations where a project may be repeated. Another advantage of using simulations is safety. Safety considerations for many jobs require participants to be trained in simulated conditions. For example, emergency medical technicians risk injury and even death if they do not learn the needed techniques prior to encountering a real-life emergency.

Although a variety of simulation techniques are used to evaluate learning, the two most common are technology and task simulation. A technology simulation uses a combination of electronic and mechanical devices to reproduce real-life situations. These simulations are used in conjunction with programs to develop operational and diagnostic skills. Expensive examples are simulated "patients" or a simulation of a nuclear power plant operator. Other, less expensive devices have been developed to simulate equipment operation.

A task simulation involves a participant's performance in a simulated task. For example, a customer service associate must demonstrate the task of creating a new account. This task simulation serves as the evaluation.

## Case Studies

A perhaps less effective but still popular technique of measuring learning is the case study. A case study presents a detailed description of a problem and usually contains a list of several questions posed to the participant. The participant is asked to analyze the case and determine the best course of action. The problem should reflect conditions in the real world and in the content of the project.

The difficulty in using a case study lies in objectively evaluating the participant's performance. Many possible courses of action are available, making an objective, measurable performance rating of successful knowledge and understanding difficult.

## Role-Playing and Skill Practice

Role plays, sometimes referred to as skill practice, require participants to practice a newly learned skill as they are observed by others. Participants are assigned roles and given specific instructions, which sometimes include an ultimate course of action. The participant then practices the skill with other individuals to accomplish the desired objectives. This exercise is intended to simulate real-world conditions to the greatest extent possible. Difficulty sometimes arises when other participants make the practice unrealistic by not reacting the way individuals would in an actual situation. To help overcome this obstacle, trained role players (the actual characters portrayed in the role play) may be used in all roles except that of the participant. For example, some pharmaceutical companies use real physicians when teaching their salespeople to call on physicians to sell new drugs. This requires additional costs but provides a more objective evaluation of a participant's knowledge.

## Informal Assessments

Many projects include activities, exercises, or problems that must be explored, developed, or solved. Some of theses are constructed in the form of interactive exercises, while others require individual problem-solving skills. When these tools are integrated into the learning activity, they can be effective in gathering learning data.

A commonly used informal method is participant self-assessment. Participants are provided an opportunity to assess their acquisition of skills and knowledge. In some situations, a project leader or a facilitator provides an assessment of the learning that has taken place. Although this approach is subjective, it may be appropriate when project leaders or facilitators work closely with participants.

In many projects, it is sufficient to allow an informal check of learning to provide some assurance that participants have acquired the skills and knowledge needed to implement the project, or that the requisite changes in attitude have occurred. The appropriateness of this approach may depend on other levels of evaluation that are being pursued. For example, if a Level 3 (application and implementation) evaluation is planned, conducting a comprehensive Level 2 evaluation might not be as critical.

An informal assessment of learning is usually sufficient. Moreover, if resources are scarce, a comprehensive evaluation at all levels becomes quite expensive. Informal assessments provide an alternative approach to measuring learning when inexpensive, low-key measurements are all that is needed.

## Administrative Issues

Several administrative issues must be addressed in measuring learning. Each is briefly discussed next and should be part of the overall plan for administering learning measurement.

### Reliability and Validity

Two important issues with regard to test design are validity and reliability. Validity is the extent to which an instrument measures what it is designed to measure. Reliability is the extent to which an instrument is stable or consistent over time. In essence, any instrument used to collect data should be both valid (measure what it should measure) and reliable (consistent over time). An instrument is reliable if the same data were collected at different times, with nothing intervening to cause the respondent to change his or her knowledge, and the response is the same. Significant deviations indicate that an instrument is unreliable. Ideally, an instrument should be both reliable and valid. It is not possible for an instrument to be valid if it is not reliable. These two criteria become important when a human resource action (job status change) is taken as a result of a person failing a learning measurement or a specific test. For example, if an individual is promoted, denied promotion, provided an increase in pay, or assigned a job because of his or her performance on the test, the instrument must be defensible. In the vast majority of project work, however, the consequences of not passing the test will not be so severe. The concepts of validity and reliability and how to check for adequate levels of the two is beyond the scope of this book. Other sources are available to provide detail.[5]

### Consistency

Tests, exercises, and assessments for measuring learning must be administered consistently from one group to another to effectively measure and compare learning between groups. Consistency refers to the time required to respond, the actual learning conditions in which the participants complete the process, the resources available to them, and the amount of assistance from other members of the group. These concerns can easily be addressed in the instructions.

When formal testing is used, participants should be monitored as they complete the test. This ensures that individuals work independently and also that someone is there to provide assistance or answer questions as needed. This may not be an issue in all situations, but it needs to be addressed in the evaluation plan.

## Pilot Testing

Pilot testing an instrument with a small group to ensure that the instrument is both valid and reliable is advisable. A pilot test provides an opportunity to resolve any confusion that might exist about the instructions, questions, and statements. When a pilot test is taken, it should be timed to see how long individuals take to complete it. Also, the individuals taking the pilot test should provide input regarding alternative ways to ask the questions, the flow of information, and any other suggestions for improvement. At a minimum, a test should be piloted for content. All too often, a test or survey is administered that does not cover the content presented that supports implementation.

## Scoring and Reporting

Scoring instructions need to be developed for the measurement process so that the person evaluating the responses will be objective and consistent in scoring. Ideally, the potential for bias from the individual scoring the instrument should be completely eliminated by providing proper scoring instructions and other information necessary to guarantee an objective evaluation.

In some situations, the participants are provided with the results immediately, particularly with self-scoring tests or with group-based scoring mechanisms. In other situations, the results may not be known until later. In these situations, a method for providing data on scores should be built into the evaluation plan unless it has been predetermined that participants are not to know the scores. The worst-case scenario is to promise participants test scores and then deliver them late or not at all.

## Confronting Test Failure

Test failure may not be an issue, particularly if the data are collected informally through a self-assessment process. However, when more rigorous and formal methods are used and individuals do not demonstrate the required competency to pass the test, some consideration must be given to confronting these failures. An important principle is to ensure that the test and the testing procedures are defensible. As described earlier, a test must be both reliable and valid, and the cutoff score for passing must be defensible. Written guidelines should be developed to address these issues, and participants should know them in advance. The outcomes and consequences should be discussed with the individuals. A retest may be allowed, if appropriate, as long as all individuals are treated consistently.

## Using Learning Data

Data must be used to add value and improve processes. Among the appropriate uses of learning data are the following:

- Provide individual feedback to build confidence.
- Validate that learning has been acquired.
- Provide additional support to ensure successful implementation.
- Evaluate project leaders/facilitators.
- Build a database for project comparisons.
- Improve the project, program, or process.

## Final Thoughts

This chapter discusses some of the key issues involved in measuring learning—an important ingredient in project success. Even if it is accomplished informally, learning must be assessed to determine the extent to which the participants in a project learn new skills, techniques, processes, tools, and procedures. By measuring learning, facilitators and project leaders can ascertain the degree to which participants are capable of successfully executing the project plan. Measuring learning provides an opportunity to make adjustments quickly so that improvements can be made or additional interventions can be introduced to facilitate project success. While learning measures indicate potential success with implementation, a better measure—at Level 3, application and implementation—is covered in the next chapter.

# Chapter 6

# APPLICATION AND IMPLEMENTATION

Many projects fail because of breakdowns in implementation. Project team members and participants just don't do what they should, when they should, at the frequency they should. Measuring application and implementation is critical to understanding the success of project implementation. Without successful implementation, positive business impact will not occur—and no positive return will be achieved.

This chapter explores the most common ways to evaluate the application and implementation of projects, processes, and programs. The possibilities vary from the use of questionnaires to observation, and include such methods as action planning. In addition to describing the techniques to evaluate implementation, this chapter addresses the challenges and benefits of each technique.

## Why Measure Application and Implementation?

Measuring application and implementation is absolutely necessary. For some projects, it is the most critical data set because it provides an understanding of the degree to which successful project implementation occurs, and of the barriers and enablers that influence success.

### Information Value

As briefly discussed in Chapter 2, the value of information increases as progress is made through the chain of impact, from reaction (Level 1) to ROI (Level 5). Thus, information concerning application and implementation (Level 3) is more valuable to the client than are reaction and learning data. This is not to discount the importance of the first two levels, but to emphasize the importance of moving up the chain of impact. Measuring the extent to which a project is implemented provides critical data about its success, and about factors that can contribute to greater success as the project is fully implemented.

The Level 1 and Level 2 measures occur during a project's early stages, when more attention and focus are placed on the participants' direct involvement in the project. Measuring application and implementation occurs after the project has been implemented and captures the success of moving the project forward through participants' on-the-job use of knowledge about the project. Essentially, this measure reflects the degree to which the project is implemented by those who are charged with its success. This is the first step in transitioning to a new state, behavior, or process. Understanding the success of the transition requires measuring application and implementation.

## Project Focus

Because many projects and programs focus directly on implementation and application or new behaviors and processes, a project sponsor often speaks in these terms and has concerns about these measures of success. The sponsor of a major project designed to transform an organization will be greatly concerned with implementation and application, and will want to know the extent to which key stakeholders adjust to and implement the desired new behaviors, processes, and procedures.

## Problems and Opportunities

If the chain of impact breaks at this level, little or no corresponding impact data will be available. Without impact there is no ROI. This breakdown most often occurs because participants in the project encounter barriers, inhibitors, and obstacles (covered later) that deter implementation. A dilemma arises when reactions to the project are favorable and participants learn what is intended, but they fail to overcome the barriers and don't manage to accomplish what is necessary.

When a project goes astray, the first question usually asked is, "What happened?" More importantly, when a project appears to add no value, the first question should be, "What can we do to change its direction?" In either scenario, it is important to identify the barriers to success, the problems in implementation, and the obstacles to application. At Level 3, measuring implementation and application, these problems are addressed, identified, and examined. In many cases, the stakeholders directly involved in the process can provide important recommendations for making changes or using a different approach in the future.

When a project is successful, the obvious question is, "How can we repeat this or improve it in the future?" The answer to this question is also found at Level 3. Identifying the factors that contribute directly to the success of the project is critical. Those same items can be used to replicate the process and produce enhanced results in the future. When key stakeholders identify those issues, they make the project successful and provide an important case history of what is necessary for success.

## Reward Effectiveness

Measuring application and implementation allows the sponsor and project team to reward those who do the best job of applying the processes and implementing the project. Measures taken at this level provide clear evidence of success and achievement, and provide a basis for performance reviews. Rewards often have a reinforcing value, helping to keep employees on track and communicating a strong message for future improvement.

# Challenges

Collecting application and implementation data brings into focus key challenges that must be addressed for success at this level. These challenges often inhibit an otherwise successful evaluation.

## Linking with Learning

Application data should be linked closely with the learning data discussed in the previous chapter. Essentially, project leaders need to know what has been accomplished, what has been done differently, and what activities have been implemented, based on what the individuals learned to do. This level measures the extent to which participants accurately took what they learned and applied it to their jobs.

## Building Data Collection into the Project

Application data are collected after the project's implementation. Because of the time lag between project implementation and data collection, it is difficult to secure a high quality and quantity of data. Consequently, one of the most effective ways to ensure that data are collected is to build data collection into the project from the beginning. Data collection tools positioned as application tools must be built in as part of the implementation. By analogy, consider that many software applications contain overlay software that shows a user performance profile. Essentially, the software tracks the user invisibly, capturing the steps, pace, and difficulties encountered while using the software. When the process is complete, a credible data set has been captured, simply because project leaders built it into the process at the beginning.

## Ensuring a Sufficient Amount of Data

Whether collecting data by questionnaire or through action plans, interviews, or focus groups, poor response rates are a problem in most organizations. Having individuals participate in the data collection process is a challenge. To ensure that adequate amounts of high-quality data are available, a serious effort is needed to improve response rates.

Because many projects are planned on the basis of the ROI methodology, it is expected that sponsors will collect impact data, monetary values, and the project's actual ROI. This need to "show the money" sometimes results in less emphasis being placed on measuring application and implementation. In many cases, it may be omitted or slighted in the analysis. But it is through focused effort on process and behavior change that business impact will occur. Therefore, emphasis must be placed on gathering data that deal with application and implementation. As with General Electric's workout processes, although added value may have been the goal, attention was placed on changing processes, procedures, and tasks, and on removing barriers. Doing things differently can result in substantial benefits, but knowing the degree to which things are done differently is essential to guaranteeing those benefits.

## Addressing Application Needs at the Outset

During the needs assessment (detailed in Chapter 3) the question is asked, "What is being done on the job, or not being done, that's inhibiting the business measure?" When this question is answered adequately, a connection is made between the solution and the business measure. When this issue is addressed, the activities or behaviors that need to change are identified, serving as the basis of the data collection. The bottom line is that too many evaluations focus on either impact measures, which define the business measure to collect, or on learning, which uncovers what people do not know. More focus is needed at Level 3, which involves the tasks, processes, procedures, and behaviors that need to be in place for successful implementation on the job.

# Measurement Issues

When measuring the application and implementation of projects and programs, several key issues should be addressed, which are largely similar to those encountered when measuring reaction and learning. (A few issues may differ slightly because of the later time frame for collecting this type of data.)

## Methods

A variety of methods are available when collecting data at Level 3. These include traditional surveys and questionnaires and methods based on observation, interviews, and focus groups. Other powerful methods include action planning, in which individuals plan their parts of the implementation, and follow-up sessions. Data collection methods are described in more detail later in this chapter.

## Objectives

As with the other levels, the starting point for data collection is the objectives set for project application and implementation. Without clear objectives, collecting data would be difficult. Objectives define what activity is expected. (Chapter 3 discusses the basic principles for developing these objectives.)

## Areas of Coverage

To a certain extent, the areas of coverage for this process parallel the areas identified in Chapter 5. The later time frame for data collection changes the measurement to a post-project measure rather than a predictive measure. The key point is that this level focuses on activity or action, not on the ability to act (Level 2) and not on the consequences (Level 4). The sheer number

### Table 6-1 Examples of Coverage Areas for Application

| Action | Explanation | Example |
|---|---|---|
| Increase | Increasing a particular activity or action | Increase the frequency of use of a particular skill |
| Decrease | Decreasing a particular activity or action | Decrease the number of times a particular process must be checked |
| Eliminate | Stopping a particular task or activity | Eliminate the formal follow-up meeting, and replace it with a virtual meeting |
| Maintain | Keeping the same level of activity for a particular process | Continue to monitor the process with the same schedule previously used |
| Create | Designing or implementing a new procedure, process, or activity | Create a procedure for resolving the differences between two divisions |
| Use | Using a particular process, procedure, skill, or activity | Use the new skill in situations for which it was designed |
| Perform | Carrying out a particular task, process, or procedure | Conduct a post-audit review at the end of each activity |
| Participate | Becoming involved in various activities, projects, or programs | Submit a suggestion for reducing costs |
| Enroll | Signing up for a particular process, program, or project | Enroll in a career advancement program |
| Respond | Reacting to groups, individuals, or systems | Respond to customer inquiries within 15 minutes |
| Network | Facilitating relationships with others who are involved in or have been affected by the project | Continue networking with contacts on (at minimum) a quarterly basis |

of activities to measure can be mind-boggling. Table 6-1 shows examples of coverage areas for application, which will vary from project to project.

## Data Sources

The sources of data mirror those identified in Chapter 4. Essentially, all key stakeholders are potential sources of data. Perhaps the most important sources of data are the users of the solutions, those directly involved in the application and implementation of the project or program. Good sources may also be the project team or team leaders charged with the implementation. In some cases, the source may be the organizational records or system.

## Timing

The timing of data collection can vary significantly. Because this is a follow-up after the project launch, the key issue is determining the best time for a post-implementation evaluation. The challenge is to analyze the nature and scope of the application and implementation, and to determine the earliest time that a trend and pattern will evolve. This occurs when the application of skills becomes routine and the implementation is making significant progress. This is a judgment call. Going in as early as possible is important so that potential adjustments can still be made. At the same time, leaders must wait long enough so that behavior changes are allowed to occur and so that the implementation can be observed and measured. In projects spanning a considerable length of time, several measures may be taken at three- to six-month intervals. Using effective measures at well-timed intervals will provide successive input on implementation progress, and clearly show the extent of improvement.

Convenience and constraints also influence the timing of data collection. If the participants are conveniently meeting to observe a milestone or special event, this would be an excellent opportunity to collect data. Sometimes, constraints are placed on data collection. Consider, for example, the time constraint that sponsors may impose. If they are anxious to have the data to make project decisions, they may request the data collection moved to an earlier time than ideal.

## Responsibilities

Measuring application and implementation involves the responsibility and work of others. With data collection occurring later than in Levels 1 and 2, an important issue may surface in terms of who is responsible for this follow-up. Many possibilities exist, ranging from project staff and sponsors to an external, independent consultant. This matter should be addressed in the planning stages so that no misunderstanding arises as to the distribution of responsibilities. More importantly, those who are responsible should fully understand the nature and scope of their accountabilities and what is needed to collect the data.

## Data Collection Methods

Some of the techniques previously mentioned that are available to collect application and implementation data are easy to administer and provide quality data. Other techniques are more robust, providing greater detail about success but raising more challenges in administration.

## Using Questionnaires to Measure Application and Implementation

Questionnaires have become a mainstream data collection tool for measuring application and implementation because of their flexibility, low cost, and ease of administration. The discussion in Chapter 4 about questionnaires designed to measure reaction and perceived value applies equally to questionnaires developed to measure application and implementation. One of the most difficult tasks is determining the specific issues to address in a follow-up questionnaire. Figure 6-1 presents content items necessary for capturing application, implementation, and impact information (Level 3 and Level 4 data).

☐ Progress with objectives
☐ Action plan implementation
☐ Relevance/importance
☐ Perception of value
☐ Use of materials
☐ Knowledge/skill enhancement
☐ Skills used
☐ Changes with work/actions
☐ Improvement/accomplishments
☐ Define Measure
☐ Provide the Change
☐ Unit Value
☐ Basis
☐ Total Impact
☐ List Other Factors
☐ Improvement linked with project
☐ Confidence Estimate

Optional unless business impact and ROI analysis are pursued

☐ Linkage with output measures
☐ Other benefits
☐ Barriers
☐ Enablers
☐ Management support
☐ Other solutions
☐ Recommendations for other audiences/participants
☐ Suggestions for improvement
☐ Other comments

**Figure 6-1 Questionnaire Content Checklist**

## Using Interviews, Focus Groups, and Observation

Interviews and focus groups can be used during implementation or on a follow-up basis to collect data on implementation and application. However, the steps needed to design and administer these instruments apply to Levels 1 and 2 and will not be presented here. Other resources cover this area quite well.[1]

For this level of data collection, observing participants on the job and recording any changes in behavior and specific actions taken is an often used method. While observation is also used in collecting learning data, a fundamental difference is that participants do not necessarily know they are being observed when observation is used to collect application data. Participant observation is often used in sales and sales support projects. The observer may be a member of the project staff, the participant's manager, a member of a peer group, or an external resource such as a mystery shopper. The most common observer, and probably the most practical one, is a member of the project staff. Technology also lends itself as a tool to assist with observations. Recorders, video cameras, and computers play an important roll in capturing application data.

## Using Action Plans

In some cases, follow-up assignments can be used to develop implementation and application data. A typical follow-up assignment requires the participant to meet a goal or complete a task or project by a set date. A summary of the results of the completed assignment provides further evidence of the project's success.

The action plan is the most common type of follow-up assignment. With this approach, participants are required to develop action plans as part of the project. Action plans contain the detailed steps necessary to accomplish specific objectives related to the project. The process is one of the most effective ways to enhance project support and build the sense of ownership needed for successful project application and implementation.

The action plan is typically prepared on a printed form that shows what is to be done by whom, and by what date the objectives should be accomplished. The action plan approach is a straightforward, easy-to-use method for determining how participants will change their behaviors on the job and achieve success with project implementation. The approach produces data that answers questions such as:

- What on-the-job improvements have been realized since the project was implemented?
- Are the improvements linked to the project?
- What may have prevented participants from accomplishing specific action items?

**Table 6-2  Action Planning Checklist**

---

- Communicate the action plan requirement early
- Describe the action planning process at the beginning of the project
- Teach the action planning process
- Allow time to develop the plan
- Secure the project leader's approval of the action plan
- Require participants to assign a monetary value to each improvement*
- Ask participants to isolate the effects of the project*
- Ask participants to provide a confidence estimate, when appropriate*
- Require action plans to be presented to the group (when possible)
- Explain the follow-up mechanism
- Collect action plans at the predetermined follow-up time
- Summarize the data

---

*Optional for impact analysis

Collectively, these data can be used to assess the success of project implementation and to make decisions regarding modification.

The action plan process can be an integral part of project implementation and is not necessarily considered an add-on or optional activity. To gain maximum effectiveness from the evaluation data collected from action plans, attempt to implement the steps listed in Table 6-2.

## Conducting Follow-up Sessions

A final way to collect application and implementation data is the follow-up session. A follow-up session is an intended regrouping of the project team to assess the project status while continuing to move the project forward. Follow-up sessions provide the project team with a forum for discussing the effectiveness of the project, and they are also ideal for discussing application barriers and developing strategies to overcome them.

# Barriers to Application

One of the important reasons for collecting application and implementation data is to uncover barriers and enablers. Although both groups are important, barriers can kill a project. The barriers must be identified and actions must be taken to minimize, remove, or go around them. Barriers are a serious problem that exists in every project. When they can be removed or minimized, the project can be implemented. When barriers are identified, they become important reference points for change and improvement. Typical barriers that will stifle the success of projects include

- My immediate manager does not support the project.
- We have no opportunity to use the project skills, knowledge, or information.
- Technology was not available for the project.
- Resources are not available to implement the project.
- The project is not appropriate for our work unit.
- Another project got in the way.
- The culture in our work group does not support the project.
- We have no time to implement the project.
- My job changed and this no longer applies.
- We didn't see a need to implement the project.

The important point is to identify any barriers and to use the data in meaningful ways to make the barriers less of a problem.

## Application Data Use

Data become meaningless if they are not used properly. As we move up the chain of impact, the data become more valuable in the minds of sponsors, key executives, and others who have a strong interest in the project. Although data can be used in dozens of ways, the following are the principal uses for data after they are collected:

- To report and review results with various stakeholders
- To adjust project design and implementation
- To identify and remove barriers
- To identify and enhance enablers
- To recognize individuals who have contributed to project success
- To reinforce in current and future project participants the value of desired actions
- To improve management support for projects
- To market future projects

## Final Thoughts

Measuring application and implementation is critical in determining the success of a project or program. This essential measure not only determines the success achieved, but also identifies areas where improvement is needed and where success can be replicated in the future. This chapter presents a variety of techniques to collect application data, ranging from observation to use of questionnaires and action plans. The method chosen must match the scope of the project. Understanding success with application is important in providing evidence that business needs should be met, but it is only through measurement at Level 4, impact and consequences, that a direct link between the project and business impact can be made.

## Chapter 7

# IMPACT AND CONSEQUENCES

Most sponsors regard business impact data as the most important data type because of its connection to business success. For many projects, poor performance in business measures (the business need) is what would have initiated the project. Impact evaluation data close the loop by showing a project's success in meeting the business needs. This chapter examines a variety of business impact measures and the specific processes needed to collect the measures within a project, but first it addresses the reasons why impact data are measured.

## Why Measure Business Impact?

Several rationales support the collection of business impact data related to a project.

### Higher-Level Data

Following the assumption that higher-level data create more value for key stakeholders, business impact measures offer more valuable data. Impact data are the consequence of the application and implementation of a project. They represent the bottom-line measures positively influenced when a project is successful. For some stakeholders, these are the most valuable data.

The chain of impact can be broken at Level 4, and it is in many projects. If the project does not drive business impact data, then the corresponding results may be less than satisfactory. In extreme cases, the project can meet with success at the lower levels but fail at Level 4. Participants may react positively to the program; may learn successfully to implement the project; and at Level 3 they may follow the correct implementation steps or use the skills needed to implement the project. However, when the business impact measure (which is anticipated to be influenced by the project) does not change, the project does not add value. What could cause this? There are two possibilities. First, the business alignment for the project may not have been completed properly, which would keep it from being the right solution. Although the project may have been implemented, it has driven activity and not results. The second possibility is that other factors are driving the business measure. Although the project could be connected to the measure, other influences may be affecting the business measure in a direction opposite than desired by project planners. So it may appear at first glance that the project has no value, but in reality it could. This brings into focus the importance of isolating the effects of a project. The business data may be disappointing, but they would be even more disappointing without the project. The important process of isolating the effects of the project is presented in Chapter 8.

## A Business Driver for Projects

For most projects, business impact data represent the initial drivers for the project. The problem of deteriorating (or poorer than expected) performance or the opportunity for improvement of a business measure usually leads to a project. If the business needs defined by business measures are the drivers for a project, then the key measure for evaluating the project is the business measure. The extent to which measures have changed is the principal determinant of project success.

## "The Money" for Sponsors

From the perspective of the sponsor, business impact data reflect key payoff measures. These are the measures often desired by the sponsor and the ones that the sponsor wants to see changed or improved. They often represent hard, indisputable facts that reflect performance that is critical to the business and operating unit level of the organization. Business impact leads to "the money"—to the actual return on investment in the project. Without credible business impact data linked directly to the project, it would be difficult, if not impossible, to establish a credible monetary value for the project. This makes this level of data collection one of the most critical.

## Easy to Measure

One unique feature of business impact data is that they are often easy to measure. Hard and soft data measures at this level often reflect key measures that are plentiful throughout an organization. It is not unusual for an organization to have hundreds or even thousands of measures reflecting specific business impact items. The challenge is to connect the objectives of the project to the appropriate business measures. This is more easily accomplished at the beginning of the project.

# Collecting Effective Impact Measures

## Data Categories

Chapter 3 defined four data categories (hard, soft, tangible, and intangible). In addition to being classified as hard or soft and tangible or intangible, data can be categorized at several different levels, as shown in Figure 7-1. The figure illustrates that some data are considered strategic and are linked to the corporate level of an organization. Other data are more operational, and are linked to the business unit level. Still others are considered tactical in nature and scope, and are used at the operating level of an organization.

Examples of data categorized at the strategic level include financial, people-oriented, and internal versus external data. At the business unit level, classifications—such as output, quality, cost, time, job satisfaction, and customer satisfaction—are critical categories. At the tactical level, the categories are greater in number and include: productivity, efficiency, cost control, quality, time, attitudes, and individual and team performance. The importance is not in the classification of data itself but in the awareness of the vast array of data available. Regardless of their categories, these data are consequence measures (Level 4) of project success. The challenge is to find the data items connected directly to the project.

## Metric Fundamentals

When determining the type of measures to use, reviewing metric fundamentals can be helpful. The first important issue is identifying what makes an effective measure. Table 7-1 shows some of the criteria of an effective measure. These are issues that should be explored when examining any type of measure.

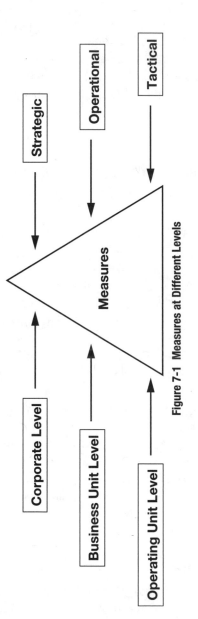

Figure 7-1 Measures at Different Levels

### Table 7-1 Criteria for Effective Measures

| Criteria: Effective Measures Are | Definition: The Extent to Which a Measure... |
| --- | --- |
| Important | Connects to strategically important business objectives rather than to what is easy to measure |
| Complete | Adequately tracks the entire phenomenon rather than only part of the phenomenon |
| Timely | Tracks at the right time rather than being held to an arbitrary date |
| Visible | Is visible, public, openly known, and tracked by those affected by it, rather than being collected privately for management's eyes only |
| Controllable | Tracks outcomes created by those affected by it who have a clear line of sight from the measure to results |
| Cost-effective | Is efficient to track using existing data or data that are easy to monitor without requiring new procedures |
| Interpretable | Creates data that are easy to make sense of and that translate into employee action |
| Simplicity | Simple to understand from each stakeholder's perspective |
| Specific | Is clearly defined so that people quickly understand and relate to the measure |
| Collectible | Can be collected with no more effort than is proportional to the measure's usefulness |
| Team-based | Will have value in the judgment of a team of individuals, not in the judgment of just one individual |
| Credible | Provides information that is valid and credible in the eyes of management |

Source: Adapted from Kerr, Steve, "On the Folly of Rewarding A, While Hoping for B," *Academy of Management Journal*, vol. 18 (1995): 769–783; and Andrew Mayo, *Measuring Human Capital*. London: The Institute of Chartered Accountants, June 2003.

These criteria serve as a screening checklist as measures are considered, developed, and ultimately added to the list of possibilities. In addition to meeting criteria, the factual basis of the measure should be stressed. In essence, the measure should be subjected to a fact-based analysis, a level of analysis never before applied to decisions about many projects, even when these decisions have involved huge sums of money. Distinguishing between the various "types" of facts is beneficial. As shown below, the basis for facts ranges from common sense to what employees "say" to actual data:

- *No facts.* Common sense tells us that employees will be more productive if they have a stake in the profits of a company.
- *Unreliable facts.* Employees say they are more likely to stay with a company if they are offered profit sharing.
- *Irrelevant facts.* We have benchmarked three world-class companies with variable pay plans: a bank, a hotel chain, and a defense contractor. All reported good results.
- *Fact-based.* Employee turnover in call centers is increasing operational costs.[1]

## Scorecards

In recent years, interest has increased in developing documents that reflect appropriate measures in an organization. Scorecards like those used in sporting events provide a variety of measures for top executives. In their landmark book *The Balanced Scorecard* Robert Kaplan and David Norton explore the concept of the scorecard for use by organizations.[2] Kaplan and Norton suggest that data can be organized in the four categories of process, operational, financial, and growth.

What exactly is a scorecard? The *American Heritage Dictionary* defines a scorecard from two perspectives:

1. A printed program or card enabling a spectator to identify players and record the progress of a game or competition.
2. A small card used to record one's own performance in sports.

Scorecards are varied in type, ranging from Kaplan and Norton's balanced scorecard to the scored set in the president's management agenda that uses a traffic-light grading system (green for success, yellow for mixed results, red for unsatisfactory). Top executives place great emphasis on scorecards, regardless of type. In some organizations, the scorecard concept has filtered down to functional business units, and each unit of the business has been required to develop a scorecard. A growing number of executives in different functions have developed scorecards to reflect their segments of the business.

The scorecard approach is appealing because it provides a quick comparison of key business impact measures and examines the status of the organization. As a management tool, scorecards can be important in shaping and improving or maintaining the performance of the organization through the implementation of projects or programs. Scorecard measures often link to particular projects. In many situations, it was a scorecard deficiency measure that initially prompted the project.

## Identifying Specific Measures Linked to Projects

An important issue that often surfaces when considering ROI applications is the understanding of specific measures that are often driven by specific projects. Although no standard answers are available, Table 7-2 represents a summary of typical payoff measures for specific types of projects. The measures are quite broad for some projects. For example, a reward systems project can pay off in a variety of measures, as in improved productivity, enhanced sales and revenues, improved quality, cycle-time reduction, and even direct cost savings. Essentially, the project should drive the measure that the reward is designed to influence. In other projects, the influenced measures are quite narrow. For example, in labor-management cooperation programs, the payoffs are typically in reduced grievances, fewer work stoppages, and improved employee satisfaction. Orientation programs typically pay off in measures of early turnover (turnover in the first ninety days of employment), initial job performance, and productivity. The measures that are influenced depend on the objectives and the design of the project.

The table also illustrates the immense number of applications of this methodology and the even larger set of measures that can be driven or influenced. In most of these situations, assigning monetary values to these measures (as the benefits of a given program are compared to the costs) and developing the ROI become reasonable tasks.

A word of caution: Presenting specific measures linked to a typical project may give the impression that these are the only measures influenced. In practice, a given project can have many outcomes, and this can make calculation of the ROI a difficult process. The good news is that most projects are driving business measures. The monetary values are based on what is being changed in the various business units, divisions, regions, and individual workplaces. These are the measures that matter to senior executives. The difficulty often comes in ensuring that the connection to the program exists. This is accomplished through a variety of techniques to isolate the effects of the program on the particular business measures, as will be discussed in Chapter 8.

# Business Performance Data Monitoring

Data are available in every organization to measure business performance. Monitoring performance data enables management to measure performance

### Table 7-2 Typical Measures in ROI Application

| ROI Applications | |
| --- | --- |
| **Project** | **Key Impact Measurements** |
| Absenteeism control/reduction | Absenteeism, customer satisfaction, job satisfaction, stress |
| Business coaching | Productivity/output, quality, time savings, efficiency, costs, employee satisfaction, customer satisfaction |
| Career development/career management | Turnover, promotions, recruiting expenses, job satisfaction |
| Communications | Errors, stress, conflicts, productivity, job satisfaction |
| Compensation plans | Costs, productivity, quality, job satisfaction |
| Compliance programs | Penalties/fines, charges, settlements, losses |
| Diversity | Turnover, absenteeism, complaints, allegations, legal settlements, losses |
| e-Learning | Cost savings, productivity improvement, quality improvement, cycle times, error reductions, job satisfaction |
| Employee benefits plans | Costs, time savings, job satisfaction |
| Employee relations program | Turnover, absenteeism, job satisfaction, engagement |
| Gainsharing plans | Production costs, productivity, turnover |
| Labor-management cooperation programs | Work stoppages, employee grievances, absenteeism, job satisfaction |
| Leadership development | Productivity/output, quality, efficiency, cost/time savings, employee satisfaction, engagement |
| Marketing and advertising | Sales, market share, customer loyalty, cost of sales, wallet share, customer satisfaction, branding |
| Meeting planning | Sales, productivity/output, quality, time savings, job satisfaction, customer satisfaction |
| Orientation, on-boarding | New-hire turnover, training time, productivity |
| Personal productivity/time management | Time savings, productivity, stress reduction, job satisfaction |
| Procurement | Costs, time savings, quality, stability, schedule |
| Project management | Time savings, quality improvement, budgets |
| Public policy programs | Time savings, cost savings, quality, satisfaction, image |

**Table 7-2.** *(Continued)*

| ROI Applications | |
| --- | --- |
| **Project** | **Key Impact Measurements** |
| Public relations | Image, branding, customer satisfaction, investor satisfaction |
| Recruiting source (new) | Costs, yield, early turnover |
| Retention management | Turnover, engagement, job satisfaction |
| Safety incentive plan | Accident frequency rates, accident severity rates, first aid treatments |
| Selection tool (new) | New-hire turnover, training time, productivity |
| Self-directed teams | Productivity/output, quality, customer satisfaction, turnover, absenteeism, job satisfaction |
| Sexual harassment prevention | Complaints, turnover, absenteeism, employee satisfaction |
| Six Sigma | Defects, rework, response times, cycle times, costs |
| Skill-based pay | Labor costs, turnover, absenteeism |
| Strategy/policy | Productivity/output, sales, market share, customer service, quality/service levels, cycle times, cost savings, job satisfaction |
| Stress management | Medical costs, turnover, absenteeism, job satisfaction |
| Technical training (job-related) | Productivity, sales, quality, time, costs, customer service, turnover, absenteeism, job satisfaction |
| Technology implementation | Cycle times, error rates, productivity, efficiency, customer satisfaction, job satisfaction |
| Wellness/fitness | Turnover, medical costs, accidents, absenteeism |

in terms of output, quality, costs, time, job satisfaction, customer satisfaction, and other measures. In determining the source of data in the evaluation, the first consideration should be existing databases, reports, and scorecards. In most organizations, performance data will be available that are suitable for measuring improvement resulting from a project. If such data are not available, additional record-keeping systems will have to be developed for measurement and analysis. At this point, the question of economics surfaces. Is it economical to develop the record-keeping systems necessary to evaluate a project or program? If the costs will be greater than the expected benefits, developing those systems is pointless.

## Identify Appropriate Measures

Existing performance measures should be thoroughly researched to identify those related to the proposed objectives of the project. Often, several performance measures are related to the same item. For example, the efficiency of a production unit can be measured in several ways:

- The number of units produced per hour
- The number of units produced on schedule
- The percentage of equipment used
- The percentage of equipment downtime
- The labor cost per unit of production
- The overtime required per unit of production
- Total unit cost

Each of these in its own way measures the effectiveness or efficiency of the production unit. All related measures should be reviewed to determine those most relevant to the project.

## Convert Current Measures to Usable Ones

Occasionally, existing performance measures will become integrated with other data. Keeping existing performance measures isolated from unrelated data may be difficult. In these situations, all existing related measures should be extracted and retabulated to make them more appropriate for comparison in the evaluation. At times, it may be necessary to develop conversion factors. For example, the average number of new sales orders per month may be presented regularly in the performance measures for the sales department. In addition, the sales costs per sales representative may also be presented. However, in evaluating the project, the average cost per new sale is needed. The average number of new sales orders and the average number of lost sales per sales representative are required to develop the data necessary for comparison.

## Develop New Measures

In some cases, data needed to measure the effectiveness of a project are not available, and new data are needed. The project staff must work with the client organization to develop record-keeping systems, if economically feasible. In one organization, delays of the sales staff in responding to customer requests were an issue. This issue was discovered from customer feedback. The feedback data prompted a project to reduce the response time. To help ensure the success of the project, several measures were planned, including measuring the actual time to respond to a customer request. Initially, this measure was not available. As the project was implemented, new software was used to measure the time that elapsed in responding to customer requests.

# Data Collection Methods

For many projects and programs, business data are readily available to be monitored. However, at times, data won't be easily accessible to the project team or to the evaluator. Sometimes data are maintained at the individual, work unit, or department level and may not be known to anyone outside that area. Tracking down all those data sets may be too expensive and time-consuming. When this is the case, other data collection methods may be used to capture data sets and make them available for the evaluator. Three other options described in this book are the use of action plans, performance contracts, and questionnaires.

## Using Action Plans to Develop Business Impact Data

Action plans can capture application and implementation data, as discussed in Chapter 6. They can also be a useful tool for capturing business impact data. For business impact data, the action plan is more focused and credible than using a questionnaire. The basic design principles and the issues involved in developing and administering action plans are the same for business impact data as for application and implementation data. However, a few issues are unique to business impact and ROI, and are presented here. The following steps are recommended when an action plan is developed and implemented to capture business impact data and to convert the data to monetary values.

### Set Goals and Targets

An action plan can be developed with a direct focus on business impact data. Participants develop an overall objective for the plan, which is usually the primary objective of the project. In some cases, a project may have more than one objective, which requires additional action plans. In addition to the objective, the improvement measure and the current levels of performance are identified. This information requires the participant to anticipate the application and implementation of the project and to set goals for specific performances that can be realized. The action plan is completed during project implementation, often with the input, assistance, and facilitation of the project team. The evaluator or project leader actually approves the plan, indicating that it meets the requirements of being Specific, Motivational, Achievable, Realistic, and Time-based (SMART). The plan can be developed in a one- to two-hour time frame and often begins with action steps related to the implementation of the project. These action steps are Level 3 activities that detail the application and implementation. All these steps build support for and are linked to business impact measures.

### Define the Unit of Measure

The next important issue is to define the actual unit of measure. In some cases, more than one measure may be used, which will subsequently be contained in additional action plans. The unit of measure is necessary to break down the process into the simplest steps so that its ultimate value can be determined. The unit may be output data—such as an additional unit manufactured or package delivered—or it can be sales and marketing data—such as additional sales revenue or a 1 percent increase in market share. In terms of quality, the unit can be one reject, one error, or one defect. Time-based units are usually measured in minutes, hours, days, or weeks. Other units are specific to their particular type of data, such as one grievance, one complaint, one absence, or one less person receiving welfare payments. The important point is to break down impact data into the simplest terms possible.

### Place a Monetary Value on Each Improvement

During project implementation, participants are asked to locate, calculate, or estimate the monetary value of each improvement outlined in their plans. The unit value is determined using a variety of methods, including standard values, expert input, external databases, and estimates. The process used in arriving at the value is described in the instructions for the action plan. When the actual improvement occurs, participants use these values to capture the annual monetary benefits of the plan. For this step to be effective, it is helpful to understand the ways values can be assigned to the data (as discussed in Chapter 9).

In the worst-case scenario, participants are asked to calculate the values themselves, although use of standard values and consultation with an expert are better courses of action. When it is necessary for participants themselves to make the calculations, they must explain the basis of them.

### Implement the Action Plan

Participants implement the action plan during project implementation, which often lasts for weeks or months following the launch of the project. The participants complete planned actions as described on the action plan, and the subsequent business impact results are achieved.

### Provide Specific Improvements

At the end of the specified follow-up period—usually three months, six months, nine months, or one year—the participants indicate the specific improvements made, usually expressed as a daily, weekly, or monthly amount. This determines the actual amount of change observed, measured, or recorded. Participants must understand the need for accuracy as data are recorded. In most cases, only the changes are recorded, as these amounts are needed to calculate the monetary value of the project. In other cases, before-and-after data may be recorded, allowing the evaluator to calculate the difference.

### Isolate the Effects of the Project

Although the action plan is initiated because of the project, the actual improvements reported on the action plan may be influenced by other factors. Consequently, the project should not be given full credit for the improvement. For example, an action plan to implement a new system in a division could only be given partial credit for a business improvement because other variables may have affected the impact measures. Although several ways are available to isolate the effects of a project, participant estimation is usually most appropriate in the action planning process. Consequently, participants are asked to estimate the percentage of the improvement actually related to a particular project. This question can be asked on the action plan form or in a follow-up questionnaire. Sometimes it is beneficial to precede this question with a request to identify the entire range of factors that could have influenced the results. This allows participants to think through the relationships before actually allocating a portion to the particular project under evaluation.

### Provide a Confidence Level for Estimates

The process to isolate the amount of the improvement actually related to the project is not usually precise. Participants are asked to indicate their level of confidence in their estimates. Using a scale of 0 to 100 percent—where 0 indicates the values are completely false and 100 percent indicates the values are absolutely certain—participants have a way to express their uncertainty with their estimates.

### Collect Action Plans at Specified Time Intervals

Because a high response rate is essential, several steps may be necessary to ensure the action plans are completed and returned. Participants usually see the importance of the process and develop their plans in detail at the beginning of the project. Some organizations send follow-up reminders by mail or e-mail; others phone participants to check their progress. Others offer assistance in developing the final plan. These steps may require additional resources, which must be weighed against the importance of having more data. Specific ways to improve response rates are discussed in Chapter 6.

### Summarize the Data and Calculate the ROI

If developed properly, each action plan should have annualized monetary values associated with improvements. Also, each individual should have indicated the percentage of the improvement directly related to the project. Finally, participants should have provided a confidence percentage to reflect their uncertainty with the process and the subjective nature of some of the data that may be provided.

Because this process involves estimates it may appear to be inaccurate, although adjustments during analysis can make the process credible and more accurate. These adjustments reflect the guiding principles that form the basis of the ROI methodology, as outlined in Table 2-1. The adjustments are made in five steps as follows:

**Step 1:** If participants provide no data, assume they had no improvement to report. (This is a very conservative approach.)

**Step 2:** Check each value for realism, usability, and feasibility. Discard extreme values and omit them from analysis.

**Step 3:** Because the improvement is annualized, assume the project had no improvement after the first year (for short-term projects). (Chapter 9 discusses projects that add value after two and three years.)

**Step 4:** Adjust the improvement calculated in Step 3, using the confidence level multiplied by the confidence percentage. The confidence level is actually a percentage of error suggested by the participants. For example, a participant indicating 80 percent confidence with the process is reflecting a possibility of 20 percent error. In a $10,000 estimate with an 80 percent confidence factor, the participant is suggesting a value in the range of $8,000 to $12,000 (i.e., a range between 20 percent less and 20 percent more). To be conservative, use the lower number, and multiply the confidence factor by the value of the improvement.

**Step 5:** Finally, adjust the new values by the percentage of the improvement related directly to the project, using multiplication to isolate the effects of the project.

Total the monetary values determined in these five steps to arrive at the final project benefit. Because these values are already annualized, the total of these benefits becomes the annual benefits for the project. Place this value in the numerator of the ROI formula to calculate the ROI.

## Using Performance Contracts to Measure Business Impact

Another technique for collecting business impact data is the performance contract. The performance contract is essentially a slight variation of the action plan. Based on the principle of mutual goal setting, a performance contract is a written agreement between a participant and the participant's manager. The participant agrees to improve performance in an area of mutual concern related to the project. The agreement is in the form of a goal to accomplish during the project or after the project's completion. The agreement details what is to be accomplished, at what time, and with what results.

Although the steps can vary according to the organization and the specific kind of contract, a common sequence of events follows:

1. The employee (participant) becomes involved in project implementation.
2. The participant and his or her immediate manager agree on a measure or measures for improvement related to the project (What's in it for me?).
3. Specific, measurable goals for improvement are set, following the SMART requirements discussed on page **106**.

4. In the early stages of the project, the contract is discussed and plans are developed to accomplish the goals.

5. During project implementation, the participant works to meet the deadline set for contract compliance.

6. The participant reports the results of the effort to his or her manager.

7. The manager and participant document the results and forward a copy, with appropriate comments, to the project team.

The process of selecting the area for improvement is similar to the process used in an action plan. The topic can cover one or more of the following areas:

- Routine performance related to the project, including specific improvement in measures such as production, efficiency, and error rates
- Problem solving, focused on such problems as an unexpected increase in workplace accidents, a decrease in efficiency, or a loss of morale
- Innovative or creative applications arising from the project, which could include the initiation of improvements in work practices, methods, procedures, techniques, and processes
- Personal development connected to the project, such as learning new information and acquiring new skills to increase individual effectiveness

The topic of the performance contract should be stated in terms of one or more objectives that are

- Written
- Understandable by all involved
- Challenging (requiring an unusual effort to achieve)
- Achievable (something that can be accomplished)
- Largely under the control of the participant
- Measurable and dated

The performance contract objectives are accomplished by following the guidelines for action plans presented earlier, and the methods for analyzing data and reporting progress are essentially the same as those used to analyze action plan data.

## Using Questionnaires to Collect Business Impact Measures

As described in the previous chapters, the questionnaire is one of the most versatile data collection tools and can be appropriate for collecting Level 1, 2,

3, and 4 data. Essentially, the design principles and content issues are the same as at other levels, except that questionnaires developed for a business impact evaluation will include additional questions to capture those data specific to business impact.

The use of questionnaires for impact data collection brings both good news and bad news. The good news is that questionnaires are easy to implement and low in cost. Data analysis is efficient, and the time required to provide the data is often minimal, making questionnaires among the least disruptive of data collection methods. The bad news is that the data can be distorted and inaccurate, and are sometimes missing. The challenge is to take all the steps necessary to ensure that questionnaires are complete, accurate, and clear, and that they are returned.

Unfortunately, questionnaires are the weakest methods of data collection. Paradoxically, they are the most commonly used because of their advantages. Of the first one hundred case studies published on the ROI methodology, roughly 50 percent used questionnaires as a method of data collection. They are popular, convenient, low-cost, and have become a way of life. The challenge is to improve them. The philosophy in the ROI methodology is to take processes that represent the weakest method and make them as credible as possible. Here the challenge is to make questionnaires credible and useful by ensuring that they collect all the data needed, that participants provide accurate and complete data, and that return rates are in at least the 70 to 80 percent range.

The reason return rates must be high is explained in Guiding Principle 6 of the ROI methodology outlined in Table 2-1: no data, no improvement. If an individual provides no improvement data, it is assumed that the person had no improvement to report. This is a very conservative principle but necessary to bring the credibility needed. Consequently, using questionnaires will require effort, discipline, and personal attention to ensure proper response rates. Chapter 3 presented suggestions for ensuring high response rates for Level 1 data collection. The same techniques should be considered here. It is helpful to remember that this is the least preferred method for collecting Level 4 data, and it is used only when other methods do not work (i.e., when business performance data cannot be easily monitored, when action plans are not feasible, or when performance contracting is not suitable).

## Selecting the Appropriate Method for Each Level

The data collection methods presented in this and earlier chapters offer a wide range of opportunities for collecting data in a variety of situations.

Eight aspects of data collection should be considered when deciding on the most appropriate method of collecting any type of data.

### Type of Data

One of the most important issues to consider when selecting the data collection method is the type of data to be collected. Some methods are more appropriate for business impact. Follow-up questionnaires, observations, interviews, focus groups, action planning, and performance contracting are best—sometimes exclusively—suited for application data. Performance monitoring, action planning, and questionnaires can easily capture business impact data.

### Investment of Participants' Time

Another important factor when selecting the data collection method is the amount of time participants must spend with data collection and evaluation systems. Time requirements should always be minimized, and the method should be positioned so that it is a value-added activity. Participants must understand that data collection is a valuable undertaking, and not an activity to be resisted. Sampling can be helpful in keeping total participant time to a minimum. Methods like performance monitoring require no participant time, whereas others, such as conducting interviews and focus groups, require a significant investment in time.

### Investment of Managers' Time

The time that a participant's manager must allocate to data collection is another issue in method selection. This time requirement should always be minimized. Methods like performance contracting may require significant involvement from the manager before and after project implementation, whereas other methods, such as participants' completion of a questionnaire, may not require any manager time.

### Cost of Method

Cost is always a consideration when selecting the method. Some data collection methods are more expensive than others. For example, interviews and observations are expensive, whereas surveys, questionnaires, and performance monitoring are usually inexpensive.

### Disruption of Normal Work Activities

The issue that generates perhaps the greatest concern among managers is the degree of work disruption that data collection will create. Routine work processes should be disrupted as little as possible. Data collection techniques like performance monitoring require very little time and cause little distraction from normal activities. Questionnaires generally do not disrupt the work environment and can often be completed in just a few minutes, perhaps even after normal work hours. At the other extreme, techniques, such as the focus group and interview may disrupt the work unit.

### Accuracy of Method

The accuracy of the technique is another factor to consider when selecting the method. Some data collection methods are more accurate than others. For example, performance monitoring is usually very accurate, whereas questionnaires are subject to distortion and may be unreliable. If on-the-job behavior must be captured, observation is clearly one of the most accurate methods. There is often a trade-off in the accuracy and costs of a method.

### Utility of an Additional Method (Source or Time Frame)

Because many different methods to collect data exist, using too many methods is tempting. Multiple data collection methods add time and cost to the evaluation, and may result in very little added value. Utility refers to the value added by each additional data collection method. When more than one method is used, this question should always be addressed. Does the value obtained from the additional data warrant the extra time and expense of the method? If the answer is no, the additional method should not be implemented. The same issue must be addressed when considering multiple sources and time frames.

### Cultural Bias of Data Collection Method

The culture or philosophy of the organization can dictate which data collection methods are best to use. For example, if an organization or audience is accustomed to using questionnaires, they will work well within the culture of that organization. If, however, an organization tends to overuse questionnaires, this may not be the best choice for collecting project data. Some organizations routinely use third-party observation. However, others view the technique as invasive—a clear deterrent to using observation when evaluating a project.

## Measuring the Hard to Measure

The focus of this chapter is on capturing the measures that are easy to collect and easy to measure. These represent the classic definitions of hard data and soft data—or, tangible data and intangible data. Much attention today is focused on the very hard to measure—on some of the classic soft items that are even softer than customer satisfaction and job satisfaction. Although this subject is discussed at length in Chapter 10, The Intangible Measures, a few comments are appropriate here.

## Everything Can Be Measured

Contrary to the thinking of some professionals, everything can be measured. Any item, issue, or phenomenon that is important to an organization can be measured. Even images, perceptions, and ideas in a person's mind can be measured. The thorny issue is usually in identifying the best way and the available resources to do the measuring. Although the image of an organization in the community or the way that customers become aware of a brand can be measured accurately, doing so takes time and money.

A case in point is the project launched by Nissan Motor Company in the 1980s when it located its first auto manufacturing plant in North America. Nissan executives were concerned about how a Japanese automaker would be regarded in a traditional Southern community. (This came at a time when common attitudes toward Japanese automakers were less amicable than today.) The project involved extensive surveying in the communities that would host a Nissan plant. The results were impressive, and demonstrate that you can measure anything if you can define it and spend the money to measure it.

## Perceptions Are Important

Some soft, or intangible, items are not based on perceptions, but others are. For example, consider innovation. An important component of innovation in a company is image or perception. Some measures reflect innovation of a company in its processes, products, and services (e.g., number of new patents, number of new products). However, concepts like brand awareness are based strictly on perception (i.e., on what a person knows or perceives about an item, product, or service). In the past, perceptions were considered irrelevant and not valuable, but today many decisions are based on perceptions. Consider perceptions about service quality from the customer's viewpoint—these perceptions often drive tremendous organizational changes. Employees' perceptions of their employer often drive huge investments in projects to improve job satisfaction, organizational commitment, and engagement.

Therefore, perceptions are very important and must be part of the measurement plan for the hard to measure.

## Every Measure Can Be Converted to Money, but Not Every Measure Should Be

In parallel with the adage, "Everything can be measured," so, too, can everything be valued. Every measure can be converted to monetary value. The concern has to do with credibility and resources. This is the definition that accorded intangibles in this book—they are measures that cannot credibly be converted to money with minimum resources (listed as Guiding Principle 11 in Table 2-1). Knowing when to pursue conversion to money and when not to is important; specific rules are available to guide you in making this decision. These rules are presented in Chapter 9.

## Special Emphasis on Intangibles

Important emphasis must be placed on intangibles, on measuring the hard to measure and on valuing the hard to value. This book includes an entire chapter on intangibles in which more examples and techniques are given to measure the hard to measure and address the issue of converting to money.

# Final Thoughts

Business impact data are critical to address an organization's business needs. These data lead the evaluation to the "money." Although perceived as difficult to find, business impact data are readily available and very credible. After describing the types of data that reflect business impact, this chapter provides an overview of several data collection approaches that can be used to capture business data. Some methods are gaining greater acceptance for use in capturing impact data. Performance monitoring, follow-up questionnaires, action plans, and performance contracts are used regularly to collect data for an impact analysis. This chapter focuses on methods to collect data on project impact and consequences. Linking these consequences directly to the project requires the important step of isolating the effects of the program (covered in the next chapter).

# Chapter 8

# ISOLATION OF PROJECT IMPACT

Reporting improvement in business impact measures is an important step in a project evaluation that leads to the money. Invariably, however, the question comes up (as it should): How much of this improvement was the result of the project? Unfortunately, the answer is rarely given with any degree of accuracy and confidence. Although the change in performance may in fact be linked to the project, other, non–project-related factors may have contributed to the improvement as well. If this issue is not addressed, the results reported will lack credibility. This chapter explores useful techniques for isolating the effects of the project. These techniques have been used in some of the most successful organizations as they attempt to measure the ROI from projects and programs.

## Why the Concern over This Issue?

In almost every project, multiple factors influence the business measures targeted by a project. Determining the effect of each factor attributed to the project is imperative. Without this isolation, the project's success cannot be confirmed; moreover, the effects of the project may be overstated if the change in the business impact measure is attributed entirely to the project. If this issue is ignored, the impact study may be considered invalid and inconclusive. This puts pressure on evaluators and project leaders to demonstrate the actual effects of their projects on business improvement as opposed to other possible factors.

### Reality

Isolating the effects of projects on business measures has led to some important conclusions. First, other influences are almost always present. In almost every situation, multiple factors generate business results. The rest of the world does not stand still while a project is being implemented. Other processes and programs are also operating to improve the same metrics targeted by the implemented project.

Next, if the project effects are not isolated, no business link can be established. Without steps taken to document the project's contribution, there is no proof that the project actually influenced the measures. The evidence will show only that the project *might* have made a difference. Results have improved, but other factors may have influenced the data.

Also, the outside factors and influences have their own protective owners. These owners will insist that it was their processes that made the difference. Some of them will probably be certain that the results are due entirely to their efforts. They may present a compelling case to management, stressing their achievements.

Finally, isolating the effects of the project on impact data is a challenging task. For complex projects in particular, the process is not easy, especially when strong-willed owners of other processes are involved. Fortunately, a variety of approaches are available to facilitate the procedure.

## Myths

The myths surrounding the isolation of project effects create confusion and frustration with the process. Some researchers, professionals, and consultants go so far as to suggest that such isolation is not necessary. Here are the most common myths:

1. **Our project is complementary to other processes; therefore, we should not attempt to isolate the effects of the project.** A project often complements other factors at work, all of which together drive results. If the sponsor of a project needs to understand its relative contribution, the isolation process is the only way to do it. If accomplished properly, it will reveal how the complementary factors interact to drive improvements.

2. **Other project leaders do not address this issue.** Some project leaders do not grapple with the isolation problem because they wish to make a convincing case that all of the improvement is directly related to their own processes. Most customer surveys that are filled out after a purchase or the opening of a new account ask why the purchase was made. This is one way organizations try to isolate the results of multiple variables. They want to know which of their processes or systems persuaded the customer to make the purchase.

3. **If we cannot use a research-based control group, we should not attempt this procedure.** Although an experimental research design

using randomly assigned control and experimental groups is the most reliable approach to identifying causes and effects, it is inapplicable to the majority of situations. Consequently, other methods must be used to isolate the effects of a project. The challenge is to find a method that is effective and whose results are reproducible, even if it is not as credible as the group comparison method.

4. **The stakeholders will understand the link to business impact measures; therefore, we do not need to attempt to isolate the effects of the project.** Unfortunately, stakeholders try to understand only what is presented to them. The absence of information makes it difficult for them to understand the business links, particularly when others are claiming full credit for the improvement.

5. **Estimates of improvement provide no value.** It may be necessary to tackle the isolation process using estimates from those who understand the process best. Although this should be done only as a last alternative, it can provide value and credibility, particularly once the estimates have been adjusted for error in order to reduce subjectivity.

6. **Ignore the issue; maybe the others won't think about it.** Unfortunately, audiences are becoming more sophisticated on this topic, and they are aware of the presence of multiple influences. If no attempt is made to isolate the effects of the project, the audience will assume that the other factors have had a major effect, perhaps the only effect. A project's credibility can deteriorate quickly. One has only to look at the recent business literature to understand why isolating project effects is so important. The best seller *Freakonomics*[1] addresses the issue with its controversial explanation for the reduction in crime rates.

These myths underscore the importance of addressing the isolation. The emphasis on isolation is not meant to suggest that a project is implemented independently and exclusively of other processes. Obviously, all groups should be working as a team to produce the desired results. However, when funding is parceled among different functions or organizations—with different owners—there is always a struggle to show, and often to understand, the connection between their activities and the results. If you do not undertake this process, others will—leaving your project with reduced budgets, resources, and respect.

## Case Study

Perhaps no example better emphasizes the importance of isolating the effects of a project than a situation described in Levitt and Dubner's best-selling book *Freakonomics*.

In the early 1990s the crime rate had been rising relentlessly, and it seemed to foreshadow the end of the world as we knew it. Death by gunfire, intentional and otherwise, had become commonplace, as had carjacking, crack dealing, robbery, and rape. Violent crime had become a gruesome, constant companion. And things were about to get even worse, according to all the experts.

The cause was the so-called super-predator: a scrawny, big-city teenager with a cheap gun in his hand and nothing in his heart. Thousands just like him were out there, a generation of killers preparing to send the country into total chaos.

In 1995 criminologist James Alan Fox wrote a report for the U.S. attorney general grimly detailing the forthcoming spike in murders by teenagers. Fox proposed optimistic and pessimistic scenarios. In the optimistic scenario, he predicted, the rate of teen homicides would rise another 15 percent over the next decade; in the pessimistic scenario, it would more than double.

Other criminologists as well as political scientists and similarly informed forecasters laid out the same horrible picture, as did President Clinton.

Then, instead of going up and up and up, crime began to fall and fall and fall. The reversal was startling in several respects, with every category of crime falling in every part of the country. It was persistent, with incremental decreases seen year after year. And it was entirely unanticipated—especially by the "experts," who had predicted the very opposite.

The magnitude of the reversal was also astounding. The teenage murder rate fell more than 50 percent over five years. By 2000 the overall murder rate in the United States had dropped to its lowest level in 35 years, as had the rate of just about every other category of crime, from assault to car theft.

Even though the experts had failed to anticipate the crime drop, they now hurried to explain it. Most of their theories sounded perfectly logical. It was the roaring 1990s economy, they said, that helped turn back crime. It was the proliferation of gun control laws, they said. It was the result of the innovative policing strategies put in place in New York City, where the number of murders would fall from 2,245 in 1990 to 596 in 2003.

These theories were not only logical; they were also *encouraging*, for they attributed the crime drop to specific recent human initiatives. If it was gun control, clever police strategies, and better-paying jobs that was quelling crime, then the power to stop criminals had been within our reach all along. And it would continue to be.

These theories were accepted seemingly without question. They became the conventional wisdom. There was only one problem: they were not true.

Another factor, it seemed, had greatly contributed to the massive crime drop of the 1990s. It had begun to take shape more than 20 years earlier and involved a young woman in Dallas. Norma McCorvey dramatically altered the course of criminal history without intending to. All she had wanted was an abortion. She was a poor, uneducated, unskilled, alcoholic, drug-using, 21-year-old woman who had already given up two children for adoption and now, in 1970, found herself pregnant again. But in Texas, as in all but a few states at that time, abortion was illegal. McCorvey's cause was taken up by people far more powerful than her. They made her the lead plaintiff in a class action lawsuit seeking to legalize abortion. The defendant was Henry Wade, the Dallas County district attorney. The case ultimately made it to the U.S. Supreme Court, by which time McCorvey's name had been changed to Jane Roe to shield her identity. On January 22, 1973, the Court ruled in favor of Ms. Roe, thereby legalizing abortion throughout the country. By this time, of course, it was far too late for Ms. McCorvey/Roe to have her abortion; she had given birth and put the child up for adoption.

So how did *Roe v. Wade* help trigger, a generation later, the greatest crime drop in recorded history? Decades of studies have shown that a child born into an adverse family environment is far more likely than other children to become a criminal. And the millions of women most likely to obtain abortions in the wake of *Roe v. Wade*—poor, unmarried, teenage mothers for whom illegal abortions had been too expensive or too hard to get—were common models of adversity. They were the very women whose children, if born, would have been much more likely to become criminals. But because of *Roe v. Wade*, these children *weren't* being born. This powerful ruling would have a drastic, delayed effect: in the years when these children, had they been born, would have entered their criminal primes, the rate of crime began to plummet.

It wasn't gun control or a strong economy or new police strategies that finally blunted the American crime wave. It was, among these and other factors, that the pool of potential criminals had dramatically shrunk.

Now, as the crime experts (the former doomsayers) spun their new theories on the reversal to the media, how many times did they cite legalized abortion as a cause? Zero.

The authors provide much detail explaining how they attempted to isolate the effects of the various influences on the crime rate reduction. Their arguments, analysis, and data are credible; however, as you might expect, their conclusion is not without its share of critics. Some found the analysis to be distasteful and perhaps racist. However, these economists were merely trying to report the data in the most credible way, attempting to isolate the effects of many complicated factors interacting in this situation to improve a particular measure.

# Preliminary Issues

The cause-and-effect relationship between a project and performance can be confusing and difficult to prove, but it can be demonstrated with an acceptable degree of accuracy. The challenge is to develop one or more specific techniques to isolate the effects of the project early in the process, usually as part of an evaluation plan conducted before the project begins. Up-front attention ensures that appropriate techniques will be used with minimal cost and time commitments. Two important issues in isolating the effects of a project are covered next, followed by specific methods.

## Chain of Impact

Before presentation of the methods, examining the chain of impact implicit in the different levels of evaluation will be helpful. Measurable results from a project should be derived from the application of the project (Level 3 data). Successful application of the project should stem from project participants learning to do something different, something necessary to implement the project (Level 2 data). Successful learning will usually occur when project participants react favorably to the project's content and objectives (Level 1 data). Without this preliminary evidence, isolating the effects of a project is difficult.

To be sure, if there is an adverse reaction, no learning, or no application, it cannot be concluded that any business impact improvements were caused by the project. From a practical standpoint, this requires data collection at four levels for an ROI calculation (Guiding Principle 1 in Table 2-1). Although this requirement is a prerequisite to isolating the effects of a project, it does not establish a direct connection, nor does it pinpoint the extent of the improvement caused by the project. It does show, however, that without improvements at previous levels, making a connection between the ultimate outcome and the project is difficult or impossible.

## Identify Other Factors: A First Step

As a first step in isolating a project's impact on performance, all key factors that may have contributed to the performance improvement should be identified. This step communicates to interested parties that other factors may have influenced the results, underscoring that the project is not the sole source of improvement. Consequently, the credit for improvement is shared among several possible variables and sources—an approach that is likely to garner the respect of the client. Several potential sources are available for identifying major influencing variables:

- The sponsor
- Participants in the project
- The project team
- The immediate managers of participants
- Subject matter experts
- Other process owners
- Experts on external issues
- Middle and top management

The importance of identifying all of the factors is underscored by an example. The Royal Bank of Canada has a sophisticated system for identifying the reasons customers make product decisions. At the point of sale, the purchaser records the reasons for the sale; was it the price, the product design, the advertising, or the referral from a satisfied customer? This system, owned by the marketing department, is designed to isolate the factors underlying the success of various marketing programs. However, it omits factors outside marketing. In essence, it assumes that 100 percent of the improvement in product sales can be attributed to a marketing influence. It ignores the effect of the economy, competition, information technology, reward systems, learning and development, job design, and other factors that could have had an important influence. Without identifying all the factors, the credibility of the analysis will suffer. Thus, competing factions within that organization had to address changing the system so that other factors are considered in the analysis.

Taking the time to focus on outside variables that may have influenced performance adds accuracy and credibility to the process. Project team leaders should go beyond this initial step and use one or more of the following techniques to isolate the impact of the project.

## Isolation Methods

Just as there are many data collection methods available for collecting data at different levels, a variety of methods are also available to isolate the effects of a project.

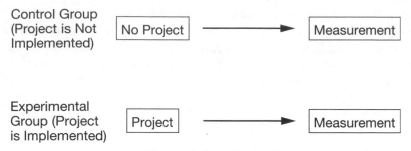

Figure 8-1  Use of Control Groups

## Control Groups

The most accurate approach for isolating the impact of a project is an experimental design with control groups. This approach involves the use of an experimental group that goes through the implementation of the project and a control group that does not. The two groups should be as similar in composition as possible and, if feasible, participants for each group should be randomly assigned. When this is achievable and the groups are subjected to the same environmental influences, any difference in performance between the two groups can be attributed to the project.

As illustrated in Figure 8-1, the control group and experimental group do not necessarily require pre-project measurements. Measurements can be taken during the project and after the project has been implemented, with the difference in performance between the two groups indicating the amount of improvement that is directly related to the project.

One caution should be observed: the use of control groups may create the impression that the project leaders are reproducing a laboratory setting, which can cause a problem for some executives and administrators. To avoid this perception, some organizations conduct a pilot project using participants as the experimental group. A similarly constituted nonparticipant comparison group is selected but does not receive any communication about the project. The terms *pilot project* and *comparison group* are a little less threatening to executives than *experimental group* and *control group*.

The control group approach has some inherent problems that can make it difficult to apply in practice. The first major problem is the selection of the groups. From a theoretical perspective, having identical control and experimental groups is next to impossible. Dozens of factors can affect performance, some individual and others contextual. On a practical basis, it is best to select the four to six variables that will have the greatest influence on performance. Essentially, this involves the 80/20 rule or the Pareto principle.

The 80/20 rule is aimed at selecting the factors that might account for 80 percent of the difference. The Pareto principle requires working from the most important factor down to cover perhaps four or five issues that capture the vast majority of the factors having influence.

Another major problem is that the control group process is not suited to many situations. For some types of projects, withholding the program from one particular group while implementing it with another may not be appropriate. This is particularly true where critical solutions are needed immediately; management is typically not willing to withhold a solution from one area to see how it works in another. This limitation keeps control group analyses from being implemented in many instances. However, in practice, many opportunities arise for a natural control group to develop even in situations where a solution is implemented throughout an organization. If it takes several months for the solution to encompass everyone in the organization, enough time may be available for a parallel comparison between the initial group and the last group to be affected. In these cases, ensuring that the groups are matched as closely as possible is critical. Such naturally occurring control groups can often be identified in the case of major enterprise-wide program implementations. The challenge is to address this possibility early enough to influence the implementation schedule to ensure that similar groups are used in the comparison.

Another problem is contamination, which can develop when participants involved in the project group (experimental group) communicate with people in the control group. Sometimes, the reverse situation occurs, where members of the control group model the behavior of the project group. In either case, the experiment becomes contaminated as the influence of the project is carried over to the control group. This hazard can be minimized by ensuring that the control and project groups are at different locations, are on different shifts, or occupy different floors of the same building. When this is not possible, it should be explained to both groups that one group will be involved in the project now and the other will be involved at a later date. Appealing to participants' sense of responsibility and asking them not to share information with others may help prevent contamination.

A closely related problem involves the passage of time. The longer a control versus experimental group comparison operates, the greater the likelihood that other influences will affect the results; more variables will enter into the situation, contaminating the results. On the other end of the scale, enough time must pass to allow a clear pattern to emerge distinguishing the two groups. Thus, the timing of control group comparisons must strike a delicate balance between waiting long enough for performance differences to show, but not so long that the results become contaminated.

Still another problem occurs when the different groups function under different environmental influences. This is usually the case when groups are at different locations. Sometimes the selection of the groups can prevent this problem from occurring. Another tactic is to use more groups than necessary and discard those groups that show some environmental differences.

A final problem is that the use of control and experimental groups may appear too research oriented for most business organizations. For example, management may not want to take the time to experiment before proceeding with a program, in addition to the selective withholding problem discussed earlier. Because of these concerns, some project managers will not entertain the idea of using control groups.

Because the use of control groups is an effective approach for isolating impact, it should be considered when a major ROI impact study is planned. In these situations, isolating the project impact with a high level of accuracy is essential, and the primary advantage of the control group process is accuracy.

## Trend Line Analysis

Another useful technique for approximating the impact of a project is trend line analysis. In this approach, a trend line is drawn to project the future, using previous performance as a base. When the project is fully implemented, actual performance is compared with the trend line projection. Any improvement in performance beyond what the trend line predicted can be reasonably attributed to project implementation. While this is not a precise process, it can provide a reasonable estimate of the project's impact.

Figure 8-2 shows a trend line analysis from the shipping department of a book distribution company. The percentage reflects the level of actual shipments compared with scheduled shipments. Data reflect conditions before and after project implementation in July. As shown in the figure, an upward trend for the data began prior to project implementation. Although the project apparently had an effect on shipment productivity, the trend line shows that some improvement would have occurred anyway, based on the trend that had previously been established. Project leaders may have been tempted to measure the improvement by comparing the six-month average for shipments prior to the project (87.3 percent) to the six-month average after the project (94.4 percent), which would yield a 7.1 percent difference. However,

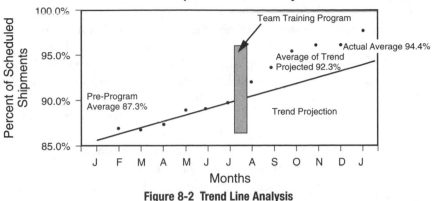

**Figure 8-2 Trend Line Analysis**

a more accurate comparison is the six-month average after the project versus the trend line (92.3 percent), a difference of 2.1 percent. Using this more conservative measure increases the accuracy and credibility of the process in terms of isolating the impact of the project.

To use this technique, two conditions must be met:

• It can be assumed that the trend that developed prior to the project would have continued if the project had not been implemented to alter it (i.e., had the project not been implemented, this trend would have continued on the same path). The process owner(s) should be able to provide input to confirm this assumption. If the assumption does not hold, trend line analysis cannot be used. If the assumption is a valid one, the second condition is considered.

• No other new variables or influences entered the process during project implementation. The key word here is *new*; the understanding is that the trend has been established from the influences already in place, and no additional influences have entered the process beyond the project. If such is not the case, another method will have to be used. Otherwise, the trend line analysis presents a reasonable estimate of the impact of this project.

Pre-project data must be available in order for this technique to be used, and the data should show a reasonable degree of stability. If the variance of the data is high, the stability of the trend line will be an issue. If the stability cannot be assessed from a direct plot of the data, more detailed statistical analyses can be used to determine if the data are stable enough to allow a projection. The trend line can be projected directly from historical data using a simple formula that is available in many calculators and software packages, such as Microsoft Excel.

A primary disadvantage of the trend line approach is that it is not always accurate. This approach assumes that the events that influenced the performance variable prior to project implementation are still in place, except for the effects of the implementation (i.e., the trends established prior to the project will continue in the same relative direction). Also, it assumes that no new influences entered the situation during the course of the project. This may not be the case.

The primary advantage of this approach is that it is simple and inexpensive. If historical data are available, a trend line can quickly be drawn and the differences estimated. While not exact, it does provide a quick general assessment of project impact.

## Forecasting Methods

A more analytical approach to isolation is the use of forecasting methods that predict a change in performance variables. This approach represents a mathematical interpretation of the trend line analysis when other variables enter the situation at the time of implementation. With this approach, the output measure targeted by the project is forecast based on the influence of variables that have changed during the implementation or evaluation period for the project. The actual value of the measure is compared with the forecast value, and the difference reflects the contribution of the project.

A major disadvantage to this approach emerges when several variables enter the process. The complexity multiplies, and the use of sophisticated statistical packages designed for multiple variable analyses is necessary. Even with this assistance, however, a good fit of the data to the model may not be possible. Unfortunately, some organizations have not developed mathematical relationships for output variables as a function of one or more inputs, and without them the forecasting method is difficult to use.

## Estimates

The most common method of isolating the effects of a project is to use estimates from some group of individuals. Although this is the weakest method, it is practical in many situations and it can enhance the credibility of the analysis if adequate precautions are taken. The beginning point in using this method is ensuring that the estimates are provided by the most reliable source, which is often the participant—not a higher-level manager or executive removed from the process. The individual who provides this information must understand the different factors and, particularly, the influence of the project on those factors. Essentially, there are four categories of input: The participants directly involved in the project are the first source considered. Managers are another possible source. Customers provide credible estimates in particular situations, and external experts may provide insight into causes for improvement. These sources are described in more detail next.

### Participant's Estimate of Impact

An easily implemented method of isolating the impact of a project is to obtain information directly from participants during project implementation. The usefulness of this approach rests on the assumption that participants are capable of determining or estimating how much of the performance improvement is related to the project implementation. Because their actions have led to the improvement, participants may provide highly accurate data. Although an estimate, the value they supply is likely to carry considerable weight with management because they know that the participants are at the center of the change or improvement. The estimate is obtained by defining the improvement and then asking participants the series of questions in Table 8-1.

Table 8-2 illustrates this approach with an example of one participant's estimation. Participants who do not provide answers to the questions in Table 8-1 are excluded from the analysis. Erroneous, incomplete, and extreme information should also be discarded before the analysis. To obtain a conservative estimate, the confidence percentage can be factored into each of the values. The confidence percentage is a reflection of the error in the estimate. Thus, an 80 percent confidence level equates to a potential error range of plus or minus 20 percent. In this approach, the estimate is multiplied by the level of confidence using the lower side of the range. In the example, the participant

**Table 8-1 Questions for Participant Estimation**

---

What is the link between these factors and the improvement?

What other factors have contributed to this improvement in performance?

What percentage of this improvement can be attributed to the implementation of this project?

How much confidence do you have in this estimate, expressed as a percentage? (0% = no confidence, 100% = complete confidence)

What other individuals or groups could provide a reliable estimate of this percentage to determine the amount of improvement contributed by this project?

---

**Table 8-2 Example of a Participant's Estimation**

| Factor Causing Improvement | Percentage of Improvement Caused | Confidence (%) | Adjusted Percentage of Improvement |
|---|---|---|---|
| Project | 60 | 80 | 48 |
| Process changes | 15 | 70 | 10.5 |
| Environmental changes | 5 | 60 | 3 |
| Compensation changes | 20 | 80 | 16 |
| Other | — | — | — |
| Total | 100 | | |

allocates 60 percent of the improvement to the project and has a level of confidence in the estimate of 80 percent. The confidence percentage is multiplied by the estimate to produce a usable project value of 48 percent. This adjusted percentage is then multiplied by the actual amount of the improvement (post-project minus pre-project value) to isolate the portion attributed to the project. For example, if errors declined 10 per week, 4.8 of the reduced errors would be attributed to the project. The adjusted improvement is now ready for conversion to monetary value and, ultimately, use in the ROI calculation.

Although the reported contribution is an estimate, this approach offers considerable accuracy and credibility. Five adjustments are effectively applied to the participant estimate to produce a conservative value:

1. Participants who do not provide usable data are assumed to have observed no improvements.
2. Extreme data values and incomplete, unrealistic, or unsupported claims are omitted from the analysis, although they may be included in the "other benefits" category.
3. For short-term projects, it is assumed that no benefits are realized from the project after the first year of full implementation. For long-term projects, several years may pass after project implementation before benefits are realized.
4. The amount of improvement is adjusted by the portion directly related to the project, expressed as a percentage.
5. The improvement value is multiplied by the confidence level, expressed as a percentage, to reduce the amount of the improvement in order to reflect the potential error.

As an enhancement of this method, the level of management above the participants may be asked to review and concur with each participant's estimate.

In using participants' estimates to measure impact, several assumptions are made:

1. The project encompasses a variety of different activities, practices, and tasks all focused on improving the performance of one or more business measures.

2. One or more business measures were identified prior to the project and have been monitored since the implementation process. Data monitoring has revealed an improvement in the business measure.

3. There is a need to associate the project with a specific amount of performance improvement and determine the monetary impact of the improvement. This information forms the basis for calculating the actual ROI.

Given these assumptions, the participants can specify the results linked to the project and provide data necessary to develop the ROI. This can be accomplished using a focus group, an interview, or a questionnaire.

### Manager's Estimate of Impact

In lieu of, or in addition to, participant estimates, the participants' manager may be asked to provide input concerning the project's role in improving performance. In some settings, the managers may be more familiar with the other factors influencing performance and therefore may be better equipped to provide estimates of impact. The questions to ask managers, after identifying the improvement ascribed to the project, are similar to those asked of the participants.

Managers' estimates should be analyzed in the same manner as the participant estimates, and they may also be adjusted by the confidence percentage. When participants' and managers' estimates have both been collected, the decision of which estimate to use becomes an issue. If there is a compelling reason to believe that one estimate is more credible than the other, then that estimate should be used. The most conservative approach is to use the lowest value and include an appropriate explanation. Another option is to recognize that each estimate source has a unique perspective and that an average of the two may be appropriate, with equal weight placed on each input. It is recommended that input be obtained from both participants and their managers.

In some cases, upper management may provide an estimate of the percentage of improvement attributable to a project. After considering other factors that could contribute to the improvement—such as technology, procedures, and process changes—they apply a subjective factor to represent the portion of the results that should be attributed to the project. Despite its subjective nature, this input by upper management is usually accepted by the individuals who provide or approve funding for the project. Sometimes, their comfort level with the processes used is the most important consideration.

### Customer Input on Project Impact

An approach that is useful in some narrowly focused project situations is to solicit input on the impact of a project directly from customers. Customers are asked why they chose a particular product or service or are asked to explain how their reaction to the product or service has been influenced by individuals or systems involved in the project. This technique often focuses directly on what the project is designed to improve. For example, after the implementation of a customer service project involving an electric utility, market research data showed that the level of customer dissatisfaction with response time was 5 percent lower compared with the rate before the project implementation. Because response time was reduced by the project and no other factor was found to contribute to the reduction, the 5 percent improvement in customer satisfaction was attributed to the project.

Routine customer surveys provide an excellent opportunity to collect input directly from customers concerning their reactions to new or improved products, services, processes, or procedures. Pre- and post-project data can pinpoint the improvements spurred by a new project.

Customer input should be elicited using current data collection methods; the creation of new surveys or feedback mechanisms is to be avoided. This measurement process should not add to the data collection systems in use. Customer input may constitute the most powerful and convincing data if it is complete, accurate, and valid.

### Internal or External Expert Input

External or internal experts can sometimes estimate the portion of results that can be attributed to a project. With this technique, experts must be carefully selected based on their knowledge of the process, project, and situation. For example, an expert in quality might be able to provide estimates of how much change in a quality measure can be attributed to a quality project and how much can be attributed to other factors.

This approach has its drawbacks, however. It can yield inaccurate data unless the project and the setting in which the estimate is made are quite similar to the program with which the expert is familiar. Also, this approach may lack credibility if the estimates come from external sources and do not involve those close to the process.

This process has the advantage that its reliability is often a reflection of the reputation of the expert or independent consultant. It is a quick and easy form of input from a reputable expert or consultant. Sometimes top management has more confidence in such external experts than in its own staff.

### Estimate Credibility: The Wisdom of Crowds

The following story is a sample of the tremendous amount of research showing the power of input from average individuals. It is taken from James Surowicki's best-selling book, *The Wisdom of Crowds*.

One day in the fall of 1906, British scientist Francis Galton left his home in the town of Plymouth and headed for a country fair. Galton was 85 years old and was beginning to feel his age, but he was still brimming with the curiosity that had won him renown—and notoriety—for his work on statistics and the science of heredity. On that particular day, Galton's curiosity turned to livestock.

Galton's destination was the annual West of England Fat Stock and Poultry Exhibition, a regional fair where the local farmers and townspeople gathered to appraise the quality of each other's cattle, sheep, chickens, horses, and pigs. Wandering through rows of stalls examining workhorses and prize hogs may seem like a strange way for a scientist to spend an afternoon, but there was certain logic to it. Galton was a man obsessed with two things: the measurement of physical and mental qualities and breeding. And what, after all, is a livestock show but a large showcase for the effects of good and bad breeding?

Breeding mattered to Galton because he believed that only a very few people had the characteristics necessary to keep societies healthy. He had devoted much of his career to measuring those characteristics, in fact, in an effort to prove that the vast majority of people did not possess them. His experiments left him with little confidence in the intelligence of the average person, "the stupidity and wrong-headedness of many men and women being so great as to be scarcely credible." Galton believed, "Only if power and control stayed in the hands of the select, well-bred few, could a society remain healthy and strong."

As he walked through the exhibition that day, Galton came across a weight judging competition. A fat ox had been selected and put on display, and many people were lining up to place wagers on what the weight of the ox would be after it was slaughtered and dressed. For sixpence, an individual could buy a stamped and numbered ticket and fill in his or her name, occupation, address, and estimate. The best guesses would earn prizes.

Eight hundred people tried their luck. They were a diverse lot. Many of them were butchers and farmers, who were presumably expert at judging the weight of livestock, but there were also quite a few people who had no insider knowledge of cattle. "Many non-experts competed," Galton wrote later in the scientific journal Nature. "The average competitor was probably as well fitted for making a just estimate of the dressed weight of the ox, as an average voter is of judging the merits of most political issues on which he votes."

Galton was interested in figuring out what the "average voter" was capable of because he wanted to prove that the average voter was capable of very little. So he turned the competition into an impromptu experiment. When the contest was over and the prizes had been awarded, Galton borrowed the tickets from the organizers and ran a series of statistical tests on them. Galton arranged the guesses (totaling 787—13 were discarded because they were illegible) in order from highest to lowest and plotted them to see if they would form a bell curve. Then, among other things, he added up all of the contestants' estimates and calculated the mean. That number represented, you could say, the collective wisdom of the Plymouth crowd. If the crowd were viewed as a single person, that would be the person's guess as to the ox's weight.

Galton had no doubt that the average guess of the group would be way off the mark. After all, mix a few very smart people with some mediocre people and a lot of dumb people, and it seems likely that you would end up with a dumb answer. But Galton was wrong. The crowd had guessed that the slaughtered and dressed ox would weigh 1,197 pounds. In fact, after it was slaughtered and dressed, the ox weighed 1,198 pounds. In other words, the crowd's judgment was essentially perfect. The "experts" were not even close. Perhaps breeding didn't mean so much after all. Galton wrote later: "The result seems more creditable to the trustworthiness of a democratic judgment than it might have been expected." That was something of an understatement.

What Francis Galton stumbled on that day in Plymouth was a simple but powerful truth: under the right circumstances, groups are remarkably intelligent, and are often smarter than the smartest people in them. Groups do not need to be dominated by exceptionally intelligent people in order to be smart. Even if most of the people within a group are not especially informed or rational, collectively they can reach a wise decision.[2]

## Calculate the Impact of Other Factors

It is sometimes possible, although not appropriate in all cases, to calculate the impact of factors (other than the project) that account for part of the improvement and then credit the project with the remaining part. That is, the project assumes credit for improvement that cannot be attributed to other factors.

An example will help explain this approach. In a consumer lending project for a large bank, a significant increase in consumer loan volume occurred after a project was implemented. Part of the increase in volume was attributed to the project, and the remainder was due to the influence of other factors in place during the same time period. Two additional factors were identified: (1) an increase in marketing and sales promotion; and (2) falling interest rates.

With regard to the first factor, as marketing and sales promotion increased, so did consumer loan volume. The contribution of this factor was estimated using input from several internal experts in the marketing department. As for the second factor, industry sources were used to estimate the relationship between consumer loan volume and interest rates. These two estimates together accounted for a modest percentage of the increase in consumer loan volume. The remaining improvement was attributed to the project.

This method is appropriate when the other factors can be easily identified and the appropriate mechanisms are in place to calculate their impact on the improvement. In some cases, estimating the impact of outside factors is just as difficult as estimating the impact of the project, limiting this approach's applicability. However, the results can be reliable if the procedure used to isolate the impact of other factors is sound.

## Select the Technique

With all of these techniques available to isolate the impact of a project, selecting the most appropriate ones for a specific project can be difficult. Some techniques are simple and inexpensive; others are time-consuming and costly. In choosing among them, the following factors should be considered:

- Feasibility of the technique
- Accuracy associated with the technique
- Credibility of the technique with the target audience
- Specific cost to implement the technique
- Amount of disruption in normal work activities resulting from the technique's implementation
- Participant, staff, and management time required for the technique

The use of multiple techniques or multiple sources of data input should be considered since two sources are usually better than one. When multiple sources are used, a conservative method should be used to combine the inputs. The reason is that a conservative approach builds acceptance. The target audience should always be provided with an explanation of the process and the subjective factors involved. Multiple sources allow an organization to experiment with different strategies and build confidence in the use of a particular technique. For example, if management is concerned about the accuracy of participants' estimates, the combination of a control group arrangement and participant estimates could be useful for checking the accuracy of the estimation process.

It is not unusual for the ROI of a project to be extremely large. Even when a portion of the improvement is allocated to other factors, the magnitude can still be impressive in many situations. The audience should understand that even though every effort has been made to isolate the project's impact, it remains an imprecise figure that is subject to error. It represents the best estimate of the impact given the constraints, conditions, and resources available. Chances are it is more accurate than other types of analysis regularly used in other functions within the organization.

## Final Thoughts

Isolating the effects of a project is an important step in answering the question of how much of the improvement in a business measure was caused by the project. The techniques presented in this chapter are the most effective approaches available to answer this question and are used by some of the most progressive organizations. Too often results are reported and linked to a project with no attempt to isolate the exact portion of the outcome associated with the project. This leads to an invalid report trumpeting project success. If professionals wish to improve their images and are committed to meeting their responsibility to obtain results, the need for isolation must be addressed early in the process for all major projects. Once this important step is completed, the gathered data must be converted to monetary values. The process for converting data to monetary values is detailed in the next chapter.

# Chapter 9

# SHOW ME THE MONEY
## CONVERTING DATA TO MONEY

To show the real money, the improvement in business measures that is attributable to the project (after the effects of the project have been isolated) must be converted to monetary values, which are then compared with project costs. This represents the ultimate level in the five-level evaluation framework presented in Chapter 2. This chapter explains how business leaders develop the monetary values used to calculate ROI.

## Why Convert Data to Monetary Values?

The need to convert data to monetary amounts is not always clearly understood by project leaders. A project can be shown to be a success just by providing business impact data showing the amount of change directly attributable to the project. For example, a change in quality, cycle time, market share, or customer satisfaction could represent a significant improvement linked directly to a new project. For some projects, this may be sufficient. However, many sponsors require the actual monetary value, and more project leaders are taking this extra step of converting data to monetary values.

### Value Equals Money

For some stakeholders, the most important value is money. As described in Chapter 1, there are many different types of value. However, monetary value is becoming one of the primary criteria of success as the economic benefits of projects are pursued. Executives, sponsors, clients, administrators, and other leaders in particular are concerned with the allocation of funds and want to see evidence of the contribution of a project in terms of monetary value. Any other outcome for these key stakeholders would be unsatisfactory.

## Impact Is More Understandable

For some projects, the impact is more understandable when stated in terms of monetary value. Consider for example, the impact of a major project to improve the creativity of an organization's employees and thereby enhance the innovation of the organization. Suppose this project involved literally all employees and had an impact on all parts of the organization. Across all departments, functions, units, and divisions, employees were being more creative, suggesting new ideas, taking on new challenges, driving new products—in short, helping the organization in a wide variety of ways. The only way to understand the value of such a project is to convert the individual efforts and their consequences to monetary values. Totaling the monetary values of all the innovations would provide some sense of the value of the project.

Consider the impact of a leadership development program directed at all of the middle managers in an organization. As part of the program, the managers were asked to select at least two measures of importance to them and to indicate what would need to change or improve for them to meet their specific goals. The measures could number in the dozens, if not hundreds. When the program's impact was studied, a large number of improvements were identified but were hard to quantify. Converting them to monetary values allowed the improvements to be expressed in the same terms, enabling the outcomes to be more clearly reported.

Monetary value is necessary to determine ROI. As described in earlier chapters, an expression of a monetary value is needed to compare against costs in order to develop the benefits/costs ratio, the ROI (as a percentage), and the payback period.

## Converting to Monetary Values Is Similar to Budgeting

Professionals and administrators are typically occupied with budgets and are expected to develop budgets for projects with an acceptable degree of accuracy. They are also comfortable with handling costs. When it comes to benefits, however, many are not comfortable, even though some of the same techniques used in developing budgets are used to determine benefits. Some of the benefits of the project will take the form of cost savings or cost reductions, and this can make identification of the costs or value easier for some projects. The monetary benefit resulting from a project is a natural extension of the budget.

## Monetary Value Is Vital to Organizational Operations

With global competitiveness and the drive to improve the efficiency of operations, awareness of the costs related to particular processes and activities is essential. In the 1990s this emphasis gave rise to activity-based costing (ABC) and activity-based management. ABC is not a replacement for traditional, general ledger accounting. Rather, it is a translator or medium between cost accumulations, or the specific expenditure account balances in the general ledger, and the end users who must apply cost data in decision making. In typical cost statements, the actual cost of a process or problem is not readily discernible. ABC converts inert cost data to relevant, actionable information. ABC has become increasingly useful for identifying improvement opportunities and measuring the benefits realized from performance initiatives on an after-the-fact basis.[1] Over 80 percent of the ROI impact studies conducted show projects benefiting the organization through cost savings (cost reductions or cost avoidance). Consequently, understanding the cost of a problem and the payoff of the corresponding solution is essential to proper management of the business.

## Monetary Values Are Necessary to Understand Problems and Cost Data

In any business, costs are essential to understanding the magnitude of a problem. Consider, for example, the cost of employee turnover. Traditional records and even those available through activity-based costing will not indicate the full value or cost of the problem. A variety of estimates and expert inputs may be necessary to supplement cost statements to arrive at a definite value. The good news is that organizations have developed a number of standard procedures for identifying undesirable costs. For example, Wal-Mart has calculated the cost of one truck sitting idle at a store for one minute, waiting to be unloaded. When this cost is multiplied by the hundreds of deliveries per store and the result then multiplied by five thousand stores, the cost becomes huge.

# Key Steps in Converting Data to Money

Converting data to monetary values involves five steps for each data item:

1. **Focus on a unit of measure.** First, a unit of measure must be defined. For output data, the unit of measure is the item produced (e.g., one item assembled), service provided (e.g., one package shipped), or sale completed. Time measures could include the time to complete a project, cycle time, or customer response time, and the unit here is usually expressed in terms of minutes, hours, or days. Quality is another common measure, with a unit defined as one error, reject, defect, or reworked item. Soft data measures vary, with a unit of improvement expressed in terms of absences, turnover, or a change in the customer satisfaction index. Specific examples of units of measure are

   - One student enrolled
   - One loan approved
   - One reworked item
   - One voluntary turnover
   - One hour of cycle time
   - One customer complaint
   - One patient served
   - One less day of incarceration (Prison)

   - One FTE employee
   - One grievance
   - One hour of downtime
   - One hour of employee time
   - One person removed from welfare
   - One point increase in customer satisfaction

2. **Determine the value of each unit.** Now comes the challenge: placing a value ($V$) on the unit identified in the first step. For measures of productivity, quality, cost, and time, the process is relatively easy. Most organizations maintain records or reports that can pinpoint the cost of one unit of production or one defect. Soft data are more difficult to convert to money. For example, the monetary value of one customer complaint or a one-point change in an employee attitude may be difficult to determine. The techniques described in this chapter provide an array of approaches for making this conversion. When more than one value is available, the most credible or lowest value is generally used in the calculation.

3. **Calculate the change in performance data.** The change in output data is calculated after the effects of the project have been isolated from other influences. This change ($\Delta$) is the performance improvement that is directly attributable to the project, represented as the Level 4 impact measure. The value may represent the performance improvement for an individual, a team, a group of participants, or several groups of participants.

4. **Determine the annual amount of change.** The $\Delta$ value is annualized to develop a value for the total change in the performance data for one year $(\Delta P)$. Using annual figures is a standard approach for organizations seeking to capture the benefits of a particular project, even though the benefits may not remain constant throughout the year. For a short-term solution, first-year benefits are used even when the project produces benefits beyond one year. This approach is considered conservative. More will be discussed about this later.

5. **Calculate the annual value of the improvement.** The total value of improvement is calculated by multiplying the annual performance change $(\Delta P)$ by the unit value $(V)$ for the complete group in question. For example, if one group of participants is involved in the project being evaluated, the total value will include the total improvement for all participants providing data in the group. This value for annual project benefits is then compared with the costs of the project to calculate the BCR, ROI, or payback period.

An example from a labor-management cooperation program at a manufacturing plant describes the five-step process of converting data to monetary values. This project was developed and implemented after the initial needs assessment and analysis revealed that a lack of teamwork was causing an excessive number of labor grievances. Labor grievances were managed using a four-stage process. The number of grievances resolved at stage 2 was selected as an output measure. Table 9-1 shows the steps in assigning a monetary value to the data, resulting in a total project impact of $546,000.

## Standard Monetary Values

Most hard data items (output, quality, cost, and time) have standard values. A standard value is a monetary value assigned to a unit of measurement that is accepted by key stakeholders. Standard values have been developed because these are often the measures that matter to the organization. They reflect problems, and their conversion to monetary values shows their impact on the operational and financial well-being of the organization.

For the last two decades, quality programs have typically focused only on the cost of quality. Organizations have been obsessed with placing a value on mistakes or the payoff from avoiding these mistakes. This assigned value—the standard cost of an item—is one of the critical outgrowths of the quality management movement. In addition, a variety of

### Table 9-1 Converting Labor Grievance Data to Monetary Values

Setting: Labor-management cooperation project in a manufacturing plant

Step 1: *Define the unit of measure.*
The unit is defined as one grievance reaching stage 2 in the four-stage grievance resolution process.

Step 2: *Determine the value (V) of each unit.*
According to internal experts (i.e., the labor relations staff), the cost of an average grievance reaching stage 2 was estimated at $6,500, when time and direct costs are considered ($V = \$6,500$).

Step 3: *Calculate the change ($\Delta$) in performance data.*
Six months after the project was completed, total grievances per month reaching stage 2 had declined by 10. Seven of the 10 grievance reductions were related to the project, as determined by first-level supervisors (see Chapter 8, "Isolation of Project Impact").

Step 4: *Determine an annual amount for the change ($\Delta P$).*
Using the six-month average of seven grievances per month yields an annual improvement value of 84 ($\Delta P = 12 \times 7 = 84$).

Step 5: *Calculate the annual monetary value of the improvement.*
Annual value $= \Delta P \times V$

$$= 84 \times \$6,500$$
$$= \$546,000$$

process improvement programs—such as reengineering, reinventing the corporation, transformation, and continuous process improvement—have included a component in which the cost of a particular measure is determined. Finally, the development of a variety of cost control, cost containment, and cost management systems—such as activity-based costing—have forced organizations, departments, and divisions to place costs on activities and, in some cases, relate those costs directly to the revenues or profits of the organization.

The following discussion describes how measures of output, quality, and time can be converted to standard values.

## Converting Output Data to Money

When a project results in a change in output, the value of the increased output can usually be determined from the organization's accounting or operating records. For organizations operating on a profit basis, this value is typically the marginal profit contribution of an additional unit of production or service provided. An example is a team within a major appliance manufacturing firm that was able to boost the production of small refrigerators after a comprehensive work cell redesign project; the unit of improvement is the profit margin associated with one refrigerator. For organizations that are performance driven rather than profit driven, this value is usually reflected in the savings realized when an additional unit of output is realized for the same input. For example, in the visa section of a government office, one additional visa application may be processed at no additional cost; an increase in output translates into a cost savings equal to the unit cost of processing a visa application.

The formulas used to calculate this contribution depend on the type of organization and the nature of its record keeping. Most organizations have standard values readily available for performance monitoring and goal setting. Managers often use marginal cost statements and sensitivity analyses to pinpoint values associated with changes in output. If the data are not available, the project team must initiate or coordinate the development of appropriate values.

One of the more important measures of output is productivity, particularly in a competitive organization. Today, most organizations competing in the global economy do an excellent job of monitoring productivity and placing a value on it. For example, consider the Snapper lawn mower factory in McDonough, Georgia. Ten years ago it produced 40 models of outdoor equipment items; now it makes 145. Ten years ago all of the manufacturing processes were performed by humans. Today robots do the welding, lasers cut parts, and computers control the steel stamping process. Productivity at the factory is three times what it was 10 years ago, and the workforce has been cut by half.[2] At Snapper, each factory worker's output is measured every hour, every day, every month, and every year. And everyone's performance is posted publicly every day for all to see. Production at the Snapper plant is rescheduled every week according to the pace of store sales across the nation. A computer juggles work assignments and balances the various parts of the assembly process. At Snapper, productivity is not only important, it is measured and valued. Snapper knows the value of improving productivity by an infinitesimal amount; the president knows that the factory must be efficient to compete in a global market with low-cost products. This requires that the performance of every factory worker be measured every hour of every day.

The benefit of converting output data to money using standard values is that these calculations are already available for the most important data items. Perhaps no area has as much experience with standard values as the sales and marketing area. Table 9-2 shows a sampling of the sales and marketing measures that are routinely calculated and reported as standard values.[3]

Table 9-2 Examples of Standard Values from Sales and Marketing

| Metric | Definition | Conversion Notes |
|---|---|---|
| Sales | The sale of the product or service recorded in a variety of different ways: by product, by time period, by customer | The data must be converted to monetary value by applying the profit margin for a particular sales category. |
| Profit margin (%) | $\frac{\text{Price-Cost}}{\text{Cost}}$ for the product, customer, and time period | Factored to convert sales to monetary value-add to the organization. |
| Unit margin | Unit price less unit cost | This shows the value of incremental sales. |
| Channel margin | Channel profits as a percentage of channel selling price | This would be used to show the value of sales through a particular marketing channel. |
| Retention rate | The ratio of customers retained to the number of customers at risk of leaving | The value is the saving of the money necessary to acquire a replacement customer. |
| Churn rate | Ratio of customers leaving to the number who are at risk of leaving | The value is the saving of the money necessary to acquire a new customer. |
| Customer profit | The difference between the revenues earned from and the cost associated with the customer relationship during the specified period | The monetary value added is the profit obtained from customers. It all goes toward the bottom line. |
| Customer value lifetime | The present value of the future cash flows attributed to the customer relationship | Bottom line; as customer value increases, it adds directly to the profits. Also, as a customer is added, the incremental value is the customer lifetime average. |
| Cannibalization rate | The percentage of new product sales taken from existing product lines | This is to be minimized, as it represents an adverse effect on existing product, with the value added being the loss of profits due to the sales loss. |
| Workload | Hours required to service clients and prospects | This includes the salaries, commissions, and benefits from the time the sales staff spend on the workloads. |

**Table 9-2** *(Continued)*

| Metric | Definition | Conversion Notes |
|---|---|---|
| Inventories | The total amount of product or brand available for sale in a particular channel | Since inventories are valued at the cost of carrying the inventory, costs involve space, handling, and the time value of money. Insufficient inventory is the cost of expediting the new inventory or the loss of sales because of the inventory outage. |
| Market share | Sales revenue as a percentage of total market sales | Actual sales are converted to money through the profit margins. This is a measure of competitiveness. |
| Loyalty | The length of time the customer stays with the organization, the willingness to pay a premium, and the willingness to search | This is calculated as the additional profit from the sale or the profit on the premium |

Adapted from *Marketing Metrics: 50+ Metrics Every Executive Should Master* by Paul W. Farris, Neil T. Bendle, Phillip E. Pfeifer, and David J. Ribstein. (Upper Saddle River, NJ: Wharton School Publishing, 2006), p. 46–47.

## Calculating the Cost of Quality

Quality and the cost of quality are important issues in most manufacturing and service organizations. Because many projects are designed to increase quality, the project team may have to place a value on the improvement of certain quality measures. For some quality measures, the task is easy. For example, if quality is measured in terms of the defect rate, the value of the improvement is the cost to repair or replace the product. The most obvious cost of poor quality is the amount of scrap or waste generated by mistakes. Defective products, spoiled raw materials, and discarded paperwork are all the result of poor quality. Scrap and waste translate directly into a monetary value. In a production environment, for example, the cost of a defective product is the total cost incurred up to the point at which the mistake is identified, minus the salvage value. In the service environment, the cost of a defective service is the cost incurred up to the point at which the deficiency is identified, plus the cost to correct the problem, plus the cost to make the customer happy, plus the loss of customer loyalty.

Employee mistakes and errors can be expensive. The costliest form of rework occurs when a product or service is delivered to a customer and must be returned for repair or correction. The cost of rework includes both labor and direct costs. In some organizations, rework costs can constitute as much as 35 percent of operating expenses.

Quality costs can be grouped into six major categories:[4]

1. *Internal failure* represents costs associated with problems detected prior to product shipment or service delivery. Typically such costs are reworking and retesting.

2. *Penalty costs* are fines or penalties incurred as a result of unacceptable quality.

3. *External failure* refers to problems detected after product shipment or service delivery. Typical items here are technical support, complaint investigation, remedial upgrades, and fixes.

4. *Appraisal costs* are the expenses involved in determining the condition of a particular product or service. Typical costs involve testing and related activities, such as product quality audits.

5. *Prevention costs* involve efforts undertaken to avoid unacceptable products or service quality. These efforts include service quality administration, inspections, process studies, and improvements.

6. *Customer dissatisfaction* is perhaps the costliest element of inadequate quality. In some cases, serious mistakes result in lost business. Customer dissatisfaction is difficult to quantify, and arriving at a monetary value may be impossible using direct methods. The judgment and expertise of sales, marketing, or quality managers are usually the best resources to draw upon in measuring the impact of dissatisfaction. More and more quality experts are measuring customer and client dissatisfaction with the use of market surveys.[5]

As with output data, the good news is that a tremendous number of quality measures have been converted to standard values. Some of these measures are

- Defects
- Rework
- Processing errors

- Date errors
- Accidents
- Grievances
- Downtime—equipment
- Downtime—system
- Delay
- Fines
- Days sales uncollected
- Queues

## Converting Employee Time Using Compensation

Reducing the workforce or saving employee time is a common objective for projects. In a team environment, a project may enable the team to complete tasks in less time or with fewer people. A major project could lead to a reduction of several hundred employees. On an individual basis, a technology project may be designed to help professional, sales, and managerial employees save time in performing daily tasks. The value of the time saved is an important measure, and determining a monetary value for it is relatively easy.

The most obvious time savings stem from reduced labor costs for performing a given amount of work. The monetary savings are found by multiplying the hours saved by the labor cost per hour. For example, a time-saving process in one organization, participants estimated, saved an average of 74 minutes per day, worth $31.25 per day or $7,500 per year, based on the average salary plus benefits for a typical participant.

The average wage, with a percentage added for employee benefits, will suffice for most calculations. However, employee time may be worth more. For example, additional costs for maintaining an employee (office space, furniture, telephones, utilities, computers, administrative support, and other overhead expenses) could be included in calculating the average labor cost. Thus, the wage rate used in the calculation can escalate quickly. In a large-scale employee reduction effort, calculating the costs of additional employees may be more appropriate for showing the value. However, for most projects, the conservative approach of using salary plus employee benefits is recommended.

Beyond reducing the labor cost per hour, time savings can produce benefits such as improved service, avoidance of penalties for late projects, and additional profit opportunities. These values can be estimated using other methods discussed in this chapter.

A word of caution is needed concerning time savings. Savings are realized only when the amount of time saved translates into a cost reduction or a profit contribution. Even if a project produces savings in manager time, monetary value is not realized unless the manager puts the time saved to productive use. Having managers estimate the percentage of time saved that is devoted to productive work may be helpful, if it is followed up with a request for examples of how the extra time was used. If a team-based project sparks a new process that eliminates several hours of work each day, the actual savings will be based on the corresponding reduction in staff or overtime pay. Therefore, an important preliminary step in figuring time savings is determining whether the expected savings will be genuine. FedEx is a primary example of assigning value to time.[6]

## Finding Standard Values

Standard values are available for all types of data. Virtually every major department will develop standard values that are monitored for that area. Typical functions in a major organization where standard values are tracked include

- Finance and accounting
- Production
- Operations
- Engineering
- IT
- Administration
- Sales and marketing
- Customer service and support
- Procurement
- Logistics
- Compliance
- Research and development
- HR

Thanks to enterprise-wide systems software, standard values are commonly integrated and made available for access by a variety of people. In some cases, access may need to be addressed to ensure that the data can be obtained by those who require them.

# When Standard Values Are Not Available

When standard values are not available, several alternative strategies for converting data to monetary are available. Some are appropriate for a specific type of data or data category, while others may be used with virtually any type of data. The challenge is to select the strategy that best suits the situation.

## Using Historical Costs from Records

Historical records often indicate the value of a measure and the cost (or value) of a unit of improvement. This strategy relies on identifying the appropriate records and tabulating the proper cost components for the item in question.

For example, suppose a large construction firm initiated a project to improve safety. The project improved several safety-related performance measures, ranging from amounts spent in response to government fines to total worker's compensation costs. From the company's records for one year of data, the average cost for each safety measure was determined. This value included the direct costs of medical payments, insurance payments and premiums, investigation services, and lost-time payments to employees, as well as payments for legal expenses, fines, and other direct services. The amount of time used to investigate, resolve, and correct the issues was also factored in. This time involved not only the health and safety staff, but other personnel as well. In addition, the costs of lost productivity, disruption of services, morale, and dissatisfaction were estimated to obtain a full cost. The corresponding costs for each item were then developed.

This example suggests the challenges inherent in maintaining systems and databases to enable the value for a particular data item to be identified. It also raises several concerns about using historical costs as a technique to convert data to money.

### *Time*

Sorting through databases, cost statements, financial records, and activity reports takes a tremendous amount of time, time that may not be available for the project. It is important to keep this part of the process in perspective. Converting data to monetary values is only one step in the ROI methodology. Time needs to be conserved.

### *Availability*

In some cases, data are not available to show all of the costs for a particular item. In addition to the direct costs associated with a measure, an equal number of indirect or invisible costs may be present that cannot be obtained easily.

### Access

Compounding the problems of time and availability is access. Monetary values may be needed from a system or record set that is under someone else's control. In a typical implementation, the project leader may not have full access to cost data. Cost data are more sensitive than other types of data and are often protected for a number of reasons, including competitive advantage. Therefore, access can be difficult and sometimes is even prohibited unless an absolute need to know can be demonstrated.

### Accuracy

Finally, the need for accuracy in this analysis should not be overlooked. A measure provided in current records may appear to be based on accurate data, but this may be an illusion. When data are calculated, estimations are involved, access to certain systems is denied, and different assumptions are made (all of which can be compounded by different definitions of systems, data, and measures). Because of these limitations, the calculated values should be viewed as suspect unless means are available to ensure that they are accurate.

Calculating monetary value using historical data should be done with caution and only when these two conditions exist:

- The sponsor has approved the use of additional time, effort, and money to develop a monetary value from the current records and reports.
- The measure is simple and can be found by searching only a few records.

Otherwise, an alternative method is preferred.

## Using Input from Experts

When it is necessary to convert data items for which historical cost data are not available, input from experts on the process might be a consideration. Internal experts can provide the cost (or value) of one unit of improvement in a measure. Individuals with knowledge of the situation and the confidence of management must be willing to provide estimates—as well as the assumptions behind the estimates. Internal experts may be found in the department in which the data originated—sales, marketing, payroll, labor relations, or any number of other functions. Most experts have their own methodologies for developing these values. So when their input is required, it is important to explain the full scope of what is needed and to provide as many specifics as possible.

If internal experts have a strong bias regarding the measure or are not available, external experts are sought. External experts should be selected based on their experience with the unit of measure. Fortunately, many experts are available who work directly with important measures, such as employee attitudes, customer satisfaction, turnover, absenteeism, and grievances. They are often willing to provide estimates of the cost (or value) of these intangibles.

External experts—including consultants, professionals, or suppliers in a particular area—can also be found in obvious places. For example, the costs of accidents can be estimated by the worker's compensation carrier, or the cost of a grievance may be estimated by the labor attorney defending the company in grievance transactions. The process of locating an external expert is similar to the external database search, which is described later.

The credibility of the expert, whether internal or external, is a critical issue if the monetary value placed on a measure is to be reliable. Foremost among the factors behind an expert's credibility is the individual's experience with the process or measure at hand. Ideally, he or she should work with this measure routinely. Also, the person must be unbiased. Experts should be neutral in connection with the measure's value and should have no personal or professional interest in it.

In addition, the credentials of external experts—published works, degrees, and other honors or awards—are important in validating their expertise. Many of these people are tapped often, and their track records can and should be checked. If their estimate has been validated in more detailed studies and was found to be consistent, this can serve as a confirmation of their qualifications in providing such data.

## Using Values from External Databases

For some measures, the use of cost (or value) estimates based on the work and research of others may be appropriate. This technique makes use of external databases that contain studies and research projects focusing on the cost of data items. Fortunately, many databases include cost studies of data items related to projects, and most are accessible on the Internet. Data are available on the costs of turnover, absenteeism, grievances, accidents, and even customer satisfaction. The difficulty lies in finding a database with studies or research germane to the particular project. Ideally, the data should originate from a similar setting in the same industry, but that is not always possible. Sometimes, data on industries or organizations in general are sufficient, with adjustments possibly required to suit the project at hand.

## Linking with Other Measures

When standard values, records, experts, and external studies are not available, a feasible alternative might be to find a relationship between the measure in question and some other measure that can be easily converted to a monetary value. This involves identifying existing relationships that show a strong correlation between one measure and another with a standard value.

A classic relationship is the correlation between job satisfaction and employee turnover. Suppose that in a project designed to improve job satisfaction, a value is needed to reflect changes in the job satisfaction index. A predetermined relationship showing the correlation between increases in job satisfaction and reductions in turnover can directly link the two measures. Using standard data or external studies, the cost of turnover can easily be determined as described earlier. Therefore, a change in job satisfaction can be immediately converted to a monetary value, or at least an approximate value. The conversion is not always exact because of the potential for error and other factors, but the estimate is sufficient for converting the data to monetary values.

Finding a correlation between a customer satisfaction measure and another measure that can easily be converted to a monetary value is sometimes possible. A strong correlation often exists between customer satisfaction and revenue. Connecting these two variables allows the monetary value of customer satisfaction to be estimated.

In some situations, a chain of relationships may establish a connection between two or more variables. A measure that may be difficult to convert to a monetary value is linked to other measures that, in turn, are linked to measures to which values can be assigned. Ultimately, these measures are traced to a monetary value typically based on profits. Figure 9-1 shows the model used by Sears.[7] The model connects job attitudes (collected directly from the employees) to customer service, which is directly related to revenue growth. The rectangles in the figure represent survey information, and the ovals represent hard data. The shaded measurements are collected and distributed in the form of Sears total-performance indicators.

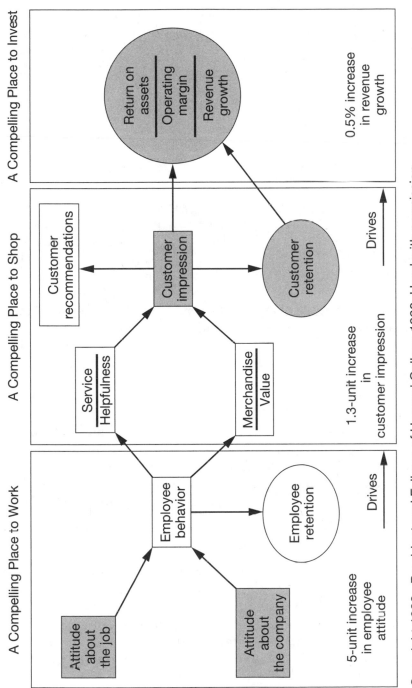

A Compelling Place to Work — A Compelling Place to Shop — A Compelling Place to Invest

**Attitude about the job**

**Attitude about the company**

Employee behavior

Employee retention

Drives

5-unit increase in employee attitude

Service / Helpfulness

Merchandise / Value

Customer recommendations

Customer impression

Customer retention

Drives

1.3-unit increase in customer impression

Return on assets / Operating margin / Revenue growth

0.5% increase in revenue growth

Copyright 1998. President and Fellows of Harvard College 1998. Used with permission.

**Figure 9-1 Relationship between Attitudes and Profits**

As the model shows, a 5-point improvement in employee attitudes leads to a 1.3-point improvement in customer satisfaction. This, in turn, drives a 0.5 percent increase in revenue growth. If employee attitudes at a local store improved by 5 points and the previous rate of revenue growth was 5 percent, the new rate of revenue growth would then be 5.5 percent.

These links between measures, often called the service-profit chain, offer a promising methodology for applying monetary values to hard-to-quantify measures.

## Using Estimates from Participants

In some cases, participants in the project should estimate the value of improvement. This technique is appropriate when participants are capable of providing estimates of the cost (or value) of the unit of measure that has improved as a result of the project. With this approach, participants should be provided with clear instructions along with examples of the type of information needed. The advantage of this approach is that the individuals who are most closely connected to the improvement are often able to provide the most reliable estimates of its value. As with isolating project effects, when estimates are used to convert measures to monetary values, adjustments are made to reduce the error in those estimates.

## Using Estimates from the Management Team

In some situations, participants in a project may be incapable of placing a value on the improvement. Their work may be so far removed from the ultimate value of the process that they cannot provide reliable estimates. In these cases, the team leaders, supervisors, or managers of participants may be able to providing estimates. Thus, they may be asked to provide a value for a unit of improvement linked to the project.

In other situations, managers are asked to review and approve participants' estimates and confirm, adjust, or reject those values. For example, suppose a project involving customer service representatives was designed to reduce customer complaints. The project did result in a reduction in complaints, but the value of a single customer complaint had to be identified to determine the value of the improvement. Although customer service representatives had knowledge of certain issues surrounding customer complaints, their scope was limited, so their managers were asked to provide a value. These managers had a broader perspective of the impact of a customer complaint.

Senior management can often provide estimates of the value of data. In this approach, senior managers concerned with the project are asked to place a value on the improvement based on their perception of its worth. This approach is used when calculating the value is difficult or when other sources of estimation are unavailable or unreliable.

## Using Project Staff Estimates

The final strategy for converting data to monetary values is using project staff estimates. Using all available information and experience, the staff members most familiar with the situation provide estimates of the value. For example, a particular project for an international oil company was designed to reduce dispatcher absenteeism and address other performance problems. Unable to identify a value using the other strategies, the consulting staff estimated the cost of an absence to be $200. This value was then used in calculating the savings from the reduction in absenteeism that followed the project implementation.

Although the project staff may be qualified to provide accurate estimates, this approach is sometimes perceived as biased. It should therefore be used only when other approaches are unavailable or inappropriate.

# Technique Selection and Finalizing Value

With so many techniques available, the challenge is selecting one or more strategies appropriate for the situation and available resources. Developing a table or list of values or techniques for the situation may be helpful. The guidelines that follow may aid in selecting a technique and finalizing the values.

## Choose a Technique Appropriate for the Type of Data

Some strategies are designed specifically for hard data, whereas others are more appropriate for soft data. Thus, the type of data often dictates the strategy. Standard values are developed for most hard data items, and company records and cost statements are used in the process. Soft data often involve the use of external databases, links with other measures, and estimates. Experts are used to convert both types of data to monetary values.

## Move from Most Accurate to the Least Accurate

The techniques in this chapter are presented in order of accuracy. Standard values are always most accurate and therefore the most credible. But, as mentioned earlier, they are not always readily available. When standard values are not available, the following sequence of operational techniques should be tried:

- Historical costs from company records
- Internal and external experts
- External databases
- Links with other measures
- Estimates

Each technique should be considered in turn based on its feasibility and applicability to the situation. The technique associated with the highest accuracy is always preferred if the situation allows.

## Consider Source Availability

Sometimes the availability of a particular source of data determines the method selection. For example, experts may be readily accessible. Some standard values are easy to find; others are more difficult. In other situations, the convenience of a technique is a major factor in the selection. The Internet, for example, has made external database searches more convenient.

As with other processes, keeping the time investment for this phase to a minimum is important so that the total effort directed to the ROI study does not become excessive. Some techniques can be implemented in much less time than others. Devoting too much time to the conversion process may dampen otherwise enthusiastic attitudes about the use of the methodology, plus drive up the costs of the evaluation.

## Use the Source with the Broadest Perspective on the Issue

According to Guiding Principle 3 in Table 2-1, the most credible data source must be used. The individual providing estimates must be knowledgeable of the processes and the issues surrounding the valuation of the data. For example, consider the estimation of the cost of a grievance in a manufacturing plant. Although a supervisor may have insight into what caused a particular grievance, he or she may have a limited perspective. A high-level manager may be able to grasp the overall impact of the grievance and how it will affect other areas. Thus, a high-level manager would be a more credible source in this situation.

## Use Multiple Techniques When Feasible

The availability of more than one technique for obtaining values for the data is often beneficial. When appropriate, multiple sources should be used to provide a basis for comparison or for additional perspectives. The data must be integrated using a convenient decision rule, such as the lowest value. The conservative approach of using the lowest value was presented as Guiding Principle 4 in Chapter 2, but this applies only when the sources have equal or similar credibility.

Converting data to monetary values has its challenges. Once the particular method has been selected and applied, several adjustments or tests are necessary to ensure the use of the most credible and appropriate value with the least amount of resources.

## Apply the Credibility Test

The discussion of techniques in this chapter assumes that each data item collected and linked to a project can be converted to a monetary value. Highly subjective data, however, such as changes in employee attitudes or a reduction in the number of employee conflicts, are difficult to convert. Although estimates can be developed using one or more strategies, such estimates may lack credibility with the target audience, which can render their use in analysis questionable.

The issue of credibility in combination with resources is illustrated in Figure 9-2. This is a logical way to decide whether to convert data to monetary values or leave them intangible. Essentially, in the absence of standard values, many other ways are available to capture the data or convert them to monetary values. However, there is a question to be answered: can it be done with minimum resources? Some of the techniques mentioned in this chapter—such as searching records or maybe even searching the Internet—cannot be performed with minimal use of resources. However, an estimate obtained from a group or from a few individuals is available with minimal use of resources. Then we move to the next question: will the executive who is interested in the project buy into the monetary value assigned to the measure with minimum explanation? If so, then it is credible enough to be included in the analysis; if not, then move it to the intangibles. The intangible benefits of a project are also important and are covered in much more detail in the next chapter.

To Convert or Not to Convert

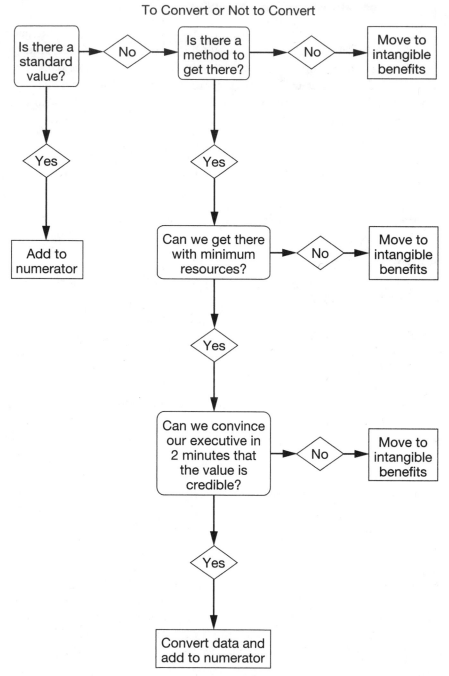

Figure 9-2  Four-Part Test: To Convert or Not to Convert?

## Consider the Possibility of Management Adjustment

In organizations where soft data are common and values are derived using imprecise methods, senior managers and administrators are sometimes offered the opportunity to review and approve the data. Because of the subjective nature of this process, management may factor (reduce) the data to make the final results more credible. In one example, senior managers at Litton Industries adjusted the value for the benefits derived from implementing self-directed teams.[8]

## Consider the Short-Term/Long-Term Issue

When data are converted to monetary values, usually one year's worth of data is included in the analysis—this is Guiding Principle 9 in Table 2-1, which states that for short-term solutions, only the first year's benefits are used. The issue of whether a project is short-term or long-term depends on the time it takes to complete or implement the project. If one group participating in the project and working through the process take months to complete it, then it is probably not short-term. Some projects literally take years to implement even for one particular group. In general, it is appropriate to consider a project short-term when one individual takes one month or less to learn what needs to be done to make the project successful. When the lag between project implementation and the consequences is relatively brief, a short-term solution is appropriate. When a project is long-term, no time limit for data inclusion is used, but the time value should be set before the project evaluation is undertaken. Input on the time value should be secured from all stakeholders, including the sponsor, champion, implementer, designer, and evaluator. After some discussion, the estimates of the time factor should be conservative and perhaps reviewed by finance and accounting. When a project is a long-term solution, forecasting will need to be used to estimate multiple years of value. No sponsor will wait several years to see how a project turns out.

## Consider an Adjustment for the Time Value of Money

Since investment in a project is made in one time period and the return is realized at a later time, some organizations adjust project benefits to reflect the time value of money using discounted-cash-flow techniques. The actual monetary benefits of the project are adjusted for the time period. The amount of adjustment, however, is usually small compared with the typical benefits of projects.

Although this may not be an issue for every project, it should be considered for each project, and some standard discount rate should be used. Consider the following example of how this is calculated. Assume that a project costs $100,000, and it is expected to take two years for the full value of the estimate to be realized. In other words, this is a long-term solution spanning two years. Using a discount rate of 6 percent, the cost for the project for the first year would be $100,000 × 106 percent = $106,000. For the second year it is $106,000 × 106 percent, or $112,360. Thus, the project cost has been adjusted for a two-year value with a 6 percent discount rate. This assumes that the project sponsor could have invested the money in some other project and obtained at least a 6 percent return on that investment.

## Final Thoughts

1. Showing the real money requires just that—money. Business impact data that have improved as a result of a project must be converted to money. Standard values make this process easier, but easy is not always an option, and other techniques must sometimes be used. However, if a measure cannot be converted with minimum resources or with no assurance of credibility, the improvement in the measure should be reported as an intangible benefit. After the data are converted to monetary values, the next step is collecting the project costs and calculating the ROI. These processes are covered in the next chapter.

# Chapter 10

# THE INTANGIBLE MEASURES

## Measuring the Hard to Measure and the Hard to Value

Project results include both tangible and intangible measures. Intangible measures are the benefits or detriments directly linked to a project that cannot or should not be converted to monetary values. By definition, and based on the guiding principles of the ROI methodology, an intangible benefit is a measure that is not converted to money (i.e., if a conversion cannot be accomplished with minimum resources and with credibility, it is considered to be an intangible). These measures are often monitored after the project has been completed. Although not converted to monetary values, they are nonetheless an important part of the evaluation process. This chapter explores the role of intangibles, how to measure them, when to measure them, and how to report them.

The range of intangible measures is almost limitless. This chapter describes just a few common and desired outcomes of projects and programs. Table 10-1 highlights 30 examples of these measures. Some measures make the list because of the difficulty in measuring them; others because of the difficulty in converting them to money. Others are on the list for both reasons. Being labeled as intangible does not mean that these items can never be measured or converted to monetary values. In one study or another, each item has been monitored and quantified in financial terms. However, in typical projects, these measures are considered intangible benefits because of the difficulty in measuring them or the difficulty in converting them to monetary values.

## Why Intangibles Are Important

Although intangible measures are not new, they are becoming increasingly important. Intangibles secure funding and drive the economy, and organizations are built on them. In every direction we look, intangibles are becoming not

## Table 10-1 Common Intangibles

| | |
|---|---|
| • Accountability | • Intellectual capital |
| • Alliances | • Innovation and creativity |
| • Attention | • Job satisfaction |
| • Awards | • Leadership |
| • Branding | • Loyalty |
| • Capability | • Networking |
| • Capacity | • Organizational commitment |
| • Clarity | • Partnering |
| • Communication | • Poverty |
| • Corporate social responsibility | • Reputation |
| • Customer service (customer satisfaction) | • Stress |
| • Employee attitudes | • Team effectiveness |
| • Engagement | • Timeliness |
| • Human life | • Sustainability |
| • Image | • Work/life balance |

only increasingly important, but also critical to organizations. Here's a recap of why they have become so important.

## Intangibles Are the Invisible Advantage

When examining the success behind many well-known organizations, intangibles are often found. A highly innovative company continues to develop new and improved products; a government agency reinvents itself; a company with highly involved and engaged employees attracts and keeps talent. An organization shares knowledge with employees, providing a competitive advantage. Still another organization is able to develop strategic partners and alliances. These intangibles do not often appear in cost statements and other record keeping, but they are there, and they make a huge difference.

Trying to identify, measure, and react to intangibles may be difficult, but the ability to do so exists. Intangibles transform the way organizations work, the way employees are managed, the way products are designed, the way services are sold, and the way customers are treated. The implications are profound, and an organization's strategy must address them. Although invisible, the presence of intangibles is felt and the results are concrete.

## We Are Entering the Intangible Economy

The intangible economy has evolved from basic changes that date to the Iron Age, which evolved into the Agricultural Age. In the late nineteenth century and during the early twentieth century the world moved into the Industrial Age. From the 1950s forward, the world has moved into the Technology and Knowledge Age, and these moves translate into intangibles. During this time, a natural evolution of technology has occurred. During the Industrial Age, companies and individuals invested in tangible assets like plants and equipment. In the Technology and Knowledge Age, companies invest in intangible assets, like brands or systems. The future holds more of the same, as intangibles continue to evolve into an important part of the overall economic system.[1]

## More Intangibles Are Converted to Tangibles

The good news is that more data once regarded as intangible are now being converted into monetary values. Because of this, classic intangibles are now accepted as tangible measures, and their value is more easily understood. Consider, for example, customer satisfaction. Just a decade ago, few organizations had a clue as to the monetary value of customer satisfaction. Now more firms have taken the extra step to link customer satisfaction directly to revenues, profits, and other measures. Companies are seeing the tremendous value that can be derived from intangibles. As this chapter will illustrate, more data are being accumulated to show monetary values, moving some intangible measures into the tangible category.

## Intangibles Drive Projects

Some projects are implemented because of the intangibles. For example, the need to have greater collaboration, partnering, communication, teamwork, or customer service will drive projects. In the public sector, the need to reduce poverty, employ disadvantaged citizens, and save lives often drives projects. From the outset, the intangibles are the important drivers and become the most important measures. Consequently, more executives include a string of intangibles on their scorecards, key operating reports, key performance indicators, dashboards, and other routine reporting systems. In some cases, the intangibles represent nearly half of all measures that are monitored.

## The Magnitude of the Investment

The Federal Reserve Bank of Philadelphia recently estimated that investment in intangible assets amounts to at least $1 trillion.[2] Only 15 percent of the value of a contemporary organization can be tied to such tangible assets as buildings and equipment. Intangible assets have become the dominant investment in businesses. They are a growing force in the economy, and measuring their values poses challenges to managers and investors. They can no longer be ignored. They must be properly identified, selected, measured, reported, and in some cases, converted to monetary values.

# Measuring and Analyzing Intangibles

In some projects, intangibles are more important than monetary measures. Consequently, these measures should be monitored and reported as part of the project evaluation. In practice, every project, regardless of its nature, scope, and content, will produce intangible measures. The challenge is to identify them effectively and report them appropriately.

## Measuring the Intangibles

From time to time it is necessary to explore the issue of measuring the difficult to measure. Responses to this exploration usually occur in the form of comments instead of questions. "You can't measure it," is a typical response. This cannot be true, because anything can be measured. What the frustrated observer suggests by the comment is that the intangible is not something you can count, examine, or see in quantities, like items produced on an assembly line. In reality, a quantitative value can be assigned to or developed for any intangible. If it exists, it can be measured. Consider human intelligence for example. Although human intelligence is vastly complex and abstract with myriad facets and qualities, IQ scores are assigned to most people and most people seem to accept them. The software engineering institute of Carnegie-Mellon University assigns software organizations a score of 1 to 5 to represent their maturity in software engineering. This score has enormous implications for the organizations' business development capabilities, yet the measure goes practically unchallenged.[3]

Several approaches are available for measuring intangibles. Intangibles that can be counted include customer complaints, employee complaints, and conflicts. These can be recorded easily, and constitute one of the most acceptable types of measures. Unfortunately, many intangibles are based on attitudes and perceptions that must be measured. The key is in the development of the instrument of measure. The instruments are usually developed around scales of 3, 5, and even 10 points to represent levels of perception. The instruments to measure intangibles consist of three basic varieties.

The first lists the intangible items and asks respondents to agree or disagree on a 5-point scale (where the midpoint represents a neutral opinion). Other instruments define various qualities of the intangible, such as its reputation. A 5-point scale can easily be developed to describe degrees of reputation, ranging from the worst rating—a horrible reputation—to the best rating—an excellent reputation. Still other ratings are expressed as an assessment on a scale of 1 to 10, after respondents review a description of the intangible.

Another instrument to measure the intangible connects it, when possible, to a measure that is easier to measure or easier to value. As shown in Figure 10-1, most hard-to-measure items are linked to an easy-to-measure item. In the classic situation, a soft measure (typically the intangible) is connected to a hard measure (typically the tangible). Although this link can be developed through logical deductions and conclusions, having some empirical evidence through a correlation analysis (as shown in the figure) and developing a significant correlation between the items is the best approach. However, a detailed analysis would have to be conducted to ensure that a causal relationship exists. In other words, just because a correlation is apparent, does not mean that one caused the other. Consequently, additional analysis, other empirical evidence, and supporting data could pinpoint the actual causal effect.

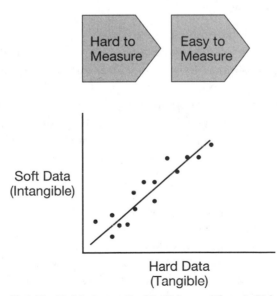

**Figure 10-1  The Link between Hard-to-Value and Easy-to-Value Items**

A final instrument for measuring the intangible is the development an index of different values. These could be a combination of both hard and soft data items that make up a particular index value. An index is a single score representing some complex factor that is constructed by aggregating the values of several different measures. Measures making up the index are sometimes weighted based on their importance to the abstract factor being measured. Some index measures are based strictly on hard data items. For example, the U.S. poverty level is based on a family income amount equal to three times the money needed to feed a family as determined by the U.S. Department of Agriculture, adjusted for inflation using the consumer price index. Sometimes an index is completely intangible, such as the customer satisfaction index developed by the University of Michigan.

Intangibles are often combined with a variety of tangibles to reflect the performance of a business unit, function, or project. Intangibles are also often associated with nonprofit, nongovernment, and public sector organizations. Table 10-2 shows the performance measures reflecting greatness at the Cleveland Orchestra. For the Cleveland Orchestra, intangibles include such items as comments from cab drivers; tangibles include ticket sales. Collectively and regardless of how difficult they are to obtain, these data sets reflect the overall performance of the orchestra.

## Converting to Money

Converting the hard to measure to monetary values is challenging to say the least. Examples in this chapter show various attempts to convert these hard-to-value measures to monetary values. When working with intangibles, the interest in the monetary contribution expands considerably. Three major groups have an interest in the monetary value. First are the sponsors who fund a particular project. They almost always seek monetary values among the measures. Second, the public is involved in some way with many intangibles. Even private sector organizations are trying to improve their image and reputation, and confidence in their organizations in the minds of the public. These days, the public is interested in the financial impacts of these organizations. They are no longer willing to accept the notion that the intangibles are enough to fund projects, particularly if they are funded by tax dollars. Third, the individuals who are actively involved with and support the project often need, and sometimes demand, that the monetary value be developed.

The approaches to convert to monetary values were detailed in Chapter 9. The specific methods used in that chapter all represent approaches that may be

**Table 10-2  Measuring Greatness at the Cleveland Orchestra**

| Superior Performance | Distinctive Impact | Lasting Endurance |
|---|---|---|
| Emotional response of audience; increase in number of standing ovations | Cleveland's style of programming increasingly copied; becoming more influential | Excellence sustained across generationsof conductors—from George Szellthrough Pierre Bou ez, Christoph von Dohnanyi, and Franz Wilser-Most |
| Wide technical range; can play any piece with excellence, no matter how difficult—from soothing and familiar classical pieces to difficult and unfamiliar modern pieces | A key point of civic pride; cab drivers say, "We're really proud of our orchestra." | Supporters donate time and money; invest in long-term success of orchestra; endowment triples |
| Increased demand for tickets; demand for more complex, imaginative programs in Cleveland, New York, and Europe | Orchestra leaders increasingly sought for leadership roles and perspectives in elite industry groups and gatherings | |
| Invited to Salzburg Festival (first time in 25 years), signifying elite status among top European orchestras | | |

Adapted from *Good to Great and the Social Sectors* by Jim Collins (Collins 2005).

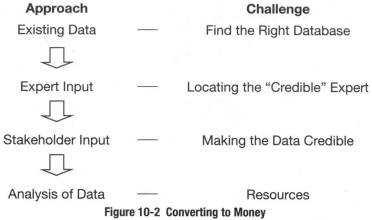

Figure 10-2  Converting to Money

used to convert the intangibles to monetary values. Although these will not be repeated here, showing the path most commonly used to capture values for the intangibles is helpful. Figure 10-2 shows the typical path of converting intangibles to monetary values, building on the methods in Chapter 9. The first challenge is to locate existing data or measure them in some way, making sure they are accurate and reliable. Next, an expert may be able to place a monetary value on the item based on experience, knowledge, credentials, and track record. Stakeholders may provide their input, although it should be factored for bias. Some stakeholders are biased in one way or the other—they want the value to be smaller or larger depending on their particular motives. These may have to be adjusted or thrown out all together. Finally, the data are converted using the conservative processes described in Chapter 9, often adjusting for the error in the process. Unfortunately, no specific rule exists for converting each intangible to monetary value. By definition, an intangible is a measure that is not converted to money. If the conversion cannot be accomplished with minimum resources and with credibility, it is left as an intangible.

## Identifying and Collecting Intangibles

Intangible measures can be taken from different sources and at different times during the project life cycle, as depicted in Figure 10-3. They can be uncovered early in the process, during the needs assessment, and their collection can be planned for as part of the overall data collection strategy. For example, one technology project has several hard data measures linked to it. Job stress, an intangible measure, is identified and monitored with no plans to convert

**Intangible Measures during the Project Life Cycle**

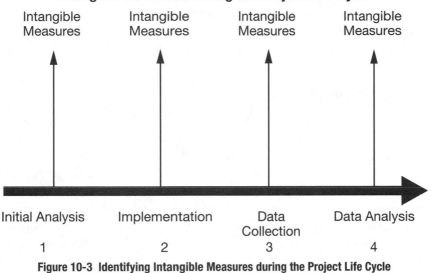

Figure 10-3  Identifying Intangible Measures during the Project Life Cycle

it to a monetary value. From the beginning, this measure is destined to be a nonmonetary, intangible benefit reported along with the ROI results.

A second opportunity to identify intangible benefits is in the planning process, when clients or sponsors of the project agree on an evaluation plan. Key stakeholders can usually identify the intangible measures they expect to be influenced by the project. For example, a change management project in a large multinational company was conducted, and an ROI analysis was planned. Project leaders, participants, participants' managers, and experts identified potential intangible measures that were perceived to be influenced by the project, including collaboration, communication, and teamwork.

A third opportunity to collect intangible measures presents itself during data collection. Although the measure may not be anticipated in the initial project design, it may surface on a questionnaire, in an interview, or during a focus group. Questions are often asked about other improvements linked to a project, and participants usually provide several intangible measures for which no plans are available to assign a value. For example, in the evaluation of a quality project, participants were asked what specifically had improved about their work area and relationships with customers as a result of the project. Participants provided more than a dozen intangible measures that managers attributed to the project.

The fourth opportunity to identify intangible measures is during data analysis and reporting, while attempting to convert data to monetary values. If the conversion loses credibility, the measure should be reported as an intangible benefit. For example, in one sales improvement project, customer satisfaction was identified early in the process as a measure of project success. A conversion to monetary values was attempted, but it lacked accuracy and credibility. Consequently, customer satisfaction was reported as an intangible benefit.

## Analyzing Intangibles

For each intangible measure identified, some evidence of its connection to the project must be shown. However, in many cases, no specific analysis is planned beyond tabulation of responses. Early attempts to quantify intangible data sometimes resulted in aborting the entire process, with no further data analysis being conducted. In some cases, isolating the effects of the project may be undertaken using one or more of the methods outlined in Chapter 9. This step is necessary when project leaders need to know the specific amount of change in the intangible measure that is linked to the project. Intangible data often reflect improvement. However, neither the precise amount of improvement nor the amount of improvement directly related to a project is always identified. Because the value of these data is not included in the ROI calculation, intangible measures are not normally used to justify another project or to justify continuing an existing project. A detailed analysis is not necessary. Intangible benefits are often viewed as additional evidence of the project's success and are presented as supportive qualitative data.

# Confronting Intangibles

There are so many intangibles that addressing them appropriately can be difficult. Many advances have been made in measuring intangibles effectively and in converting them to money. Of course, when they are converted to money, they are no longer intangible—they are tangible. This issue is not easy, but progress is being made and will continue to be made. The following section covers five areas on which organizations are focusing in measuring intangibles in the public and private sector. These measures include only a few of the examples listed in Table 10-1.

## Customer Service

Because of the importance of building and improving customer service, related measures are typically monitored to track project payoff. Several types of customer service projects have a direct influence on these measures. This

**Awareness, Attitudes, and Usage: Typical Questions**

| Type | Measures | Typical Questions |
|------|----------|-------------------|
| Awareness ⇩ | Awareness and Knowledge | Have you heard of Brand X?<br><br>What brand comes to mind when you think "luxury car?" |
| Attitudes ⇩ | Beliefs and Intentions | Is Brand X for me?<br><br>On a scale of 1 to 5, is Brand X for young people? |
| Usage ⇩ | Purchase Habits and Loyalty | Did you use Brand X this week?<br><br>What brand did you last buy? |

**Figure 10-4  Customer Service Linkage**

metric makes our list because it is perceived as difficult to measure and to convert to monetary value. However, in the last two decades, much progress has been made in this area, and some of these measures are routinely considered tangible because they are converted to money using the measures described in Chapter 9, where the technique of linking to other measures clearly illustrates the most common way in which customer service intangible measures are converted to money. This technique follows the sequence shown in Figure 10-4. The first step is to create awareness of a particular product, brand, or service. The next step is to develop attitudes that define the beliefs, opinions, and intentions regarding the product, service, or brand, and leads to usage, the final step that confirms the purchasing habits and loyalty of the customer.

This important link is ingrained in most marketing and promotion programs and processes and has led to a variety of measures that are becoming standard in the industry. Table 10-3 shows customer intangibles and underscores the array of possibilities—all aimed at developing awareness, attitudes, and usage. Perhaps the most common intangible is customer satisfaction, which is generally measured on scales of 1 to 5, 1 to 7, or 1 to 10 (although other scales are used, too). A tremendous amount of research has been accumulated about the value of satisfied customers and the loss connected with

**Table 10-3  Customer Service Intangibles**

| Metric | Definition | Issues | Purpose |
|---|---|---|---|
| Awareness | Percentage of total population who are aware of a brand | Is awareness prompted or unprompted? | Consideration of who has heard of the brand |
| Top of mind | First brand to be considered | May be subject to most recent advertising or experience | Saliency of brand |
| Knowledge | Percentage of population who know product, have recollection of its advertising | Not a formal metric.Is knowledge prompted or unprompted? | Extent of familiarity with product beyond name recognition |
| Beliefs | Customers'/consumers' view of product, generally captured via survey responses, often through ratings on a scale | Customers/consumers may hold beliefs with varying degrees of conviction | Perception of brand by attribute |
| Purchasing intentions | Probability of intention to purchase | To estimate probability of purchase, aggregate and analyze ratings of stated intentions (for example, top two boxes) | Measures pre-shopping disposition to purchase |
| Willingness to recommend | Generally measured by ratings on scale of 1 to 5 | Nonlinear in impact | Shows strength of loyalty, potential impact on others |
| Customer satisfaction | Generally measured on scale of 1 to 5, in which customers declare satisfaction with brand in general or with specific attributes | Subject to response bias; captures views of current customers, not lost customers; satisfaction is  function of expectations | Indicates likelihood of repurchase; reports of dissatisfaction show aspects requiring improvement to enhance loyalty |
| Willingness to search | Percentage of customers willing to delay purchases, change stores, or reduce quantities to avoid switching brands | Hard to capture | Indicates importance of distribution coverage |
| Loyalty | Measures include willingness to pay premium, to search, to stay | "Loyalty" itself is not a formal metric, but specific metrics do measure aspects of this dynamic. New product entries may alter loyalty levels | Indication of base future revenue stream |

Adapted from *Marketing Metrics: 50+ Metrics Every Executive Should Master* by Paul W. Farris, Neil T. Bendle, Phillip E. Pfeifer, and David J. Ribstein. (Upper Saddle River, NJ: Wharton School Publishing, 2006), p. 16.

dissatisfied customers. Using elaborate processes of decision tree analysis, probability theories, expected value, and correlations, organizations have developed detailed monetary values showing that movement in sales and profits is connected to a variety of measures. The most important measure is customer satisfaction. Within an organization, a variety of specific measures can be developed, including customer response time, sensitivity to costs and pricing issues, and creativity with customer responses. Of particular importance is the matter of timing. Providing prompt customer service is critical for most organizations. Therefore, organizations monitor the time required to respond to specific customer service requests or problems. Although reducing response times is a common objective, the measure is not usually converted to a monetary value. Thus, customer response time is usually reported as an important intangible measure.

## Innovation and Creativity

Innovation and creativity are related. Creative employees create innovative products, services, and solutions. In our knowledge- and technology-based economy, innovation, and creativity are becoming important factors in organizations' success.

### Innovation

Innovation is critical to most organizations. Just how important is innovation? Let's put it in perspective. If it were not for the intellectual curiosity of employees—thinking things through, trying out new ideas, and taking wild guesses in all the R&D labs across the country—the United States would have half the economy it has today. In a recent report on R&D, the American Association for the Advancement for Science estimated that as much as 50 percent of U.S. economic growth in the half century since the Fortune 500 came into existence is the result of advances in technology.[4]

After a few years' retrenchment and cost cutting, senior executives from a variety of industries now share the conviction that innovation—the ability to define and create new products and services and quickly bring them to market—is an increasingly important source of competitive advantage. Executives are setting aggressive performance goals for their innovation and product development organizations, targeting 20 to 30 percent improvements in such areas as time to market, development cost, product cost, and customer value.[5]

A vast disconnect lies between hope and reality, however. A recent survey of 50 companies conducted by Booz Allen Hamilton shows that companies are only marginally satisfied that their innovation organizations are delivering their maximum potential. Worse, executives say that only half the improvement efforts they launch end up meeting expectations. Several waves of improvement in innovation and product development have already substantially enhanced companies' abilities to deliver differentiated, higher-quality products to markets faster and more efficiently. However, the degree of success achieved has varied greatly among companies and among units within companies. The differences in success stem from the difficulty in managing change in the complex processes and organizations associated with innovation and product development.

Some companies have managed to assemble an integrated "innovation chain" that is truly global and allows them to outflank competitors that innovate using knowledge in a single cluster. They have been able to implement a *process* for innovating that transcends local clusters and national boundaries, becoming "meta-national innovators." This strategy of using localized pockets of technology, market intelligence, and capabilities has provided a powerful new source of competitive advantage: more higher-value innovation at lower cost.[6]

Innovation is both easy and difficult to measure. Measuring the outcomes in areas such as new products and processes, improved products and processes, copyrights, patents, inventions, and employee suggestions is easy. Many companies track these items. They can be documented to reflect the innovative profile of an organization. Unfortunately, comparing these data with previous data or benchmarking with other organizations is difficult because these measures are typically unique to each organization.

Perhaps the most obvious measure is tracking patents that are both used internally and licensed for others' use through a patent and license exchange. For example, IBM has been granted more patents than any other company in the world—more than 25,000 U.S. patents. IBM's licensing of patents and technology generates several billion dollars in profits each year. IBM and Microsoft are at the top of the list, but most organizations in the new economy monitor trademarks, patents, and copyrights as important measures of the innovative talent of their employees.

It is helpful to remember that the registration of patents stems from employees' inventive spirit. The good news is that employees do not have to be highly degreed scientists or engineers to be inventive. Although invention is often thought of in the context of technology, computing, materials, or energy, in fact it spans all disciplines and can therefore be extracted from any technological realm for application to problems in any area.[7]

Through the years, inventors have been viewed as "nerds," with much of their inventiveness explained by their quirky personality makeup. This is because history is laced with well-known inventors endowed with an eccentric personality. In fact, inventors are usually ordinary people who possess extraordinary imagination. Many modern organizations of wide-ranging focus are devoting resources to the encouragement of employee creativity from which they will gain advantage over their competition. Organizations intent on sparking ingenuity will consider innovation, monitor it, and take action to enhance it.

*Business Week* uses a widely recognized evaluation processes to develop its list of the world's most innovative companies.[8] This list of companies that produce the top 25 innovations is both comprehensive and respected. In partnership with Boston Consulting Group, the evaluation begins with a senior management survey of innovation distributed electronically to executives worldwide early in the year, targeting 1,500 global corporations determined by market capitalization. Executives are instructed to distribute the survey to their top 10 executives. The survey is also accessible on several Websites. The survey consists of 19 general questions on innovation, and questions that focus on innovation metrics. In 2006, Apple, Google, 3M, Toyota, and Microsoft composed the list's top five. Although the survey is comprehensive, it is deficient in measuring the actual monetary value attributable to innovation. Figure 10-5 shows how survey respondents measured the success of innovation. It is disappointing that only 30 percent indicated that they measure the actual ROI on innovation investments.

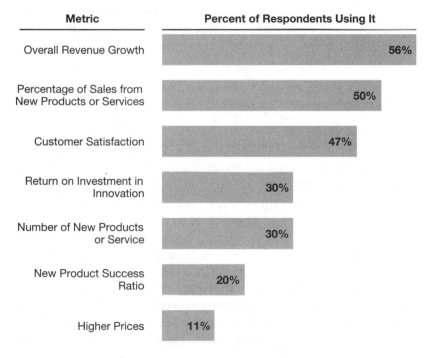

| Metric | Percent of Respondents Using It |
|---|---|
| Overall Revenue Growth | 56% |
| Percentage of Sales from New Products or Services | 50% |
| Customer Satisfaction | 47% |
| Return on Investment in Innovation | 30% |
| Number of New Products or Service | 30% |
| New Product Success Ratio | 20% |
| Higher Prices | 11% |

**Figure 10-5  Measuring the Success of Innovation**

## *Creativity*

Creativity, often considered the precursor to innovation, encompasses the creative experience, actions, and input of organizations. Measuring the creative spirit of employees may prove more difficult. An employee suggestion system, a long-time measure of the creative processes of the organization, flourishes today in many organizations and is easily measured. Employees are rewarded for their suggestions if they are approved and implemented. Tracking the suggestion rates and comparing them with other organizations is an important benchmarking item for creative capability. Other measures that can be monitored are the number of new ideas and comments. Formal feedback systems often contain creative suggestions that can lead to improved processes.

Some organizations measure the creative capabilities of employees using inventories and instruments that may be distributed at meetings and training sessions. In other organizations, a range of statements about employee creativity is included in the annual employee feedback survey. Using scaled ratings, employees either agree or disagree with the statements. Comparing actual scores of groups of employees over time reflects the degree to which employees perceive improvement in creativity in the workplace. Having consistent and comparable measures is still a challenge. Other organizations may monitor the number, duration, and participation rate of creativity training programs. The last decade has witnessed a proliferation of creativity tools, programs, and activity.

# Employee Attitudes

## *Employee Satisfaction*

An important item monitored by most organizations is employee job satisfaction. Using feedback surveys, executives can monitor the degree to which employees are satisfied with their employer's policies, work environment, and supervision and leadership; with the work itself; and with other factors. A composite rating may be developed to reflect an overall satisfaction value or an index for the organization, division, department, or region.

Whereas job satisfaction has always been an important factor in employee relations, in recent years it has taken on a new dimension because of the link between job satisfaction and other measures. The relationship between job satisfaction and the attraction and retention of employees is classic, in that firms with excellent job satisfaction ratings have better success in attracting the most desirable employees. Job satisfaction ratings high enough that companies can be titled among the "Employers of Choice" or "Best Places to Work" have gained a subtle but powerful recruiting tool. The recent heightened emphasis on the relationship between job satisfaction and employee retention owes to turnover and retention being such critical issues. These relationships are now easily developed using human capital management systems featuring modules to calculate the correlation between turnover rates and job satisfaction scores for various job groups, divisions, and departments.

Job satisfaction has taken on new dimensions in connection with customer service. Dozens of applied research projects are beginning to show a high correlation between job satisfaction scores and customer satisfaction scores. Intuitively, one understands that a more satisfied employee is likely to provide more productive, friendly, and appropriate customer service. Likewise, a disgruntled employee will provide poor service. Research has established that job attitudes (job satisfaction) relate to customer impression (customer satisfaction), which relates to revenue growth (profits). Therefore, the conclusion follows that if employee attitudes improve, revenues increase. These links, often referred to as a service profit chain, create a promising way to identify important relationships between attitudes within an organization and the profits the organization earns.

### Organizational Commitment

In recent years, organizational commitment (OC) measures have complemented or replaced job satisfaction measures. OC measures go beyond employee satisfaction to include the extent to which the employees identify with the organization's goals, mission, philosophy, values, policies, and practices. The concept of involvement and commitment to the organization is a key issue. OC more closely correlates with productivity and other performance improvement measures, whereas job satisfaction usually does not. OC is often measured in the same way as job satisfaction, using attitude surveys based on a 5-point or 7-point scale, and administered directly to employees. As organizational commitment scores (taken as a standard index) improve, a corresponding improvement in productivity should also be seen.

### Employee Engagement

A different twist to the OC measure is one that reflects employee engagement. This involves the measures that indicate the extent to which employees are actively engaged in the organization. Consider the case of the Royal Bank of Scotland Group (RBS). With more than 115,000 employees, RBS considered it a strategic imperative to measure the effectiveness of its investment in people and the impact of this investment on business performance. Consequently,

RBS built, validated, and introduced a human capital model that demonstrably links "people strategies" to performance.[9]

RBS moved beyond monitoring employee satisfaction and commitment to measuring whether employees actively improved business results. The bank did this using an employee engagement model that assesses employees' likelihood of contributing to business profits. The model linked separate elements of human resource (HR) information in a consistent way, which it then linked to key business indicators. The outputs enabled RBS to understand how to influence the bank's results through its workforce.

To test and validate its model, RBS's HR research and measurement team reviewed the array of survey instruments used in HR activities. The HR team decided to put the employee engagement model into practice in the processing and customer contact centers, where productivity measures are very important as they relate to customer service. Using the amount of work processed as a throughput measure, the team found that productivity increased in tandem with engagement levels. They were also able to establish a correlation between increasing engagement and decreasing staff turnover.

Hundreds of organizations now use engagement data, reflecting the extent to which employees are engaged and how their engagement connects with productivity and turnover.

## Leadership

Leadership is perhaps the most difficult measure to address. On the surface, it would seem easy to measure the outcome because effective leadership leads to an effective organization. However, putting a monetary value on the consequences of new leadership behavior is not as easy as it appears. Leadership can (and usually does) determine the success or failure of an organization. Without appropriate leadership behaviors throughout an organization, resources can be misapplied or wasted, and opportunities can be missed. The news and literature are laced with examples of failed leadership at the top, and accounts of mismanaged employees, shareholders, investors, and the public. Some of these high-profile failed leadership stories have been painful. At the same time, positive examples exist of leaders—for example, former General Electric CEO Jack Welch—who have won extraordinary success at many levels of their organization over a sustained period. These leaders are often documented in books, articles, and lists of admiration. They clearly make the difference in their organizations. Obviously, the ultimate measure of leadership is the overall success of the organization. Whenever overall measures of success have been achieved or surpassed, they are always attributed to great leadership—perhaps rightfully so. However, attempting to use overall success as the only measure of leadership is a cop-out in terms of accountability. Other measures must be in place to develop system-wide monitoring of leaders and leadership in the organization.

### 360° Feedback

Leadership can be measured in many different ways, perhaps the most common of which is known as 360° feedback. Here, a prescribed set of leadership behaviors desired in the organization is assessed by different sources to provide a composite of overall leadership capability and behavior. The sources often consist of the immediate manager of the leader being assessed, a colleague in the same area, the employees directly supervised by the leader, internal or external customers, and the leader's self-assessment. Combined, these assessments form a circle of influence (360°). The measure is basically an observation of behavior captured in a survey, often reported electronically. This 360° feedback has been growing rapidly in the United States, Europe, and Asia as an important way to capture overall leadership behavior change. Because the consequences of behavior change are usually measured as business impact, leadership improvement should be linked to the business in some way.

### Leadership Inventories

Another way to measure leadership is to require the management team to participate in a variety of leadership inventories, assessing predetermined leadership competency statements. The inventories reflect the extent to which a particular leadership style, approach, or even success is in place. These inventories, although popular in the 1970s and '80s, are today often being replaced by the 360° feedback process.

### Leadership Perception

It is also useful to capture the quality of leadership from the perspective of employees. In some organizations, employees regularly rate the quality of their leadership. Top executives and middle managers are typically the subjects of this form of evaluation. The measure is usually taken in conjunction with the annual feedback survey, in the form of direct statements about the executive or immediate manager with which respondents agree or disagree using a 5-point scale. This survey attempts to measure how the followers in a particular situation perceive the quality, success, and appropriateness of leadership as exercised by their managers.

## Business Impact

The outcomes of leadership development are clearly documented in many case studies involving ROI analysis. Of the thousands of studies conducted annually, leadership development ROI studies are at the top of the list—not because conducting them is easier but because of the uncertainty and the unknown aspects of investing in leadership development. Most leadership development will have an impact in a particular leader's area. Leadership development produces new skills that are applied on the job and produces improvements in the leader's particular work unit. These can vary significantly. The best way to evaluate a general leadership development program involving executives and leaders from a variety of areas is with respect to the monetary impact. When particular measures are improved, examining those measures individually makes little sense. Examining the monetary value of each measure as a whole is more worthwhile. The measures are converted to monetary values using one of the methods discussed in Chapter 9. The monetary values of the improvements from the first year are combined into a total value, ultimately leading to an ROI calculation. Leadership development programs aimed at improving leadership behavior and driving business improvement often yield high payoff, with ROI values that range from 500 percent to 1,000 percent.[10] This is primarily because of the multiplicative effect as leaders are developed and changes of behavior influence important measures in the leaders' teams.

## Human Life

Seeing human life listed as an intangible may be surprising to some. It's not intangible because of the difficulty in measuring it—obviously, bodies can be counted. Human life is often considered to be intangible because of the difficulty in converting the value of life to money. Yet, this value is required in many projects and has been used in hundreds of studies. The issue spans both the private sector and the public sector.

Consider, for example, a recommendation by federal health officials that 11- and 12-year-old girls be routinely vaccinated against the sexually transmitted human papillomavirus (HPV) that causes cervical cancer. This recommendation has been endorsed by several federal health agencies, and by insurance companies. One health insurance company, Wellpoint, Inc., announced its intention to cover the vaccine.[11] What would lead Wellpoint to this decision? Insurance companies are willing to pay for the vaccine because it can reduce the number of claims, and ultimately the number of deaths, caused by cervical and vaginal cancers. Each year in the United States alone, approximately four thousand women die from cervical cancer. The HPV vaccine Gardasil is expected to dramatically reduce this number. The results are even more staggering when it is considered that one or more types of HPV will infect more than 50 percent of sexually active women in their lifetimes. On the logic of the situation, covering the vaccination pays off for insurance companies, but only if monetary values are established for the cost of treating cancer (which should exist in insurance company records), and for the cost of a death (which also should exist in company records). Compensation limits are often defined by the amount of life insurance carried by the person who dies.

The value of a life comes into question more clearly in public policy programs, as when the government acts to try to prevent death. A cost-benefit analysis can quickly show what is economically sound to attempt. An example is the valuation of a life according to the U.S. Environmental Protection Agency, which places the value at $6.1 million.[12] This estimate was developed in 2000 to evaluate the benefits of removing arsenic from drinking water. Since then, many government studies have placed a value on a human life, and the results vary considerably, ranging from $1.5 to $5.8 million. The factors involved in placing a value on a human life include the person's age, economic status, education, and earning potential. Consequently, not every life is of equal value.

The private sector is very interested in this issue because of the risks associated with everyday dangers in the safety and health sectors of the economy. Employers must be concerned about casualties that may result from on-the-job accidents, and about their liability exposure. The value of a human life is a constant concern in the arena of risk management. Consider, for example, a health care chain that is considering a new risk management procedure that would reduce the likelihood of acts of infant abduction. Although the infant may not be killed during the act of abduction, assumptions must be made about such costs. To conduct this type of analysis, the probability of infant abduction without the risk management procedure is compared to the probability of infant abduction with the procedure in place, based on assumptions made by those who understand such processes well. The cost of the risk management procedure, which would be accounted for as an extra direct expense, is known. What must be identified to make the estimate complete is the cost of an abduction. Previous liability claims can be reviewed to estimate what it would cost the hospital should an abduction occur, based on the value of the human life. When this is known, it is a matter of using the ROI methodology to determine whether the risk management procedure is economically justified. To some, this would seem absurd, and no amount of money would be considered too great to prevent the abduction or even the death of an infant. However, organizations have limits on what they can afford and are willing to pay.

As with many intangibles, this one generates others. For example, loss of life not only generates pain and suffering for the family, but can also lower morale and can even tarnish the image of an organization. For example, the energy company British Petroleum (BP) saw its stock price nose-dive when unsafe conditions led to fatalities. BP's safety record was among the worst in the industry. After an explosion on an oil platform, investors grew alarmed and began to sell shares. This obviously was an image problem that spooked investors. A damaged public image is an expensive intangible that can generate other economic impacts as well.

In summary, human life is considered an intangible primarily because of the perceived difficulty of placing a monetary value on life. However, a human life *can be valued* and human life *is being valued* routinely, making it more likely to be measured as a tangible in the future.

## Final Thoughts

Get the picture? Intangible measures are crucial to reflecting the success of a project. Although they may not carry the weight of measures expressed in monetary terms, they are nevertheless an important part of the overall evaluation. Intangible measures should be identified, explored, examined, and monitored for changes linked to projects. Collectively, they add a unique dimension to the project report because most, if not all, projects involve intangible variables. Although five common intangible measures are explored in some detail in this chapter, the coverage is woefully incomplete. The range of intangible measures is practically limitless. Now that intangible measures have been identified, the costs must be captured and the ROI calculated next. This will be covered in the next chapter.

# Chapter 11

# PROJECT COSTS AND CALCULATING ROI

This chapter explores the costs of projects and the ROI calculation. Specific costs that should be captured are identified along with economical ways in which they can be developed. One of the primary challenges addressed in this chapter is deciding which costs should be captured or estimated. For major projects, some costs are hidden and rarely counted. The conservative philosophy presented here is to account for all costs, direct and indirect. Several checklists and guidelines are included. The monetary values for the benefits of a project are combined with project cost data to calculate the return on investment. This chapter explores the various techniques, processes, and issues involved in calculating and interpreting the ROI.

## Why Monitor Costs and Measure ROI?

One of the main reasons for monitoring costs is to create budgets for projects. The initial costs of most projects are usually estimated during the proposal process and are often based on previous projects. The only way to have a clear understanding of costs so that they can be used to determine future projects and future budgets is to track them using different categories, as explained later in this chapter.

Costs should be monitored in an ongoing effort to control expenditures and keep the project within budget. Monitoring cost activities not only reveals the status of expenditures but also gives visibility to expenditures and encourages the entire project team to spend wisely. And, of course, monitoring costs in an ongoing fashion is much easier, more accurate, and more efficient than trying to reconstruct events to capture costs retrospectively. Developing accurate costs by category builds a database for understanding and predicting costs in the future.

Monitoring project costs is an essential step in developing the ROI calculation because it represents the denominator in the ROI formula. ROI has become a critical measure demanded by many stakeholders, including clients and senior executives. It is the ultimate level of evaluation, showing the actual payoff of the project, expressed as a percentage and based on the same formula as the evaluation for other types of capital investment.

A brief example will highlight the importance of costs and ROI. A new suggestion system was implemented in a large electric utility. This new plan provided cash awards for employees when they submitted a suggestion that was implemented and resulted in cost savings. This project was undertaken to help lower the costs of this publicly owned utility. As the project was rolled out, the project leaders captured reaction to ensure that the employees perceived the suggestion system as fair, equitable, motivating, and challenging. At Level 2, they measured learning to make sure that the employees understood how to document their suggestions and how and when the awards were made. Application data (Level 3) were the actual submission of the awards, and the company had the goal of a 10 percent participation rate. Level 4 data corresponded to the actual monetary value. In this case, $1.5 million was earned or saved over a two-year period.

In most organizations, the evaluation would have stopped there. The project appeared to be a success, as the goals were met at each of the four levels. Bring on the champagne! However, the costs of the project for the same two-year period totaled $2 million. Thus, the utility company spent $2 million to have $1.5 million returned. This is a negative ROI, and it would not have been recognized if the ultimate measure, the ROI, had not been developed. (Incidentally, a negative ROI might be acceptable by some executives. After all, the intangibles for the utility showed increased commitment, engagement, ownership, teamwork, cooperation, and communications. However, if the objective was a positive ROI, this system failed to achieve it, primarily because of excessive administrative costs.)

## Fundamental Cost Issues

The first step in monitoring costs is to define and address issues relating to cost control. Several rules apply to tabulating costs. Consistency and standardization are necessary. A few guidelines follow:

- Monitor all costs, even if they are not needed.
- Costs must be realistic and reasonable.

- Costs will not be precise; estimates are okay.
- Disclose all costs.

Other key issues are detailed later in this section.

## Fully Loaded Costs

Because a conservative approach is used to calculate the ROI, costs should be fully loaded, which is Guiding Principle 10 (see Chapter 2). With this approach, all costs (direct and indirect) that can be identified and linked to a particular project are included. The philosophy is simple: for the denominator, "when in doubt, put it in" (i.e., if there is any question as to whether a cost should be included, include it, even if the cost guidelines for the organization do not require it). When an ROI is calculated and reported to target audiences, the process should withstand even the closest scrutiny, when necessary, to ensure its credibility. The only way to meet this test is to include all costs. Of course, from a realistic viewpoint, if the controller or chief financial officer insists on not using certain costs, then leaving them out or reporting them in an alternative way is suggested.

## Costs Reported without Benefits

Because costs can easily be collected, they are presented to management in many ingenious ways, such as in terms of the total cost of the project, cost per day, and cost per participant. While these may be helpful for efficiency comparisons, presenting them without identifying the corresponding benefits may be problematic. When most executives review project costs, a logical question is raised: what benefit was received from the project? This is a typical management reaction, particularly when costs are perceived to be very high.

Unfortunately, many organizations have fallen into this trap. For example, in one organization, all the costs associated with a major transformation project were tabulated and reported to the senior management team. From an executive perspective, the total figure exceeded the perceived value of the project, and the executive group's immediate reaction was to request a summary of (monetary and nonmonetary) benefits derived from the overall transformation. The conclusion was that few, if any, economic benefits were achieved from the project. Consequently, budgets for similar projects were drastically reduced in the future. While this may be an extreme example, it shows the danger of presenting only half the equation. Because of this, some organizations have developed a policy of not communicating cost data unless the benefits can be captured and presented along with the costs, even if the benefits are subjective and intangible. This helps maintain a balance between the two components.

## Develop and Use Cost Guidelines

When multiple projects are being evaluated, it may be helpful to detail the philosophy and policy on costs in the form of guidelines for the evaluators or others who monitor and report costs. Cost guidelines detail specifically which cost categories are included with projects and how the data are captured, analyzed, and reported. Standards, unit cost guiding principles, and generally accepted values are included in the guidelines. Cost guidelines can range from a one-page brief to a hundred-page document in a large, complex organization. The simpler approach is better. When fully developed, cost guidelines should be reviewed and approved by the finance and accounting staff. The final document serves as the guiding force in collecting, monitoring, and reporting costs. When the ROI is calculated and reported, costs are included in summary or table form, and the cost guidelines are usually referenced in a footnote or attached as an appendix.

## Sources of Costs

It is sometimes helpful to first consider the sources of project costs. Four major categories of sources are illustrated in Table 11-1. The charges and expenses from the project team represent the major segment of costs and are usually transferred directly to the client for payment. These are often placed in subcategories under fees and expenses. A second major cost category relates to the vendors or suppliers who assist with the project. A variety of expenses, such as consulting or advisory fees, may fall in this category. A third major cost category is those expenses borne by the client organization— both direct and indirect. In many projects, these costs are not identified but nevertheless are part of the costs of the project. The final cost category involves expenses not covered in the other three categories. These include payments for equipment and services needed for the project. Finance and accounting records should track and reflect the costs from these different sources, and the process presented in this chapter can also help track these costs.

**Table 11-1 Sources of Project Costs**

| Source of Costs | Cost Reporting Issues |
|---|---|
| Project team fees and expenses | • Costs are usually accurate<br>• Variable expenses are usually underestimated |
| Vendor/suppliers fees and expenses | • Costs are usually accurate<br>• Variable expenses are usually underestimated |
| Client expenses, direct and indirect | • Direct expenses are usually not fully loaded<br>• Indirect expenses are rarely included in costs |
| Equipment, services, and other expenses | • Sometimes understated<br>• May lack accountability |

## Prorated versus Direct Costs

Usually all costs related to a project are captured and expensed to that project. However, some costs are prorated over a longer period. Equipment purchases, software development and acquisitions, and the construction of facilities are all significant costs with a useful life that may extend beyond the project. Consequently, a portion of these costs should be prorated to the project. Under a conservative approach, the expected life of the project is fixed. Some organizations will assume a period of one year of operation for a simple project. Others may consider three to five years appropriate. If a question is raised about the specific time period to be used in this calculation, the finance and accounting staff should be consulted, or appropriate guidelines should be developed and followed.

## Employee Benefits Factor

Employee time is valuable, and when time is required for a project, the costs for that time must be fully loaded, representing total compensation, including employee benefits. This means that the employee benefits factor should be included. This number is usually well-known in the organization and is used in other costing formulas. It represents the cost of all employee benefits expressed as a percentage of payroll. In some organizations, this value is as high as 50 to 60 percent. In others, it may be as low as 25 to 30 percent. The average in the United States is 38 percent.[1]

### Table 11-2 Project Cost Categories

| Cost Item | Prorated | Expensed |
| --- | --- | --- |
| **Initial analysis and assessment** | | ✓ |
| **Development of solutions** | | ✓ |
| **Acquisition of solutions** | | ✓ |
| **Implementation** | | |
| Salaries/benefits for project team time | | ✓ |
| Salaries/benefits for coordination time | | ✓ |
| Salaries/benefits for participant time | | ✓ |
| Project materials | | ✓ |
| Hardware/software | ✓ | |
| Travel/lodging/meals | | ✓ |
| Use of facilities | | ✓ |
| Capital expenditures | ✓ | |
| **Maintenance and monitoring** | | ✓ |
| **Administrative support and overhead** | ✓ | |
| **Evaluation and reporting** | | ✓ |

## Specific Costs to Include

Table 11-2 shows the recommended cost categories for a fully loaded, conservative approach to estimating project costs. Consistency in capturing all these costs is essential, and standardization adds credibility. Each category is described in this section.

### Initial Analysis and Assessment

One of the most underestimated items is the cost of conducting the initial analysis and assessment that leads to the need for the project. In a comprehensive project, this involves data collection, problem solving, assessment, and analysis. In some projects, this cost is near zero because the project is implemented without an initial assessment of need. However, as more project sponsors place attention on needs assessment and analysis in the future, this item will become a significant cost.

### Development of Project Solutions

Also significant are the costs of designing and developing the project solution. These costs include time spent in both the design and development and the purchase of supplies, technology, and other materials directly related to the solution. As with needs assessment costs, design and development costs are usually charged to the project. However, if the solution can be used in other projects, the major expenditures can be prorated.

## Acquisition Costs

In lieu of development costs, some project leaders use acquisition costs connected to the purchasing of solutions from other sources to use directly or in a modified format. The costs for these solutions include the purchase price, support materials, and licensing agreements. Some projects have both acquisition costs and solution development costs. Acquisition costs can be prorated if the acquired solutions can be used in other projects.

## Implementation Costs

The largest cost segment in a project is associated with implementation and delivery. The time (salaries and benefits), travel, and other expenses of those involved in the project in any way should be included. These costs can be estimated using average or midpoint salary values for corresponding job classifications. When a project is targeted for an ROI calculation, participants can provide their salaries directly in a confidential manner. Project materials, such as field journals, instructions, reference guides, case studies, surveys, and participant workbooks, should be included in the implementation costs, along with license fees, user fees, and royalty payments. Supporting hardware, software, CD-ROMs, and videos should also be included.

The cost for the use of facilities needed for the project should be included. For external meetings, this is the direct charge for the conference center, hotel, or motel. If the meetings are conducted in-house, the conference room represents a cost for the organization, and the cost should be estimated and incorporated— even if it is uncommon to include facilities costs in other cost reporting. If a facility or building is constructed or purchased for the project, it is included as a capital expenditure, but is prorated. The same is true for the purchase of major hardware and software when they are considered capital expenditures.

## Maintenance and Monitoring

Maintenance and monitoring involve routine expenses necessary to maintain and operate the project. These are ongoing expenses that allow the new project solution to continue. They may involve staff members and additional expenses, and they may be significant for some projects.

## Support and Overhead

The cost of support and overhead includes the additional costs not directly charged to the project—any project cost not considered in the above calculations. Typical items are the cost of administrative/clerical support, telecommunication expenses, office expenses, salaries of client managers, and other fixed costs. Usually, this is provided in the form of an estimate allocated in some convenient way.

## Evaluation and Reporting

The total evaluation cost completes the fully loaded costs. Activities under evaluation costs include developing the evaluation strategy, designing instruments, collecting data, analyzing data, preparing a report, and communicating the results. Cost categories include time, materials, purchased instruments, surveys, and any consulting fees.

# Cost Classifications

Project costs can be classified in two basic ways. One is with a description of the expenditures, such as labor, materials, supplies, or travel. These are expense account classifications, which are standard with most accounting systems. The other way to classify costs is to use the categories in the project steps, such as initial analysis, development, implementation, maintenance, overhead, and evaluation. An effective system monitors costs by account category according to the description of those accounts, but also includes a method for accumulating costs for the process steps. Many systems stop short of this second step, grouping. Although the first grouping adequately states the total project costs, it does not allow for a useful comparison with other projects to provide information on areas where costs might be excessive.

# The ROI Calculation

The term *return on investment* for projects and programs is occasionally misused, sometimes intentionally. In this misuse, a very broad definition for ROI is given that includes any benefit from the project. ROI becomes a vague concept in which even subjective data linked to a program are included. In this book, the return on investment is defined more precisely and represents an actual value determined by comparing project costs to benefits. The two most common measures are the benefits/costs ratio (BCR) and the ROI formula. Both are presented along with other approaches to calculate the return or payback.

The formulas presented in this chapter use annualized values so that the first-year impact of the investment can be calculated for short-term projects. Using annualized values is becoming an accepted practice for developing the ROI in many organizations. This approach is a conservative way to develop the ROI, since many short-term projects have added value in the second or third year. For long-term projects, longer time frames should be used. For example, in an ROI analysis of a project involving major software purchases, a five-year time frame was used. However, for short-term projects that take only a few weeks to implement (such as a leadership development program), first-year values are appropriate.

In selecting the approach to measure ROI, the formula used and the assumptions made in arriving at the decision to use this formula should be communicated to the target audience. This helps prevent misunderstandings and confusion surrounding how the ROI value was developed. Although several approaches are described in this chapter, two stand out as preferred methods: the benefits/costs ratio and the basic ROI formula. These two approaches are described next.

## Benefits/Costs Ratio

One of the original methods for evaluating projects was the benefits/costs ratio. This method compares the benefits of the project with the costs, using a simple ratio. In formula form,

$$BCR = \frac{\text{Project benefits}}{\text{Project costs}}$$

In simple terms, the BCR compares the annual economic benefits of the project with the costs of the project. A BCR of 1 means that the benefits equal the costs. A BCR of 2, usually written as 2:1, indicates that for each dollar spent on the project, two dollars were returned in benefits.

The following example illustrates the use of the BCR. A behavior modification project designed for managers and supervisors was implemented at an electric and gas utility. In a follow-up evaluation, action planning and business performance monitoring were used to capture the benefits. The first-year payoff for the program was $1,077,750. The total, fully loaded implementation costs were $215,500. Thus, the ratio was

$$BCR = \frac{\$1,077,750}{\$215,500} = 5{:}1$$

For every dollar invested in the project, five dollars in benefits were returned.

## ROI Formula

Perhaps the most appropriate formula for evaluating project investments is net program benefits divided by costs. This is the traditional financial ROI and is directly related to the BCR. The ROI ratio is usually expressed as a percentage where the fractional values are multiplied by 100. In formula form,

$$ROI(\%) = \frac{\text{Net project benefits}}{\text{Project costs}} \times 100$$

Net project benefits are project benefits minus costs. Another way to calculate ROI is to subtract 1 from the BCR and multiply by 100 to get the ROI percentage. For example, a BCR of 2.45 is the same as an ROI value of 145 percent (1.45 × 100%). This formula is essentially the same as the ROI for capital investments. For example, when a firm builds a new plant, the ROI is developed by dividing annual earnings by the investment. The annual earnings are comparable to net benefits (annual benefits minus the cost). The investment is comparable to the fully loaded project costs.

An ROI of 50 percent means that the costs were recovered and an additional 50 percent of the costs were returned. A project ROI of 150 percent indicates that the costs have been recovered and an additional 1.5 times the costs are returned.

An example illustrates the ROI calculation. Public- and private-sector groups concerned about literacy have developed a variety of projects to address the issue. Magnavox Electronics Systems Company was involved in one literacy project that focused on language and math skills for entry-level electrical and mechanical assemblers. The results of the project were impressive. Productivity and quality alone yielded an annual value of $321,600.

The total, fully loaded costs for the project were just $38,233. Thus, the return on investment was

$$ROI = \frac{\$321,600 - \$38,233}{\$38,233} \times 100 = 741\%$$

For each dollar invested, Magnavox received $7.40 in return after the costs of the consulting project were recovered.

Investments in plants, equipment, subsidiaries, or other major items are not usually evaluated using the benefits/costs method. Using the ROI formula to calculate the return on project investments essentially places these investments on a level playing field with other investments whose valuation uses the same formula and similar concepts. The ROI calculation is easily understood by key management and financial executives who regularly work with investments and their ROIs.

## Monetary Benefits

Profits can be generated through increased sales or cost savings. In practice, there are more opportunities for cost savings than for profits. Cost savings can be realized when improvements in productivity, quality, efficiency, cycle time, or actual cost reduction occur. In a review of almost five hundred studies, the vast majority of them were based on cost savings. Approximately 85 percent of the studies used a payoff based on cost savings from output, quality, efficiency, time, or a variety of soft data measures. The others used a payoff based on sales increases, where the earnings were derived from the profit margin. Cost savings are important for nonprofits and public-sector organizations, where opportunities for profit are often unavailable. Most projects or programs are connected directly to cost savings; ROIs can still be developed in such settings.

The formula provided above should be used consistently throughout an organization. Deviations from or misuse of the formula can create confusion, not only among users but also among finance and accounting staff. The chief financial officer (CFO) and the finance and accounting staff should become partners in the implementation of the ROI methodology. The staff must use the same financial terms as those used and expected by the CFO. Without the support, involvement, and commitment of these individuals, the wide-scale use of ROI will be unlikely.

### Table 11-3 Misused Financial Terms

| Term | Misuse | CFO Definition |
|---|---|---|
| ROI | Return of information<br>Return of intelligence | Return on investment |
| ROE | Return on expectation<br>Return on events | Return on equity |
| ROA | Return on anticipation | Return on assets |
| ROCE | Return on client expectation | Return on capital employed |
| ROP | Return on people | ? |
| ROR | Return on resources | ? |
| ROT | Return on technology | ? |
| ROW | Return on web | ? |
| ROM | Return on marketing | ? |
| ROO | Return on objectives | ? |
| ROQ | Return on quality | ? |

Table 11-3 shows some financial terms that are misused in literature. Terms such as *return on intelligence* (or *information*), abbreviated as ROI, do nothing but confuse the CFO, who assumes that ROI refers to the return on investment described above. Sometimes *return on expectations* (ROE), *return on anticipation* (ROA), and *return on client expectations* (ROCE) are used, also confusing the CFO, who assumes the abbreviations refer to return on equity, return on assets, and return on capital employed, respectively. The use of these terms in the payback calculation of a project will also confuse and perhaps lose the support of the finance and accounting staff. Other terms such as *return on people, return on resources, return on technology,* and *return on web* are often used with almost no consistency in terms of financial calculations. The bottom line: don't confuse the CFO. Consider this person an ally, and use the same terminology, processes, and concepts when applying financial returns for projects.

## ROI Targets

Specific expectations for ROI should be developed before an evaluation study is undertaken. Although no generally accepted standards exist, four strategies have been used to establish a minimum expected requirement, or hurdle rate, for the ROI of a project or program. The first approach is to set the ROI using the same values used for investing in capital expenditures, such as equipment, facilities, and new companies. For North America, Western Europe, and most of the Asian Pacific area, including Australia and New Zealand, the cost of capital is quite low, and the internal hurdle rate for ROI is usually in the 15–20 percent range. Thus, using this strategy, organizations would set the expected ROI for a project at the same value expected from other investments.

A second strategy is to use an ROI minimum target value that is above the percentage expected for other types of investments. The rationale is that the ROI process for projects and programs is still relatively new and often involves subjective input, including estimations. Because of this, a higher standard is required or suggested.

A third strategy is to set the ROI value at a break-even point. A 0 percent ROI represents break even; this is equivalent to a BCR of 1. This approach is used when the goal is to recapture the cost of the project only. This is the ROI objective for many public-sector organizations, where all of the value and benefit from the program come through the intangible measures, which are not converted to monetary values. Thus, an organization will use a break-even point for the ROI based on the reasoning that it is not attempting to make a profit from a particular project.

A fourth, and often the recommended, strategy is to let the client or program sponsor set the minimum acceptable ROI value. In this scenario, the individual who initiates, approves, sponsors, or supports the project establishes the acceptable ROI. Almost every project has a major sponsor, and that person may be willing to specify an acceptable value. This links the expectations for financial return directly to the expectations of the sponsor.

# Other ROI Measures

In addition to the traditional ROI formula, several other measures are occasionally used under the general heading of return on investment. These measures are designed primarily for evaluating other financial measures but sometimes work their way into project evaluations.

## Payback Period (Break-Even Analysis)

The payback period is commonly used for evaluating capital expenditures. With this approach, the annual cash proceeds (savings) produced by an investment are compared against the original cash outlay for the investment to determine the multiple of cash proceeds that is equal to the original investment. Measurement is usually in terms of years and months. For example, if the cost savings generated from a project are constant each year, the payback period is determined by dividing the original cash investment (including development costs, expenses, etc.) by the expected or actual annual savings. The net savings are found by subtracting the project expenses.

To illustrate this calculation, assume that the initial cost of a project is $100,000 and the project has a three-year useful life. Annual net savings from the project are expected to be $40,000. Thus, the payback period is

$$\text{Payback period} = \frac{\text{Total investment}}{\text{Annual savings}} = \frac{\$100,000}{\$40,000} = 2.5 \text{ years}$$

The project will "pay back" the original investment in 2.5 years.

The payback period method is simple to use but has the limitation of ignoring the time value of money. It has not enjoyed widespread use in the evaluation of project investments.

## Discounted Cash Flow

Discounted cash flow is a method of evaluating investment opportunities in which certain values are assigned to the timing of the proceeds from the investment. The assumption behind this approach is that a dollar earned today is more valuable than a dollar earned a year from now, based on the accrued interest possible from investing the dollar.

There are several ways of using the discounted-cash-flow concept to evaluate a project investment. The most common approach uses the net present value of an investment. The savings each year are compared with the outflow of cash required by the investment. The expected annual savings are discounted based on a selected interest rate, and the outflow of cash is discounted by the same interest rate. If the present value of the savings exceeds the present value of the outlays, after the two have been discounted by the common interest rate, the investment is usually considered acceptable by management. The discounted-cash-flow method has the advantage of ranking investments, but it requires calculations that can become difficult. Also, for the most part, it is very subjective.

## Internal Rate of Return

The internal rate of return (IRR) method determines the interest rate necessary to make the present value of the cash flow equal zero. This represents the maximum rate of interest that could be paid if all project funds were borrowed and the organization was required to break even on the project. The IRR considers the time value of money and is unaffected by the scale of the project. It can be used to rank alternatives and to accept or reject decisions when a minimum rate of return is specified. A major weakness of the IRR method is that it assumes all returns are reinvested at the same internal rate of return. This can make an investment alternative with a high rate of return look even better than it really is and make a project with a low rate of return look even worse. In practice, the IRR is rarely used to evaluate project investments.

# Final Thoughts

ROI, the final evaluation level, compares costs with benefits. Costs are important and should be fully loaded in the ROI calculation. From a practical standpoint, some costs may be optional and depend on the organization's guidelines and philosophy. However, because of the scrutiny ROI calculations typically receive, all costs should be included, even if this goes beyond the requirements of the organization's policy. After the benefits are collected and converted to monetary values and the project costs are tabulated, the ROI calculation itself is easy. Plugging the values into the appropriate formula is the final step. This chapter presented the two basic approaches for calculating return: the ROI formula and the benefits/costs ratio. Each has its advantages and disadvantages. Alternatives to the standard ROI determination were also briefly discussed.

Now that the process has been fully laid out, the next chapter details how to forecast the value of a project, including its ROI.

# Chapter 12

# THE BUSINESS CASE
## FORECASTING VALUE, INCLUDING ROI

Confusion sometimes exists about when to develop the ROI. The traditional approach, described in previous chapters, is to base ROI calculations on business impact obtained after the project or program is implemented, using business performance measures converted to monetary values. This chapter illustrates that ROI can be calculated at earlier stages—even before the project or program is initiated.

## Why Forecast ROI?

Although ROI calculations based on post-project data are the most accurate, sometimes it is important to know the forecast before the project is initiated or before final results are tabulated. Certain critical issues drive the need for a forecast before the project is completed, or even pursued.

### Expensive Projects

In addition to reducing uncertainty, forecasting may be appropriate for costly projects. In these cases, implementation is not practical until the project has been analyzed to determine the potential ROI. For example, if the project involves a significant amount of effort in design, development, and implementation, a client may not want to expend the resources—not even for a pilot test—unless some assurance of a positive ROI can be given. In another example, an expensive equipment purchase may be necessary to launch a process or system. An ROI may be necessary prior to purchase, to ensure that the monetary value of the process outcomes outweigh the cost of equipment and implementation. While there may be trade-offs in deploying a lower-profile, lower-cost pilot, the pre-project ROI is still important, and may prompt some clients to stand firm until an ROI forecast is produced.

## High Risks and Uncertainty

Sponsors want to remove as much uncertainty as possible from the project and act on the best data available. This concern sometimes pushes the project to a forecast ROI, even before any resources are expended to design and implement it. Some projects are high-risk opportunities or solutions. In addition to being expensive, they may represent critical initiatives that can make or break an organization. Or the situation may be one where failure would be disastrous, and where there is only one chance to get it right. In these cases, the decision maker must have the best data possible, and the best data possible often include a forecast ROI.

For example, one large restaurant chain developed an unfortunate reputation for racial insensitivity and discrimination. The fallout brought many lawsuits and caused a public relations nightmare. The company undertook a major project to transform the organization—changing its image, attitudes, and actions. Because of the project's high stakes and critical nature, company executives requested a forecast before pursuing the project. They needed to know not only whether this major program would be worthwhile financially, but also what specifically would change, and how specifically the program would unfold. This required a comprehensive forecast involving various levels of data, up to and including the ROI.

## Post-Project Comparison

An important reason for forecasting ROI is to see how well the forecast holds up under the scrutiny of post-project analysis. Whenever a plan is in place to collect data on a project's success, comparing actual results to pre-project expectations is helpful. In an ideal world, a forecast ROI would have a defined relationship with the actual ROI—or at least one would lead to the other, after adjustments. The forecast is often an inexpensive process because it involves estimates and assumptions. If the forecast becomes a reliable predictor of the post-project analysis, then the forecast ROI might substitute for the actual ROI. This could save money on the use of post-project analysis.

## Compliance

More than ever, organizations are requiring a forecast ROI before they undertake major projects. For example, one organization requires any project with a budget exceeding $500,000 to have a forecast ROI before it grants project approval. Some units of government have enacted legislation that requires project forecasts. With increasing frequency, formal policy and legal structures are reasons to develop ROI forecasts.

Collectively, these reasons are leading more organizations to develop ROI forecasts so their sponsors will have an estimate of projects' expected payoff.

## The Trade-offs of Forecasting

The ROI can be developed at different times and with different levels of data. Unfortunately, the ease, convenience, and costs involved in capturing a forecast ROI create trade-offs in accuracy and credibility. As shown in Table 12-1, there are five distinct time intervals during a project when the ROI can be developed. The relationship between the timing of the ROI and the factors of credibility, accuracy, cost, and difficulty is also shown in this table.

- A **pre-project forecast** can be developed using estimates of the impact of the project This approach lacks credibility and accuracy, but is the least expensive and least difficult to calculate. Because of the interest in pre-project forecasting, this scenario is expanded.

**Table 12-1 Time Intervals when ROI Can Be Developed**

| ROI with | Data Collection Timing (Relative to Project) | Credibility | Accuracy | Cost to Develop | Difficulty |
|---|---|---|---|---|---|
| 1. Pre-project data | Before project | Not very credible | Not very accurate | Inexpensive | Not difficult |
| 2. Reaction data | During project | | | | |
| 3. Learning data | During project | | | | |
| 4. Application data | After project | | | | |
| 5. Business impact data | After project | Very credible | Very accurate | Expensive | Very difficult |

- **Reaction data** can be extended to develop an anticipated impact, including the ROI. In this case, participants anticipate the chain of impact as a project is implemented and drives specific business measures. This is done after the project has begun. While accuracy and credibility increase from the pre-project basis, this approach lacks the credibility and accuracy desired in many situations. However, it is easily accomplished and is a low-cost option.

- In projects where there is a substantial learning component, **learning data** can be used to forecast the ROI. This approach is applicable only when formal testing shows a relationship between test scores and subsequent business performance. When this correlation is available (it is usually developed to validate the test), test data can be used to forecast subsequent performance. The performance can then be converted to monetary impact, and the ROI can be developed. This has less potential as a forecasting tool.

- When frequency of skills or knowledge use is critical, the **application and implementation** of those skills or knowledge can be converted to a value using a concept called *utility analysis*. While this is particularly helpful in situations where competencies are being developed and values are placed on improving competencies, it has limited applications in most projects.

- Finally, the ROI can be developed from **business impact data** converted directly to monetary values and compared to the cost of the program. This is not a forecast; but is a post-project evaluation—the basis for other ROI calculations in this book. It is the preferred approach, but because of the pressures outlined above, examining ROI calculations at other times and with other levels is sometimes necessary.

This chapter discusses in detail pre-project ROI forecasting and ROI forecasting based on reactions. In less detail, ROI forecasts developed from learning and application data are also discussed.

# Pre-Project ROI Forecasting

Perhaps one of the most useful ways to convince a sponsor that a project is beneficial is to forecast the ROI for the project. The process is similar to the post-project analysis, except that the extent of the impact must be estimated along with the project costs.

## Basic Model

Figure 12-1 shows the basic model for capturing the data necessary for a pre-project forecast, a modified version of the post-program ROI process model presented in Chapter 2. In the pre-project forecast, the project outcomes are estimated, rather than being collected after project implementation. Data collection is kept simple, and relies on interviews, focus groups, or surveys of experts. Tapping into benchmarking studies or locating previous studies may also be helpful.

Beginning at the reaction level, anticipated or estimated reactions are captured. Next, the anticipated learning that must occur is developed, followed by the anticipated application and implementation data. Here, the estimates focus on what must be accomplished for the project to be successful. These items may be based on the objectives at each of these levels. Finally, the impact data are estimated by experts. These experts may include subject matter experts, the supplier, or potential participants in the project. In this model, the levels build on each other. Having data estimated at Levels 1, 2, and 3 enhances the quality of the estimated data at Level 4 (impact), which is needed for the analysis.

The model shows that there is no need to isolate the effects of a project as in the post-project model. The individual providing the data is asked the following question: "How much will the business impact measure change as a result of the project?" This question ties the change in the measure directly to the project; thus, isolation is not needed. This approach makes this process easier than the post-evaluation model, where isolating project impact is always required.

Converting data to money is straightforward using a limited number of techniques. Locating a standard value or finding an expert to make the estimate is the logical choice. Analyzing records and databases are less likely alternatives at the forecasting stage. Securing estimates from stakeholders is the technique of last resort.

Estimating the project's costs should be an easy step because costs can easily be anticipated on the basis of previous or similar projects, factoring in reasonable assumptions about the project. To achieve a fully loaded cost profile, include all cost categories.

The anticipated intangibles are merely speculation in forecasting but can be reliable indicators of which measures may be influenced in addition to those included in the ROI calculation. At this point, it is assumed that these measures will not be converted to money.

The formula used to calculate the ROI is the same as that used in the post-analysis. The net monetary value from the data conversion is included

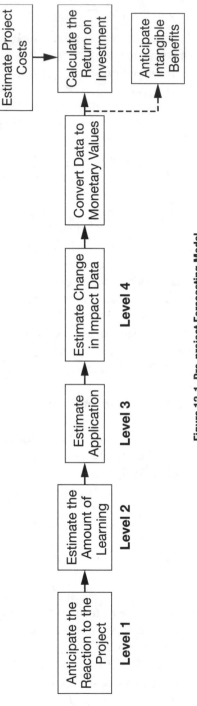

**Figure 12-1  Pre-project Forecasting Model**

204

as the numerator, and the estimated cost of the project is inserted as the denominator. The projected cost-benefit analysis can be developed along with the ROI. The specific steps to develop the forecast are detailed next.

## Basic Steps to Forecast ROI

Eighteen detailed steps are necessary to develop a credible pre-project ROI forecast using expert input:

1. **Understand the situation.** Individuals providing input to the forecast and conducting the forecast must have a good understanding of the present situation. This is typically a requirement for selecting the experts.

2. **Predict the present.** The project is sometimes initiated because a particular business impact measure is not doing well. However, such measures often lag the present situation; they may be based on data that are several months old. Also, these measures are based on dynamic influences that may change dramatically and quickly. It may be beneficial to estimate where the measure is now, based on assumptions and current trends. Although this appears to be a lot of work, it does not constitute a new responsibility for most of the experts, who are often concerned about the present situation. Market share data, for example, are often several months old. Trending market share data and examining other influences driving market share can help organizations understand the current situation.

3. **Observe warnings.** Closely tied to predicting the present is making sure that warning signs are observed. Red flags signal that something is going against the measure in question, causing it to go in an undesired direction or otherwise not move as it should. These often raise concerns that lead to projects. These are early warnings that things may get worse; they must be factored into the situation as forecasts are made.

4. **Describe the new process, project, program, or solution.** The project must be completely and clearly described to the experts so they fully understand the mechanics of what is to be implemented. The description should include the project scope, the individuals involved, time factors, and whatever else is necessary to express the magnitude of the project and the profile of the solution.

5. **Develop specific objectives.** These objectives should mirror the levels of evaluation and should include reaction objectives, learning

objectives, application objectives, and impact objectives. Although these may be difficult to develop, they are developed as part of the up-front analysis described in Chapter 3. Objectives provide clear direction toward the project's end. The cascading levels represent the anticipated chain of impact that will occur as the project is implemented.

6. **Estimate what participants will think about the project.** In this step, the experts are trying to understand participants' reaction: Will they support the project? How will they support it? What may cause participants to become unsupportive? The response is important because a negative reaction can cause a project to fail.

7. **Estimate what the participants will learn.** To some extent, every project will involve learning, and the experts will estimate what learning will occur. Using the learning objectives, the experts will define what the participants will learn as they enter the project, identifying specific knowledge, skills, and information the participants must acquire or enhance during the project.

8. **Anticipate what participants should accomplish in the project.** Building on the application objectives, the experts will identify what will be accomplished as the project is implemented successfully. This step details specific actions, tasks, and processes that will be taken by the individuals. Steps 6, 7, and 8—based on reaction, learning, and application—provide important information that serves as the basis for the next step, estimating improvement in business impact data.

9. **Estimate the improvement in business impact data.** This is a critical step in that the data generated are needed for the financial forecast. The experts will provide the estimate—in either absolute numbers or percentages—of the monetary change in the business impact measure ($\Delta P$). While accuracy is important, it is also important to remember that a forecast is no more than an estimate based on the best data available at a given point. This is why the next step is included.

10. **Apply the confidence estimate.** Because the estimate attained in the previous step is not very accurate, an error adjustment is needed. This is developed by deriving a confidence estimate on the value identified in Step 9. The experts are asked to indicate the confidence they have in the previous data. The confidence level is expressed as a percentage, with 0 indicating "no confidence" and 100 percent indicating "certainty." This becomes a discount factor in the analysis.

11. **Convert the business impact data to monetary values.** Using one or more methods described in Chapter 9, the data are converted to money. If the impact measure is a desired improvement such as productivity, the value represents the gain obtained by having one more unit of the measure. If it is a measure that the organization is trying to reduce—like downtime, mistakes, or complaints—the value is the cost that the organization incurs as a result of one incident. For example, the cost of unwanted employee turnover may be 1.5 times annual pay. This value is noted with the letter $V$.

12. **Develop the estimated annual impact of each measure.** The estimated annual impact is the first-year improvement directly related to the project. In formula form, this is expressed as $\Delta I = \Delta P \times V \times 12$ (where $\Delta I$ = annual change in monetary value, $\Delta P$ = annual change in performance of the measure, and $V$ = the value of that measure). If the measure is weekly or monthly, it must be converted to an annual amount. For example, if three lost-time accidents will be prevented each month, the time saved represents a total of 36.

13. **Factor additional years into the analysis for projects that will have a significant useful life beyond the first year.** For these projects, the factor should reflect the diminished benefit of subsequent years. The client or sponsor of the project should provide some indication of the amount of the reduction and the values developed for the second, third, and successive years. It is important to be conservative by using the smallest numbers possible.

14. **Estimate the fully loaded project costs.** In this step, use all the cost categories described in Chapter 11, and denote the value as $C$ when including it in the ROI equation. Include all direct and indirect costs in the calculation.

15. **Calculate the forecast ROI.** Using the total projected benefits and the estimated costs in the standard ROI formula. Calculate the forecast ROI as follows:

$$\text{ROI}(\%) = \frac{\Delta I - C}{C} \times 100$$

16. **Use sensitivity analysis to develop several potential ROI values with different levels of improvement ($\Delta P$).** When more than one measure is changing, the analysis may take the form of a spreadsheet showing various output scenarios and the subsequent ROI forecasts. The break-even point will be identified.

17. **Identify potential intangible benefits.** Anticipate intangible benefits using input from those most knowledgeable about the situation on the basis of assumptions from their experience with similar projects. Remember, the intangible benefits are those benefits not converted to monetary values, but possessing value nonetheless.

18. **Communicate the ROI projection and anticipated intangibles with caution.** The target audience must clearly understand that the forecast is based on several assumptions (clearly defined), and that although the values are the best possible estimates, they may include a degree of error.

Following these eighteen steps will enable an individual to forecast the ROI.

## Sources of Expert Input

Several sources of expert input are available for estimating improvement in impact data when the project is implemented. Ideally, experience with similar projects in the organization will help form the basis of the estimates the experts make. The experts may include

- Clients and/or sponsors
- Members of project team
- Prospective participants
- Subject matter experts
- External experts
- Advocates (who can champion the project)
- Finance and accounting staff
- Analysts (if one is involved with the project)
- Executives and/or managers
- Customers

Collectively, these sources provide an appropriate array of possibilities for helping estimate the value of an improvement. Because errors may develop, ask for a confidence measure when using estimates from any source.

## Securing Input

With the experts clearly identified, three major steps must be addressed before developing the ROI. First, data must be collected from the individuals listed as experts. If the number of individuals is small (for example, one person from each of the expert groups involved), a short interview may suffice. During interviews, it is critical to avoid bias and to ask clear, succinct questions that are not leading. Questions should be framed in a balanced way to capture what may occur as well as what may not. If groups are involved, using focus groups may be suitable. For large numbers, surveys or questionnaires may be appropriate.

When the groups are diverse and scattered, the Delphi technique may be appropriate. This technique, originally developed by the Rand Corporation in the 1950s, has been used in forecasting and decision making in a variety of disciplines. The Delphi technique was originally devised to help experts achieve better forecasts than they might obtain through traditional group meetings by allowing access to the group without in-person contact. Necessary features of a Delphi procedure are anonymity, continuous iteration, controlled feedback to participants, and a physical summary of responses. Anonymity is achieved by means of a questionnaire that allows group members to express their opinions and judgments privately. Between all iterations of the questionnaire the facilitator informs the participants of the opinions of their anonymous colleagues. Typically this feedback is presented as a simple statistical summary using a mean or median value. The facilitator takes the group judgment as the statistical average in the final round.[1]

In some cases, benchmarking data may be available and can be considered as a source of input for this process. The success of previous studies may provide input essential to the project as well. It may include an extensive search of databases using a variety of search engines. The important point is to understand, as much as possible, what may occur as a result of the project.

## Conversion to Money

The measures forecast by the experts must be converted to monetary values for one, two, three, or more years depending on the nature and scope of the project. Standard values are available for many of these measures. Considering the importance of these measures, someone has probably placed monetary values on them. If not, experts are often available to convert the data to monetary values. Otherwise, existing records or databases may be appropriate sources. Another option is to ask stakeholders—perhaps some of the experts listed above—to provide these values for the forecast. This step is the only means of showing the money made from the project. Chapter 9 covered these techniques in more detail.

## Estimate Project Costs

Project cost estimates are based on the most reliable information available, and include the typical categories outlined in Table 11-2. The estimates can be based on previous projects. Although the costs are unknown, this task is often relatively easy to accomplish because of its similarity to budgeting, a process with usually routine procedures and policies in place. Dividing costs into categories representing the functional processes of the project provides additional insight into project costs. Areas often not given enough attention include analysis, assessment, evaluation, and reporting. If these elements are not properly addressed, much of the value of the project may be missed. With these costs and monetary benefits, the forecast can be made using the calculations presented in Chapter 11.

## Case Study: Forecasting ROI for a Technology Solution

Global Financial Services (GFS) was in the process of implementing contact management software to enable its sales relationship managers to track routine correspondence and communication with customers. A needs assessment and initial analysis determined the project was needed. The project would involve further detailing, selecting an appropriate software package, and implementing the software with appropriate job aids, support tools, and training. However, before pursuing the project and purchasing the software, a forecast ROI was needed. Following the steps previously outlined, it was determined that four business impact measures would be influenced by implementation of this project:

1. Increase in sales to existing customers
2. Reduction in customer complaints caused by missed deadlines, late responses, and failure to complete transactions
3. Reduction in response time for customer inquiries and requests
4. Increase in the customer satisfaction composite survey index

Several individuals provided input in examining the potential problem. With comprehensive customer contact management software in place, relationship managers should benefit from quick and effective customer communication and have easy access to customer databases. The software should also provide the functionality to develop calendars and to-do lists. Relationship managers should further benefit from features such as built-in contact management, calendar sharing, and the fact that the software is

Internet-ready. To determine the extent to which the four measures would change, input was collected from six sources:

1. Internal software developers with expertise in various software applications provided input on expected changes in each of the measures.
2. Marketing analysts supplied information on sales cycles, customer needs, and customer care issues.
3. Relationship managers provided input on expected changes in the variables if the software was used regularly.
4. The analyst who confirmed the initial need for the software provided supplemental data.
5. The sponsor provided input on what could be expected from the project.
6. The proposed vendor provided input based on previous experience.

When input is based on estimates, the actual results will usually differ significantly. However, GFS was interested in a forecast based on analysis that, although very limited, would be strengthened with the best easily available expert opinion. Input was adjusted on the basis of the estimates and other information to assess its credibility. After discussing the availability of data and examining the techniques to convert it to monetary values, the following conclusions were reached:

- The increase in sales could easily be converted to a monetary value as the average margin for sales increase is applied directly.
- The cost of a customer complaint could be based on an internal value currently in use, providing a generally accepted cost.
- Customer response time was not tracked accurately, and the value of this measure was not readily available, making it an intangible benefit.
- No generally accepted value for increasing customer satisfaction was available, so customer satisfaction impact data would be listed as an intangible benefit.

The forecast ROI calculation was developed from combined input based on the variety of estimates. The increase in sales was easily converted to monetary values using the margin rates, and the reduction in customer complaints was easily converted using the discounted value of a customer complaint. The costs for the project could easily be estimated based on input from those who briefly examined the situation. The total costs included development costs, materials, software, equipment, facilitators, facilities, and lost time for learning activities, coordination, and evaluation. This fully loaded projected cost, compared to the benefits, yielded a range of expected ROI values. Table 12-2 shows possible scenarios based on payoffs of the two measures as assessed by six experts. The ROI values range from a low of 12 percent to a high of 180 percent. The break-even point could be developed with different scenarios. With these values in hand, the decision to move forward was easy: even the worst-case scenarios were positive and the best case was expected to yield more than 10 times the ROI of the worst. As this example illustrates, the process must be simple, and must use the most credible resources available to quickly arrive at estimates.

## Forecasting with a Pilot Program

Because of inaccuracies inherent in a pre-project forecast, a better approach is to develop a small-scale pilot project with the ROI based on post-program data. This involves the following steps:

1. As in the previous process, develop Level 1, 2, 3, and 4 objectives.
2. Implement the project on a small-scale sample as a pilot project, excluding all the bells and whistles. (This keeps the project costs low without sacrificing project integrity.)
3. Fully implement the project with one or more of the groups who can benefit from the initiative.
4. Develop the ROI using the ROI process model for post-project analysis as outlined in previous chapters.
5. Based on the results of the pilot project, decide whether to implement the project throughout the organization. Data can be developed using all six of the measures outlined in this book: reaction, learning, application, impact, ROI, and intangibles.

Evaluating a pilot project and withholding full implementation until its results can be developed provides less risk than developing an ROI forecast. Wal-Mart uses this method to evaluate pilot programs before implementing them throughout its chain of four thousand U.S. stores. Using pilot groups of 18 to 30 stores called *flights,* the decision to implement a project throughout the system is based on six types of post-program data (reaction, learning, application, impact, ROI, and intangibles).

## Forecasting ROI with Reaction Data

When a reaction evaluation includes the planned applications of a project, the data can ultimately be used in an ROI forecast. ROI information can be

Table 12-2 Expected ROI Values for Different Outputs

| Expert | Potential Sales Increase | Basis | Potential Complaint Reduction (Monthly Reduction) | Basis | Expected ROI | Credibility Rating (5 = highest 1 = lowest) |
|---|---|---|---|---|---|---|
| Relationship. mgr. | 3.5% | Sales opportunity | 3 | Lower response time | 60% | 3 |
| District mgr. | 4% | Customer satisfaction | 4 | Lower response time | 90% | 4 |
| Marketing analyst | 3% | Missed opportunity | 5 | Quicker response | 120% | 4 |
| Project sponsor | 5% | Customer services | 4 | Quicker response | 77% | 4 |
| Vendor | 10% | Customer loyalty | 12 | Higher priority | 180% | 2 |
| IT Analyst | 2% | Customer relationships | 3 | Faster response | 12% | 2 |

developed with questions concerning how participants plan to implement the project and what results they expect to achieve. For example, consider a project proposed by a major pharmaceutical company. The firm was considering installing high-speed DSL lines in the homes of each of its pharmaceutical sales representatives on the premise that this would save the reps time that they could otherwise spend with their customers. However, reaction to the proposed project was not positive. The sales reps said they do most of their online work at night when speed is not such an issue, and even if they did save time, they would be unlikely to add another call to their schedule, or even be able to spend more time with customers. Although the project's goals had merit, from the standpoint of forecast monetary value, the project would not add value or improve the original measure.

## Data Collection

To forecast ROI at this level, at the beginning of a project participants are asked to state specifically how they plan to use the project and what results they expect to achieve. They are asked to convert their planned accomplishments into monetary values and show the basis for developing the values. Participants can adjust their responses with a confidence factor to make the data more credible. Next, estimates are adjusted for confidence level. When tabulating data, participants multiply the confidence levels by annual monetary values. This produces a conservative estimate for use in data analysis. For example, if a participant estimated the monetary impact of the project at $10,000 but was only 50 percent confident in his or her estimate, a $5,000 value would be used in the ROI forecast calculations.

To develop a summary of the expected benefits, discard any data that are incomplete, unusable, extreme, or unrealistic. Then total the individual data items. Finally, as an optional exercise, adjust the total value again by a factor that reflects the unknowns in the process and the possibility that participants will not achieve the results they anticipate. This adjustment factor can be estimated by the project team. In one organization, the benefits are divided by two to develop a number to use in the calculation. Finally, calculate the forecast ROI using the net benefits from the project divided by the project costs.

## Case Study: Forecasting ROI from Reaction Data

This process can best be described using an actual case. Global Engineering and Construction Company (GEC) designs and builds large commercial projects like plants, paper mills, and municipal water systems. Safety is always a critical matter at GEC and usually commands much management attention. To improve safety performance, a safety improvement project was initiated for project engineers and construction superintendents. The project solution involved policy changes, audits, and training. The project focused on safety leadership, safety planning, safety inspections, safety meetings, accident investigation, safety policies and procedures, safety standards, and worker's compensation. Safety engineers and superintendents (participants) were expected to improve the safety performance of their individual construction projects. A dozen safety performance measures used in the company were discussed and analyzed at the beginning of the project. At that time, participants completed a feedback questionnaire that probed specific action items planned as a result of the safety project and provided estimated monetary values of the planned actions. In addition, participants explained the basis for estimates and placed a confidence level on their estimates. Table 12-3 presents data provided by the participants. Only 19 of the 25 participants supplied data. (Experience has shown that approximately 50 to 90 percent of participants will provide usable data on this series of questions.) The estimated cost of the project, including participants' salaries for the time devoted to the project, was $358,900.

The monetary values of the planned improvements were extremely high, reflecting the participants' optimism and enthusiasm at the beginning of an impressive project from which specific actions were planned. As a first step in the analysis, extreme data items were omitted (one of the guiding principles of the methodology). Data such as "millions," "unlimited," and "$4 million" were discarded, and each remaining value was multiplied by the confidence value and totaled. This adjustment is one way of reducing highly subjective estimates. The resulting tabulations yielded a total improvement of $990,125 (rounded to $990,000). The projected ROI, which was based on the feedback questionnaire at the beginning of the project, is

$$\text{ROI} = \frac{\$990,000 - \$358,900}{\$358,900} \times 100 = 176\%$$

Although these projected values are subjective, the results were generated by project participants who should be aware of what they could accomplish. A follow-up study would determine the true results delivered by the group.

Table 12-3  Level 1 Data for ROI Forecast Calculations

| Participant No. | Estimated Value | Basis | Confidence Level | Adjusted |
|---|---|---|---|---|
| 1 | $80,000 | Reduction in lost-time accidents | 90% | $72,000 |
| 2 | 91,200 | OSHA Reportable injuries | 80% | 72,960 |
| 3 | 55,000 | Accident reduction | 90% | 49,500 |
| 4 | 10,000 | First-aid visits/visits to doctor | 70% | 7,000 |
| 5 | 150,000 | Reduction in lost-time injuries | 95% | 142,500 |
| 6 | Millions | Total accident cost | 100% | — |
| 7 | 74,800 | Worker's compensation | 80% | 59,840 |
| 8 | 7,500 | OSHA citations | 75% | 5,625 |
| 9 | 50,000 | Reduction in accidents | 75% | 37,500 |
| 10 | 36,000 | Worker's compensation | 80% | 28,800 |
| 11 | 150,000 | Reduction in total accident costs | 90% | 135,000 |
| 12 | 22,000 | OSHA Fines/citations | 70% | 15,400 |
| 13 | 140,000 | Accident reductions | 80% | 112,000 |
| 14 | 4 million | Total cost of safety | 95% | — |
| 15 | 65,000 | Total worker's compensation | 50% | 32,500 |
| 16 | Unlimited | Accidents | 100% | — |
| 17 | 20,000 | Visits to doctor | 95% | 19,000 |
| 18 | 45,000 | Injuries | 90% | 40,500 |
| 29 | 200,000 | Lost-time injuries | 80% | 160,000 |
| | | | **Total** | **$990,125** |

## Use of the Data

Caution is required when using a forecast ROI: The calculations are highly subjective and may not reflect the extent to which participants will achieve results. A variety of influences in the work environment and project setting can enhance or inhibit the attainment of performance goals. Having high expectations at the beginning of a project is no guarantee that those expectations will be met. Project disappointments are documented regularly.

Although the process is subjective and possibly unreliable, it does have some usefulness.

1. If the evaluation must stop at this point, this analysis provides more insight into the value of the project than data from typical reaction input, which report attitudes and feelings about a project. Sponsors and managers usually find this information more useful than a report stating that "40 percent of project team participants rated the project above average."

2. These data can form a basis for comparing different projects of the same type (e.g., safety projects). If one project forecast results in an ROI of 300 percent and a similar project forecast results in a 30 percent ROI, it would appear that one project may be more effective. The participants in the first project have more confidence in the planned implementation of the project.

3. Collecting these types of data focuses increased attention on project outcomes. Participants will understand that specific action is expected, which produces results for the project. The data collection helps participants plan the implementation of what they are learning. This issue becomes clear to participants as they anticipate results and convert them to monetary values. Even if the forecast is ignored, the exercise is productive because of the important message it sends to participants.

4. The data can be used to secure support for a follow-up evaluation. A skeptical manager may challenge the data and this challenge can be converted into support for a follow-up to see whether the forecast holds true. The only way to know whether these results will materialize is to conduct a post-project evaluation.

5. If a follow-up evaluation of the project is planned, the post-project results can be compared to the ROI forecast. Comparisons of forecast and follow-up data are helpful. If there is a defined relationship between the two, the less expensive forecast can be substituted for the more expensive follow-up. Also, when a follow-up evaluation is planned, participants are usually more conservative with their projected estimates.

The use of ROI forecasting with reaction data is increasing, and some organizations have based many of their ROI forecast calculations on this type of data. For example, Wachovia Bank routinely develops ROI forecasts with reaction data. Although they may be subjective, the calculations do add value, particularly if they are part of a comprehensive evaluation system.

## Forecasting ROI with Learning Data

Testing for changes in skills and knowledge in a project or program is a common method for measuring learning. In many situations, participants are required to demonstrate their knowledge or acquired skills during a project implementation, and their performance is expressed as a numeric value. When this type of test is developed, it must be reliable and valid. Because a test should reflect the content of the project or program, successful mastery of content should be related to improved job performance. A relationship between test scores and subsequent on-the-job performance should be evident. This relationship, expressed as a correlation coefficient, is a measure of validity for the test.

This situation provides an opportunity for an ROI calculation with learning data using valid test results. When a statistically significant relationship exists between test scores and on-the-job performance (output) and the performance can be converted to monetary values, it is possible to use test scores to estimate the ROI during the project.

This approach is best applied when significant learning takes place or when the project focuses almost entirely on developing learning solutions. The absence of validated tests can create problems because the instruments cannot be used to forecast actual performance unless their validity is ensured. Other resources provide more detail on how to conduct a forecast from learning data.[2]

## Forecasting ROI with Application Data

Although not as credible as desired, a forecast can be made on the basis of the improved competencies or skills of the project implementation team. This process uses the concept of utility analysis, which is best described in the experience of a large European bank that was seeking to develop a leadership program for its executives. Bank managers identified the specific competencies they wanted to develop. Before making the €8 million investment in the program, the senior executive team wanted to know the value it would add. The project team used utility analysis to conduct the forecast.

First, the team assessed the percentage of executives' jobs covered in the leadership competencies. To keep it simple, assume that this involved

**Table 12-4 Forecasting Using Improved Competencies**

| | |
|---|---|
| Percentage of managers' jobs covered by competencies | 40% |
| Average manager's salary | €100,000 |
| Monetary value of covered competencies (40% × €100,000) | €40,000 |
| Percentage of anticipated improvement in competencies | 10% |
| Added benefit of improved competencies in monetary terms(€40,000 × 10%) | €4,000 per manager |
| Cost of program per participant | €3,000 per manager |
| ROI | 33% |

40 percent of their job content. This amount was derived from the sample of the management team. Next the average salary was determined—say, €100,000, to keep it simple. Thus, the project could influence 40 percent of €100,000, or €40,000. The managers assessed the team's current level of performance of the competencies using a convenient scale. After reviewing the competencies and the program's objectives, the managers indicated that a 10 percent improvement could be achieved on these competencies by implementing the leadership development program. Thus, the program had a potential of improving the €40,000 portion of their salary by 10 percent, or €4,000. (In essence, it would add €4,000.) Table 12-4 provides a summary of this process. This value is compared to the proposed participant cost for the leadership program to determine the forecast on an individual basis. If the cost of the program is €3,000, the ROI is 33 percent.

Although this example is simple, it shows the concept of forecasting based on improving competencies. It could be forecasted, as in the example, or collected at application time, after the competencies have been developed and applied. However, it ignores what the managers or executives will accomplish with the competencies, so it is not as credible as a Level 4 (impact) ROI. Nevertheless, it has value and is described in more detail in other sources.[3]

## Forecasting Guidelines

With the four different forecasting time frames outlined in this chapter, it may help to follow a few guidelines known to drive the forecasting possibilities within an organization. These guidelines are based on experience in forecasting in a variety of projects and programs.[4]

1. **If you must forecast, forecast frequently.** Forecasting is an art and a science. Users can build comfort, experience, and history with the process by using it frequently.

2. **Make forecasting an essential part of the evaluation mix.** This chapter began with a list of essential reasons for forecasting. The use of forecasting is increasingly being demanded by many organizations. It can be an effective and useful tool when used properly and in conjunction with other types of evaluation data. Some organizations have targets for the use of forecasting (e.g., if a project exceeds a certain cost, it will always require a pre-project forecast). Others will target a certain number of projects for a forecast based on reaction data and use those data in the manner described. It is important to plan for the forecast and let it be a part of the evaluation mix, using it regularly.

3. **Forecast different types of data.** Although most of this chapter focuses on how to develop a forecast ROI using the standard ROI formula, forecasting the value of the other types of data is important as well. A useable, helpful forecast will include predictions about reaction and perceived value, the extent of learning, and the extent of application and implementation. These types of data are very important in anticipating movements and shifts, based on the project that is planned. It assists in developing the overall forecast and helps the project team understand the project's total anticipated impact.

4. **Secure input from those who know the process best.** As forecasts are developed, it is essential to secure input from individuals who understand the dynamics of the workplace and the measures being influenced by the project—go to the experts. This will increase not only the accuracy of the forecast, but also the credibility of the results. In other situations, it may be the analysts who are aware of the major influences in the workplace and the dynamics of those changes.

5. **Long-term forecasts will usually be inaccurate.** Forecasting works better when it covers a short time frame. Most short-term scenarios afford a better grasp of the influences that might drive the measures. In the long-term, a variety of new influences, unforeseen now, could enter the process and drastically change the impact measures. If a long-term forecast is needed, it should be updated regularly.

6. **Expect forecasts to be biased.** Forecasts will consist of data coming from those who have an interest in the issue. This is unavoidable. Some will want the forecast to be optimistic; others will have a pessimistic view. Almost all input is biased in one way or another. Every attempt should be made to minimize the bias, adjust for the bias, or adjust for the uncertainty in the process. Still, the audience should recognize the forecast as a biased prediction.

7. **Serious forecasting is hard work.** The value of forecasting often depends on the amount of effort put into the process. High-stake projects or programs need a serious approach, collecting all possible data, examining different scenarios, and making the best prediction available. It is in these situations that mathematical tools can be most valuable.

8. **Review the success of forecasting routinely.** As forecasts are made, it is imperative to revisit the forecast with post-project data to check its accuracy. This can aid in the continuous improvement of the processes. Sources could prove to be more or less credible, specific inputs may be more or less biased, certain analyses may be more appropriate than others. It is important to constantly improve the methods and approaches for forecasting within the organization.

9. **The assumptions are the most serious error in forecasting.** Of all the variables that can enter the process, assumptions offer the greatest opportunity for error. It is important for the assumptions to be clearly understood and communicated. When multiple inputs are given, each forecaster should use the same set of assumptions, if possible.

10. **Utility is the most important characteristic of forecasting.** The most important use of forecasting is providing information and input for the decision maker. Forecasting is a tool for those attempting to make decisions about project implementation. It is not a process intended to maximize the output or minimize any particular variable. It is not a process undertaken to dramatically change the way a project is implemented. It is a process to provide data for decisions.

## Final Thoughts

This chapter illustrates that ROI calculations can be developed at different times and at different evaluation levels, although most project leaders focus only on impact data for ROI calculations. Although post-project data are desired, impact data are not yet available in many situations. ROI forecasts developed before a project begins can be useful to the sponsor and are sometimes necessary before projects can be approved. Forecasts made during project implementation can be useful to management and participants, and can focus participants' attention on the economic impact of the project. However, using ROI estimates during the project may give a false sense of accuracy. As expected, pre-project ROI forecasts have the least credibility and accuracy, yet have the advantage of being inexpensive and relatively easy to develop. ROI calculations using impact data are more credible and accurate than forecasts but are expensive and difficult to develop. The reality is that forecasting is an important part of the measurement mix. It should be pursued routinely and used regularly in decision making. Whether a forecast ROI or a post-analysis ROI, the results must be reported to stakeholders. The next chapter details how and when results are communicated and who they are communicated to.

# Chapter 13

# RESULTS REPORTING

Now that we have the results in hand, what's next? Should the results be used to modify the project, change the process, demonstrate the contribution, justify new projects, gain additional support, or build goodwill? How should the data be presented? The worst course of action is to do nothing. Achieving results without communicating them is like planting seeds and failing to fertilize and cultivate the seedlings—the yield will be less than optimal. This chapter provides useful information for presenting evaluation data to various audiences in the form of both oral and written reports.

## Why the Concern about Communicating Results?

Communicating results is critical to project success. The results achieved must be conveyed to stakeholders not just at project completion but throughout the duration of the project. Continuous communication maintains the flow of information so that adjustments can be made and all stakeholders are kept up to date on the status of the project.

Mark Twain once said, "Collecting data is like collecting garbage—pretty soon we will have to do something with it." Measuring project success and gathering evaluation data mean nothing unless the findings are communicated promptly to the appropriate audiences so that they are apprised of the results and can take action in response if necessary. Communication is important for many reasons, some of which are detailed next.

## Communication Is Necessary to Make Improvements

Information is collected at different points during the process, and providing feedback to involved groups enables them take action and make adjustments if needed. Thus, the quality and timeliness of communication are critical to making improvements. Even after the project is completed, communication is necessary to make sure the target audience fully understands the results achieved, and how the results may be enhanced in future projects or in the current project, if it is still operational. Communication is the key to making important adjustments at all phases of the project.

## Communication Is Necessary to Explain the Contribution

The overall contribution of the project, as determined from the six major types of measures, is unclear at best. The different target audiences will each need a thorough explanation of the results. The communication strategy—including techniques, media, and the overall process—will determine the extent to which each group understands the contribution. Communicating results, particularly in terms of business impact and ROI, can quickly overwhelm even the most sophisticated target audiences. Communication must be planned and implemented with the goal of making sure the respective audiences understand the full contribution.

## Communication Is a Politically Sensitive Issue

Communication is one of those issues that can cause major problems. Because the results of a project may be closely linked to political issues within an organization, communicating the results can upset some individuals while pleasing others. If certain individuals do not receive the information, or if it is delivered inconsistently between groups, problems can quickly surface. Not only must the information be understood, but issues relating to fairness, quality, and political correctness make it crucial that the communication be constructed and delivered effectively to all key individuals.

## Different Audiences Need Different Information

With so many potential target audiences requiring communication on the success of a project, the communication must be individually tailored to their needs. A varied audience has varied needs. Planning and effort are necessary to ensure that each audience receives all the information it needs, in the proper format, at the proper time. A single report for presentation to all audiences is inappropriate. The scope, the format, and even the content of the information will vary significantly from one group to another. Thus, the target audience is the key to determining the appropriate method of communication.

Communication is a critical need for the reasons just cited, although it is often overlooked or underfunded in projects. This chapter presents a variety of techniques for accomplishing communication of all types for various target audiences.

# Principles of Communicating Results

The skills one must possess to communicate results effectively are almost as sensitive and sophisticated as those necessary for obtaining results. The style of the communication is as important as the substance. Regardless of the message, audience, or medium, a few general principles apply.

## Communication Must Be Timely

In general, project results should be communicated as soon as they become known. From a practical standpoint, however, it is sometimes best to delay the communication until a convenient time, such as the publication of the next client newsletter or the next general management meeting. Several questions are relevant to the timing decision. Is the audience ready for the results in view of other issues that may have developed? Is the audience expecting results? When will the delivery have the maximum impact on the audience? Do circumstances dictate a change in the timing of the communication?

## Communication Should Be Targeted to Specific Audiences

As stated earlier, communication is usually more effective if it is designed for the specific group being addressed. The message should be tailored to the interests, needs, and expectations of the target audience. The results of the project should reflect outcomes at all levels, including the six types of data presented in this book. Some of the data are developed earlier in the project and communicated during the implementation of the project. Other data are collected after project implementation and communicated in a follow-up study. The results, in their broadest sense, may incorporate early feedback in qualitative form all the way to ROI values expressed in varying quantitative terms.

## Media Should Be Carefully Selected

Certain media may be more appropriate for a particular group than others. Face-to-face meetings may be preferable to special bulletins. A memo distributed exclusively to top executives may be a more effective outlet than the company newsletter. The proper format of communication can determine the effectiveness of the process.

## Communication Should Be Unbiased and Modest in Tone

For communication to be effective, fact must be separated from fiction and accurate statements distinguished from opinions. Some audiences may approach the communication with skepticism, anticipating the presence of biased opinions. Boastful statements can turn off recipients, and most of the content will be lost. Observable phenomena and credible statements carry much more weight than extreme or sensational claims. Although such claims may get an audience's attention, they often detract from the importance of the results.

## Communication Must Be Consistent

The timing and content of the communication should be consistent with past practices. A special presentation at an unusual time during the course of the project may provoke suspicion. Also, if a particular group, such as top management, regularly receives communication on outcomes, it should continue receiving communication even if the results are not positive. Omitting unfavorable results leaves the impression that only positive results will be reported.

## Testimonials Are More Effective When They Come from Respected Individuals

Opinions are strongly influenced by other people, particularly those who are respected and trusted. Testimonials about project results, when solicited from individuals who are respected within the organization, can influence the effectiveness of the message. This respect may be related to leadership ability, position, special skills, or knowledge. A testimonial from an individual who commands little respect and is regarded as a substandard performer can have a negative impact on the message.

## The Audience's Opinion of the Project Will Influence the Communication Strategy

Opinions are difficult to change, and a negative opinion toward a project or project team may not change with the mere presentation of facts. However, the presentation of facts alone may strengthen the opinions held by those who already support the project. Presentation of the results reinforces their position and provides them with a defense in discussions with others. A project team with a high level of credibility and respect may have a relatively easy time communicating results. Low credibility can create problems when one is trying to be persuasive.

These general principles are vital to the overall success of the communication effort. They should serve as a checklist for the project team planning the dissemination of project results.

# The Process for Communicating Results

The communication of project results must be systematic, timely, and well planned, and the process must include seven components in a precise sequence. The first step is critical and consists of an analysis of the need to communicate the results from a project. Possibly, a lack of support for the project was identified, or perhaps the need for adjusting or maintaining the funding for the project was uncovered. Instilling confidence or building credibility for the project may be necessary. It is important first of all to outline the specific reasons for communicating the results.

The second step focuses on the plan for communication. Planning should include numerous agenda items to be addressed in all communications about the project. Planning also covers the actual communication, detailing the specific types of data to be communicated, and when and to which groups the communication will be presented.

The third step involves selecting the target audiences for communication. Audiences range from top management to past participants, and each audience has its own special needs. All groups should be considered in the communication strategy. An artfully crafted, targeted delivery may be necessary to win the approval of a specific group.

The fourth step is developing a report, the written material explaining project results. This can encompass a wide variety of possibilities, from a brief summary of the results to a detailed research document on the evaluation effort. Usually, a complete report is developed, and selected parts or summaries from the report are used for different media.

Media selection is the fifth step. Some groups respond more favorably to certain methods of communication. A variety of approaches, both oral and written, are available to the project leaders.

The content, in the form of detailed information, represents the sixth step. The communication is delivered with the utmost care, confidence, and professionalism.

The last step, but certainly not the least significant, is analyzing reactions to the communication. Positive reactions, negative feedback, and a lack of comments are all indicators of how well the information was received and understood. An informal analysis may be appropriate for many situations. For an extensive and more involved communication effort, a formal, structured feedback process may be necessary. The nature of the reactions could trigger an adjustment to the subsequent communication of results for the same project or provide input for adapting future project communications.

The various steps are discussed further in the following sections.

## The Need for Communication

Because there may be various reasons for communicating results, a list should be tailored to the organization and adjusted as necessary. The reasons for communicating results depend on the specific project, the setting, and the unique needs of each party. Some of the most common reasons are

- Securing approval for the project and the allocation of time and money
- Gaining support for the project and its objectives
- Securing agreement on the issues, solutions, and resources
- Enhancing the credibility of the project leader
- Reinforcing the processes used in the project
- Driving action for improvement in the project
- Preparing participants for the project
- Optimizing results throughout the project and the quality of future feedback
- Showing the complete results of the project
- Underscoring the importance of measuring results
- Explaining techniques used to measure results
- Motivating participants to become involved in the project
- Demonstrating accountability for expenditures
- Marketing future projects

There may be other reasons for communicating results, so the list should be tailored to the needs of each organization.

## The Communication Plan

Any activity must be carefully planned to achieve maximum results. This is a critical part of communicating the results of the project. The actual planning of the communication is important to ensure that each audience receives the proper information at the right time and that necessary actions are taken. Several issues are crucial in planning the communication of results:

- What will be communicated?
- When will the data be communicated?
- How will the information be communicated?
- Where will the information be communicated?
- Who will communicate the information?
- Who is the target audience?
- What are the specific actions required or desired?

The communication plan is usually developed when the project is approved. This plan details how specific information is to be developed and communicated to various groups and the expected actions. In addition, this plan details how the overall results will be communicated, the time frame for communication, and the appropriate groups to receive the information. The project leader, key managers, and stakeholders need to agree on the degree of detail in the plan.

## The Audience for Communications

The following questions should be asked about each potential audience for communication of project results:

- Are they interested in the project?
- Do they really want to receive the information?
- Has a commitment been made to include them in the communications?
- Is the timing right for this audience?
- Are they familiar with the project?
- How do they prefer to have results communicated?
- Do they know the project leader? The project team?

- Are they likely to find the results threatening?
- Which medium will be most convincing to this group?

For each target audience, three steps are necessary. To the greatest extent possible, the project leader should get to know and understand the target audience. Also, the project leader should find out what information is needed and why. Each group will have its own required amount of information; some will want detailed information while others will prefer a brief overview. Rely on the input from others to determine the audience's needs. Finally, the project leaders should take into account audience bias. Some audiences will immediately support the results, others may oppose them, and still others will be neutral. The staff should be empathetic and try to understand the basis for the differing views. Given this understanding, communications can be tailored to each group. This is critical when the potential exists for the audience to react negatively to the results.

## Basis for Selecting the Audience

The target audiences for information on project results are varied in terms of job levels and responsibilities. Determining which groups will receive a particular item of communication requires careful thought, because problems can arise when a group receives inappropriate information or is overlooked altogether. A sound basis for audience selection is to analyze the reason for the communication, as discussed earlier. Table 13-1 identifies common target audiences and the basis for audience selection. Several audiences stand out as critical. Perhaps the most important audience is the client. This group (or individual) initiates the project, reviews data, usually selects the project leader, and weighs the final assessment of the effectiveness of the project. Another important target audience is top management. This group is responsible for allocating resources to the project and needs information to help them justify expenditures and gauge the effectiveness of the efforts.

Participants need feedback on the overall success of the effort. Some individuals may not have been as successful as others in achieving the desired results. Communicating the results creates additional pressure to implement the project effectively and improve results in the future. For those achieving excellent results, the communication will serve as reinforcement. Communication of results to project participants is often overlooked, with the assumption that once the project is completed, they do not need to be informed of its success.

Communicating with the participants' immediate managers is essential. In many cases, these managers must encourage participants to implement

## Table 13-1 Common Target Audiences

| Primary Target Audience | Reason for Communication |
|---|---|
| Client, top executives | To secure approval for the project |
| Immediate managers, team leaders | To gain support for the project |
| Participants, team leaders | To secure agreement with the issues |
| Top executives | To enhance the credibility of the project leader |
| Immediate managers | To reinforce the processes used in the project |
| Project team | To drive action for improvement |
| Team leaders | To prepare participants for the project |
| Participants | To improve the results and quality of future feedback |
| Stakeholders | To show the complete results of the project |
| Client, project team | To underscore the importance of measuring results |
| Client, project support staff | To explain the techniques used to measure results |
| Team leaders | To create the desire for a participant to be involved |
| All employees | To demonstrate accountability for expenditures |
| Prospective clients | To market future projects |

the project. Also, they are key in supporting and reinforcing the objectives of the project. An appropriate return on investment strengthens the commitment to projects and enhances the credibility of the project team.

The project team must receive information about project results. Whether for small projects in which team members receive a project update, or for larger projects where a complete team is involved, those who design, develop, facilitate, and implement the project require information on the project's effectiveness. Evaluation data are necessary so that adjustments can be made if the project is not as effective as it was projected to be.

## Information Development: The Impact Study

The type of formal evaluation report to be issued depends on the degree of detail in the information presented to the various target audiences. Brief summaries of project results with appropriate charts may be sufficient for

## Table 13-2 Format of an Impact Study Report

- General information
  - Background
  - Objectives of study
- Methodology for impact study
  - Levels of evaluation
  - ROI process
  - Collecting data
  - Isolating the effects of the project
  - Converting data to monetary values
- Data analysis issues
- Costs
- Results: General information
  - Response profile
  - Success with objectives
- Results: Reaction and perceived
  - Data sources
  - Data summary
  - Key issues
- Results: Learning and confidence
  - Data sources
  - Data summary
  - Key Issues
- Results: Application and implementation
  - Data sources
  - Data summary
  - Key issues
- Results: Impact and consequences
  - General comments
  - Linkage with business measures
  - Key issues
- Results: ROI and its meaning
- Results: Intangible measures
- Barriers and enablers
  - Barriers
  - Enablers
- Conclusions and recommendations
  - Conclusions
  - Recommendations
- Exhibits

some communication efforts. In other situations, particularly those involving major projects requiring extensive funding, a detailed evaluation report is crucial. A complete and comprehensive impact study report is usually necessary. This report can then be used as the basis for more streamlined information aimed at specific audiences and using various media. One possible format for an impact study report is presented in Table 13-2.

While the impact study report is an effective, professional way to present ROI data, several cautions are in order. Since this report documents the success of a project involving a large group of employees, credit for the success must go completely to the participants and their immediate leaders. Their performance generated the success. Also, it is important to avoid boasting about results. Grand claims of overwhelming success can quickly turn off an audience and interfere with the delivery of the desired message.

The methodology should be clearly explained, along with the assumptions made in the analysis. The reader should easily see how the values were developed and how specific steps were followed to make the process more conservative, credible, and accurate. Detailed statistical analyses should be placed in an appendix.

## Media Selection

Many options are available for the dissemination of project results. In addition to the impact study report, commonly used media are meetings, interim and progress reports, organization publications, and case studies. Table 13-3 lists a variety of options to develop the content and the message.

### Meetings

If used properly, meetings are fertile ground for the communication of project results. All organizations hold a variety of meetings, and some may provide

**Table 13-3  Options for Communicating Results**

| Meetings | Detailed Reports | Brief Reports | Electronic Reporting | Mass Publications |
|---|---|---|---|---|
| Executives | Impact study | Executive summary | Website | Announcements |
| Management | Case study (internal) | Slide overview | E-mail | Bulletins |
| Stakeholders | Case study (external) | One-page summary | Blog | Newsletters |
| Staff | Major articles | Brochure | Video | Brief articles |

the proper context to convey project results. Along the chain of command, staff meetings are held to review progress, discuss current problems, and distribute information. These meetings can be an excellent forum for discussing the results achieved in a project that relates to the group's activities. Project results can be sent to executives for use in a staff meeting, or a member of the project team can attend the meeting to make the presentation.

Regular meetings with management groups are a common practice. Typically, discussions will focus on items that might be of help to work units. The discussion of a project and its results can be integrated into the regular meeting format. A few organizations have initiated the use of periodic meetings for all key stakeholders, where the project leader reviews progress and discusses next steps. A few highlights from interim project results can be helpful in building interest, commitment, and support for the project.

## Interim and Progress Reports

A highly visible way to communicate results, although usually limited to large projects, is the use of interim and routine memos and reports. Published or disseminated by e-mail on a periodic basis, they are designed to inform management about the status of the project, to communicate interim results of the project, and to spur needed changes and improvements.

A secondary reason for the interim report is to enlist additional support and commitment from the management group and to keep the project intact. This report is produced by the project team and distributed to a select group of stakeholders in the organization. The report may vary considerably in format and scope and may include a schedule of planned steps or activities, a brief summary of reaction evaluations, initial results achieved from the project, and various spotlights recognizing team members or participants. Other topics may also be appropriate. When produced in a professional manner, the interim report can boost management support and commitment.

## Routine Communication Tools

To reach a wide audience, the project leader can use internal, routine publications. Whether a newsletter, magazine, newspaper, or electronic file, these media usually reach all employees or stakeholders. The content can have a significant impact if communicated appropriately. The scope should be limited to general-interest articles, announcements, and interviews.

Results communicated through these types of media must be important enough to arouse general interest. For example, a story with the headline "Safety Project Helps Produce One Million Hours without a Lost-Time Accident" will catch the attention of many readers because it is likely they participated in the project and can appreciate the relevance of the results. Reports on the accomplishments of a group of participants may not generate interest if the audience cannot relate to the accomplishments.

For many projects, results are not achieved until weeks or even months after the project is completed. Participants need reinforcement from many sources. Communicating results to a general audience may lead to additional pressure to continue the project or introduce similar ones in the future.

Stories about participants involved in a project and the results they have achieved can help create a favorable image. Employees are made aware that the organization is investing time and money to improve performance and prepare for the future. This type of story provides information about a project that employees otherwise may be unfamiliar with, and it sometimes creates a desire in others to participate if given the opportunity.

General-audience communication can bring recognition to project participants, particularly those who excel in some aspect of the project. Public recognition of participants who deliver exceptional performance can enhance their self-esteem and their drive to continue to excel. A project can generate many human interest stories. A rigorous project with difficult challenges can provide the basis for an interesting story on participants who made the extra effort.

## E-Mail and Electronic Media

Internal and external Internet pages, company-wide intranets, and e-mails are excellent vehicles for releasing results, promoting ideas, and informing employees and other target groups of project results. E-mail, in particular, provides a virtually instantaneous means of communicating results to and soliciting responses from large groups of people. For major projects, some organizations create blogs to present results and elicit reactions, feedback, and suggestions.

## Project Brochures and Pamphlets

A brochure might be appropriate for a project conducted on a continuing basis or where the audience is large and continuously changing. The brochure should be attractive and present a complete description of the project, with a major section devoted to results obtained with previous participants, if available. Measurable results and reactions from participants, or even direct quotes from individuals, can add spice to an otherwise dull brochure.

## Case Studies

Case studies represent an effective way to communicate the results of a project. A typical case study describes the situation, provides appropriate background information (including the events that led to the project), presents the techniques and strategies used to develop the study, and highlights the key issues in the project. Case studies tell an interesting story of how the project was implemented and the evaluation was developed, including the problems and concerns identified along the way.

# Routine Feedback on Project Progress

A primary reason for collecting reaction and learning data is to provide feedback so that adjustments can be made throughout the project. For most projects, data are routinely collected and quickly communicated to a variety of groups. A feedback action plan designed to provide information to several audiences using a variety of media may be an option. These feedback sessions may point out specific actions that need to be taken. This process becomes complex and must be managed in a very proactive manner. The following steps are recommended for providing feedback and managing the overall process. Some of the steps and concepts are based on the recommendations of Peter Block in his successful book *Flawless Consulting*.[1]

- *Communicate quickly.* Whether the news is good news or bad, it should be passed on to individuals involved in the project as soon as possible. The recommended time for providing feedback is usually a matter of days and certainly no longer than a week or two after the results become known.
- *Simplify the data.* Condense the data into an easily understandable, concise presentation. This is not the appropriate situation for detailed explanations and analysis.
- *Examine the role of the project team and the client in the feedback process.* The project leader is often the judge, jury, prosecutor, defendant, and/or witness. On the other hand, sometimes the client fills

these roles. These respective functions must be examined in terms of reactions to the data and the actions that are called for.

- *Use negative data in a constructive way.* Some of the data will show that things are not going so well, and the fault may rest with the project leader or the client. In this case, the story basically changes from "Let's look at the success we've achieved" to "Now we know which areas to change."

- *Use positive data in a cautious way.* Positive data can be misleading, and if they are communicated too enthusiastically, they may create expectations that exceed what finally materializes. Positive data should be presented in a cautious way—almost in a discounting manner.

- *Choose the language of the meeting and the communication carefully.* The language used should be descriptive, focused, specific, short, and simple. Language that is too judgmental, macro, stereotypical, lengthy, or complex should be avoided.

- *Ask the client for reactions to the data.* After all, the client is the number 1 customer, and it is most important that the client be pleased with the project.

- *Ask the client for recommendations.* The client may have some good suggestions for what needs to be changed to keep a project on track, or to put it back on track should it derail.

- *Use support and confrontation carefully.* These two actions are not mutually exclusive. At times, support and confrontation are both needed for a particular group. The client may need support and yet be confronted for lack of improvement or sponsorship. The project team may be confronted regarding the problem areas that have developed, but may need support as well.

- *React to and act on the data.* The different alternatives and possibilities should be weighed carefully to arrive at the adjustments that will be necessary.

- *Secure agreement from all key stakeholders.* It is essential to ensure that everyone is willing to make any changes that may be necessary.

- *Keep the feedback process short.* Allowing the process to become bogged down in long, drawn-out meetings or lengthy documents is a bad idea. If this occurs, stakeholders will avoid the process instead of being willing participants.

Following these steps will help move the project forward and generate useful feedback, often ensuring that adjustments are supported and can be executed.

## Presentation of Results to Senior Management

Perhaps one of the most challenging and stressful types of communication is presenting an impact study to the senior management team, which also serves as the client for a project. The challenge is convincing this highly skeptical and critical group that outstanding results have been achieved (assuming they have) in a very reasonable time frame, addressing the salient points, and making sure the managers understand the process. Two potential reactions can create problems. First, if the results are very impressive, making the managers accept the data may be difficult. On the other extreme, if the data are negative, ensuring that managers don't overreact to the results and look for someone to blame is important. Several guidelines can help ensure that this process is planned and executed properly.

Arrange a face-to-face meeting with senior team members to review the results. If they are unfamiliar with the ROI methodology, this meeting is necessary to make sure they understand the process. The good news is that they will probably attend the meeting because they have never seen ROI data developed for this type of project. The bad news is that it takes precious executive time, usually about an hour, for this presentation. After the meeting with a couple of presentations, an executive summary may suffice. At this point, the senior members will understand the process, so a shortened version may be appropriate. When a particular audience is familiar with the process, a brief version may be developed, including a one- to two-page summary with charts and graphs showing the six types of measures.

The results should not be disseminated before the initial presentation or even during the session, but should be saved until the end of the session. This will allow enough time to present the process and collect reactions to it before the target audience sees the ROI calculation. Present the ROI methodology step by step, showing how the data were collected, when they were collected, who provided them, how the effect of the project was isolated from other influences, and how data were converted to monetary values. The various assumptions, adjustments, and conservative approaches are presented along with the total cost of the project, so that the target audience will begin to buy into the process of developing the ROI.

When the data are actually presented, the results are given one level at a time, starting with Level 1, moving through Level 5, and ending with the intangibles. This allows the audience to observe the reaction, learning, application and implementation, business impact, and ROI procedures. After some discussion of the meaning of the ROI, the intangible measures are presented. Allocate time for each level as appropriate for the audience. This helps to defuse potential emotional reactions to a very positive or negative ROI.

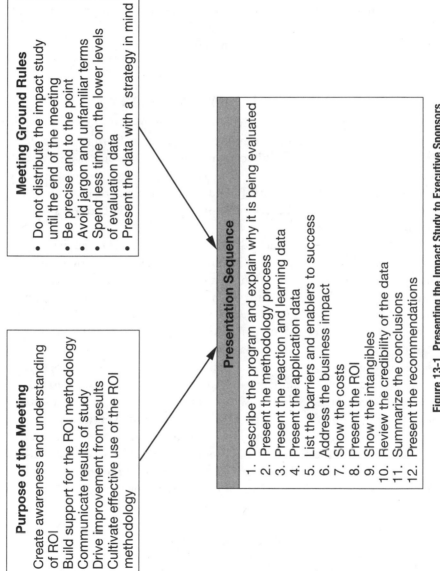

**Purpose of the Meeting**

- Create awareness and understanding of ROI
- Build support for the ROI methodology
- Communicate results of study
- Drive improvement from results
- Cultivate effective use of the ROI methodology

**Meeting Ground Rules**

- Do not distribute the impact study until the end of the meeting
- Be precise and to the point
- Avoid jargon and unfamiliar terms
- Spend less time on the lower levels of evaluation data
- Present the data with a strategy in mind

**Presentation Sequence**

1. Describe the program and explain why it is being evaluated
2. Present the methodology process
3. Present the reaction and learning data
4. Present the application data
5. List the barriers and enablers to success
6. Address the business impact
7. Show the costs
8. Present the ROI
9. Show the intangibles
10. Review the credibility of the data
11. Summarize the conclusions
12. Present the recommendations

**Figure 13-1 Presenting the Impact Study to Executive Sponsors**

Show the consequences of additional accuracy if this is an issue. The trade-off for more accuracy and validity often is more expense. Address this issue when necessary, agreeing to add more data if they are required. Collect concerns, reactions, and issues involving the process and make adjustments accordingly for the next presentation.

Collectively, these steps will help in the preparation and presentation of one of the most important meetings in the ROI methodology. Figure 13-1 shows the recommended approach to an important meeting with the sponsor.

## Reactions to Communication

The best indicator of how effectively the results of a project have been communicated is the level of commitment and support from the managers, executives, and sponsors. The allocation of requested resources and voiced commitment from top management are strong evidence of management's positive perception of the results. In addition to this macro-level reaction, a few techniques can also be helpful in measuring the effectiveness of the communication effort.

When results are communicated, the reactions of the target audiences can be monitored. These reactions may include nonverbal gestures, oral remarks, written comments, or indirect actions that reveal how the communication was received. Usually, when results are presented in a meeting, the presenter will have some indication of how they were received by the group. Usually, the interest and attitudes of the audience can be quickly evaluated. Comments about the results—formal or informal—should be noted and tabulated.

Project team meetings are an excellent arena for discussing the reaction to communicated results. Comments can come from many sources depending on the particular target audience. When major project results are communicated, a feedback questionnaire may be administered to the entire audience or a sample of the audience. The purpose of the questionnaire is to determine the extent to which the audience understood and/or believed the information presented. This is practical only when the effectiveness of the communication will have a significant impact on future actions by the project team.

## Final Thoughts

The final step in the ROI methodology, communication of results, is a crucial step in the overall evaluation process. If this step is not executed adequately, the full impact of the results will not be recognized, and the study may amount to a waste of time. The chapter began with general principles and steps for communicating project results; these can serve as a guide for any significant communication effort. The various target audiences were then discussed, with emphasis on the executive group because of its importance. A suggested format for a detailed evaluation report was also provided. The chapter presented the most commonly used media for communicating project results, including meetings, client publications, and electronic media.

A final issue regarding the ROI methodology will be discussed in the next chapter: overcoming barriers to sustaining the use of the methodology.

# Chapter 14

# IMPLEMENTING AND SUSTAINING ROI

Even the best-designed process, model, or technique is worthless unless it is effectively and efficiently integrated into the organization. Often, resistance to the ROI process arises. Some of this resistance is based on fear and misunderstanding. Some is real, based on actual barriers and obstacles. Although the ROI methodology presented in this book is a step-by-step, methodical, and simplistic procedure, it can fail if it is not integrated properly, fully accepted, and supported by those who must make it work within the organization. This chapter focuses on some of the most effective means of overcoming resistance to implementing the ROI process in an organization.

## Why the Concern about Implementing and Sustaining ROI?

With any new process or change, there is resistance. Resistance may be especially great when implementing a process as complex as ROI. To implement ROI and sustain it as an important accountability tool, the resistance must be minimized or removed. Successful implementation essentially equates to overcoming resistance. Explained below are four key reasons to have a detailed plan in place to overcome resistance.

### Resistance Is Always Present

Resistance to change is a constant. Sometimes, there are good reasons for resistance, but often it exists for the wrong reasons. The important point is to sort out both kinds of resistance and try to dispel the myths. When legitimate barriers are the basis for resistance, minimizing, or removing them altogether is the challenge.

## Implementation Is Key

As with any process, effective implementation is the key to its success. This occurs when the new technique, tool, or process is integrated into the routine framework. Without effective implementation, even the best process will fail. A process that is never removed from the shelf will never be understood, supported, or improved. Clear-cut steps must be in place for designing a comprehensive implementation process that will overcome resistance.

## Consistency Is Needed

Consistency is an important consideration as the ROI process is implemented. With consistency come accuracy and reliability . . . and accountability. The only way to make sure consistency is achieved is to follow clearly defined processes, procedures, and standards each time the ROI methodology is used. Proper effective implementation will ensure that this occurs.

## Efficiency

Cost control and efficiency will be significant considerations in any major undertaking, and the ROI methodology is no exception. During implementation, tasks must be completed efficiently and effectively. Doing so will help ensure that process costs are kept to a minimum, that time is used economically, and that the process remains affordable.

# Implementing the Process: Overcoming Resistance

Resistance shows up in varied ways: in the form of comments, remarks, actions, or behaviors. Table 14-1 lists representative comments that indicate open resistance to the ROI process. Each comment signals an issue that must be resolved or addressed in some way. A few are based on realistic barriers, whereas others are based on myths that must be dispelled. Sometimes, resistance to the process reflects underlying concerns. For example, the individuals involved may fear losing control of their processes, and others may feel vulnerable to whatever action may follow if the process is not successful. Still

**Table 14-1 Typical Objections to Use of ROI Methodology**

**Open Resistance**

1. It costs too much.
2. It takes too much time.
3. Who is asking for this?
4. This is not in my job description.
5. I did not have input on this.
6. I do not understand this.
7. What happens when the results are negative?
8. How can we be consistent with this?
9. The ROI looks too subjective.
10. Our managers will not support this.
11. ROI is too narrowly focused.
12. This is not practical.

others may be concerned about any process that brings change or requires the additional effort of learning.

Project team members may resist the ROI process and openly make comments similar to those listed in Table 14-1. It may take heavy persuasion and evidence of tangible benefits to convince team members that it is in their best interest to make the project a success. Although most clients do want to see the results of the project, they may have concerns about the information they are asked to provide and about whether their personal performance is being judged while the project is undergoing evaluation. Participants may express the very same fears listed in the table.

The challenge is to implement the methodology systematically and consistently so that it becomes normal business behavior and a routine and standard process built into projects. The implementation necessary to overcome resistance covers a variety of areas. Figure 14-1 shows actions outlined in this chapter that are presented as building blocks to overcoming resistance. They are all necessary to build the proper base or framework to dispel myths and remove or minimize barriers. The remainder of this chapter presents specific strategies and techniques devoted to each of the nine building blocks identified in Figure 14-1. They apply equally to the project team and the client organization, and no attempt is made to separate the two in this presentation. In some situations, a particular strategy would work best with the project team. In certain cases all strategies may be appropriate for both groups.

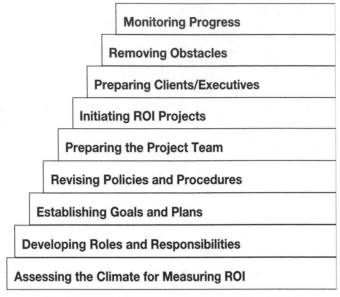

Figure 14-1  Building Blocks to Overcome Resistance

## Assessing the Climate

As a first step toward implementation, some organizations assess the current climate for achieving results. One way to do this is to develop a survey to determine current perspectives of the management team and other stakeholders (for an example go to www.showmethemoney.biz). Another way is to conduct interviews with key stakeholders to determine their willingness to follow the project through to ROI. With an awareness of the current status, the project leaders can plan for significant changes and pinpoint particular issues that need support as the ROI process is implemented.

## Developing Roles and Responsibilities

Defining and detailing specific roles and responsibilities for different groups and individuals addresses many of the resistance factors and helps pave a smooth path for implementation.

### Identifying a Champion

As an early step in the process, one or more individual(s) should be designated as the internal leader or champion for the ROI methodology. As in most change efforts, someone must take responsibility for ensuring that the process is implemented successfully. This leader serves as a champion for ROI and is usually the one who understands the process best and sees vast potential for its contribution. More important, this leader is willing to teach others and will work to sustain sponsorship.

## Developing the ROI Leader

The ROI leader is usually a member of the project team who has the responsibility for evaluation. This person holds a full-time position in larger project teams or a part-time position in smaller teams. Client organizations may also have an ROI leader who pursues the ROI methodology from the client's perspective. The typical job title for a full-time ROI leader is Manager of Measurement and Evaluation. Some organizations assign this responsibility to a team and empower it to lead the ROI effort.

In preparation for this assignment, individuals usually receive special training that builds specific skills and knowledge of the ROI process. The role of the implementation leader is quite broad and serves a variety of specialized duties. In some organizations, the implementation leader can take on many roles, ranging from problem solver to communicator to cheerleader. Leading the ROI process is a difficult and challenging assignment that requires unique skill. Fortunately, programs are available that teach these skills. For example, one such program is designed to certify individuals who will be assuming leadership roles in the implementation of the ROI methodology. For more detail, see www.showmethemoney.biz. This certification is built around 10 specific skill sets linked to successful ROI implementation, focusing on the critical areas of data collection, isolating the effects of the project, converting data to monetary value, presenting evaluation data, and building capability. This process is quite comprehensive but may be necessary to build the skills necessary for taking on this challenging assignment.

## Establishing a Task Force

Making the ROI methodology work well may require the use of a task force. A task force usually comprises a group of individuals from different parts of the project or client team who are wiling to develop the ROI methodology and implement it in the organization. The selection of the task force may involve volunteers, or participation may be mandatory depending on specific job responsibilities. The task force should represent the cross section necessary for accomplishing stated goals. Task forces have the additional advantage of bringing more people into the process and developing more ownership of and support for the ROI methodology. The task force must be large enough to cover the key areas but not so large that it becomes too cumbersome to function. Six to twelve members is a good size.

## Assigning Responsibilities

Determining specific responsibilities is critical because confusion can arise when individuals are unclear about their specific assignments in the use of the ROI methodology. Responsibilities apply to two areas. The first is the measurement and evaluation responsibility of the entire project team. Everyone involved in projects must have some responsibility for measurement and evaluation. These responsibilities include providing input on designing instruments, planning specific evaluations, analyzing data, and interpreting the results. Typical responsibilities include

- Ensuring that the initial analysis for the project includes specific business impact measures
- Developing specific application and business impact objectives for the project
- Keeping participants focused on application and impact objectives
- Communicating rationale and reasons for evaluation
- Assisting in follow-up activities to capture application and business impact data
- Providing assistance for data collection, data analysis, and reporting

Although involving each member of the project team in all these activities may not be appropriate, each individual should have at least one responsibility as part of his or her routine job duties. This assignment of responsibility keeps the ROI methodology from being disjointed and separated during projects. More important, it brings accountability to those directly involved in project implementation.

Another issue involves technical support. Depending on the size of the project team, establishing an individual or a group of technical experts to provide assistance with the ROI methodology may be helpful. When the group is established, the project team must understand that the experts have been assigned not for the purpose of relieving the team of its evaluation responsibilities, but to supplement its ROI efforts with technical expertise.

These technical experts are typically the individuals who participated in the certification and training process to build special skills. Responsibilities of the technical support group involve six key areas:

1. Designing data collection instruments
2. Providing assistance for developing an evaluation strategy
3. Analyzing data, including specialized statistical analyses
4. Interpreting results and making specific recommendations
5. Developing an evaluation report or case study to communicate over-all results
6. Providing technical support in all phases of the ROI methodology

The assignment of responsibilities for evaluation requires attention throughout the evaluation process. Although the project team must be assigned specific responsibilities during an evaluation, requiring others to serve in support functions to help with data collection is not unusual. These responsibilities are defined when a particular evaluation strategy plan is developed and approved.

## Establishing Goals and Plans

Establishing goals, targets, and objectives is critical to the implementation, particularly when several projects are planned. The establishment of goals can include detailed planning documents for the overall process and for individual ROI projects. The next sections discuss aspects of the establishment of goals and plans.

### Setting Evaluation Targets

Establishing specific targets for evaluation levels is an important way to make progress with measurement and evaluation. As emphasized throughout this book, not every project should be evaluated to ROI. Knowing in advance to which level the project will be evaluated helps in planning which measures will be needed and how detailed the evaluation must be at each level. Table 14-2 presents examples of targets set for evaluation at each level when there are many different types of projects. The setting of targets should be completed early in the process with the full support of the entire project team. If practical and feasible, the targets should also have the approval of key managers—particularly the senior management team.

Table 14-2  Evaluation Targets in a Large Organization with Many Projects

| Level | Target |
| --- | --- |
| Level 1, Reaction and Perceived Value | 100% |
| Level 2, Learning and Confidence | 80% |
| Level 3, Application and Implementation | 40% |
| Level 4, Business Impact and Consequences | 25% |
| Level 5, ROI | 10% |

## Developing a Plan for Implementation

An important part of implementation is establishing a timetable for the complete implementation of the ROI methodology. This document becomes a master plan for completion of the different elements presented earlier. Beginning with forming a team and concluding with meeting the targets previously described, this schedule is a project plan for transitioning from the present situation to the desired future situation. Items on the schedule include developing specific ROI projects, building staff skills, developing policy, and teaching managers the process. Figure 14-2 is an example of an implementation plan. The more detailed the document, the more useful it becomes. The project plan is a living, long-range document that should be reviewed frequently and adjusted as necessary. More important, those engaged in work on the ROI methodology should always be familiar with the implementation plan.

## Revising or Developing Policies and Guidelines

Another part of planning is revising or developing the organization's policy on project measurement and evaluation. The policy statement contains information developed specifically for the measurement and evaluation process. It is developed with input from the project team and key managers or stakeholders. Sometimes, policy issues are addressed during internal workshops designed to build measurement and evaluation skills. The policy statement addresses critical matters that will influence the effectiveness of the measurement and evaluation process. These may include adopting the framework presented in this book, requiring objectives at all levels for some or all projects, and defining responsibilities for the project team.

Policy statements are important because they provide guidance and direction for the staff and others who work closely with the ROI methodology.

| | J | F | M | A | M | J | J | A | S | O | N | D | J | F | M | A | M | J | J | A |
|---|---|---|---|---|---|---|---|---|---|---|---|---|---|---|---|---|---|---|---|---|
| Team Formed | ▓ | ▓ | | | | | | | | | | | | | | | | | | |
| Responsibilities Defined | | ▓ | | | | | | | | | | | | | | | | | | |
| Policy Developed | | | ▓ | | | | | | | | | | | | | | | | | |
| Targets Set | | | | ▓ | | | | | | | | | | | | | | | | |
| Workshops Developed | | | | | ▓ | ▓ | | | | | | | | | | | | | | |
| ROI Project (A) | | | | | | ▓ | | | | | | | | | | | | | | |
| ROI Project (B) | | | | | | | | | | ▓ | ▓ | ▓ | | | | | | | | |
| ROI Project (C) | | | | | | | | | | | ▓ | ▓ | ▓ | | | | | | | |
| ROI Project (D) | | | | | | | | | | | | ▓ | ▓ | ▓ | ▓ | | | ▓ | ▓ | |
| Project Teams Trained | | | | | | | | | | | | | | | | | | | | |
| Managers Trained | | | | | | | | | | | | | | | | | | ▓ | ▓ | |
| Support Tools Developed | | | | | | | ▓ | ▓ | | | | | | | | | | | | |
| Guidelines Developed | | | | | | | ▓ | | | | | | | | | | | | | |

**Figure 14-2 Implementation Plan for a Large Organization with Many Projects**

These individuals keep the process clearly focused, and enable the group to establish goals for evaluation. Policy statements also provide an opportunity to communicate basic requirements and fundamentals of performance and accountability. More than anything else, they serve as learning tools to teach others, especially when they are developed in a collaborative way. If policy statements are developed in isolation, staff and management will be denied the sense of their ownership, making them neither effective nor useful.

Guidelines for measurement and evaluation are important for showing how to use the tools and techniques, guide the design process, provide consistency in the ROI process, ensure that appropriate methods are used, and place the proper emphasis on each of the areas. The guidelines are more technical than policy statements and often include detailed procedures showing how the process is undertaken and developed. They often include specific forms, instruments, and tools necessary to facilitate the process.

# Preparing the Project Team

Project team members may resist the ROI methodology. They often see evaluation as an unnecessary intrusion into their responsibilities that absorbs precious time and stifles creative freedom. The cartoon character Pogo perhaps characterized it best when he said, "We have met the enemy, and he is us." Several issues must be addressed when preparing the project team for ROI implementation.

## Involving the Project Team

For each key issue or major decision involving ROI implementation, the project team should be involved in the process. As policy statements are prepared and evaluation guidelines developed, team input is essential. Resistance is more difficult if the team helped design and develop the ROI process. Convene meetings, brainstorming sessions, and task forces to involve the team in every phase of developing the framework and supporting documents for ROI.

## Using ROI as a Learning and Project Improvement Tool

One reason the project team may resist the ROI process is that the projects' effectiveness will be fully exposed, putting the reputation of the team on the line. They may have a fear of failure. To overcome this, the ROI methodology should be clearly positioned as a tool for learning, not a tool for evaluating project team performance (at least not during the early years of use). Team members will not be interested in developing a process that may reflect unfavorably on their performance.

Evaluators can learn as much from failures as from success. If the project is not working, it is best to find out quickly so that issues can be understood firsthand, not from others. If a project is ineffective and not producing the desired results, the failure will eventually be known to clients and the management group (if they are not aware of it already). A lack of results will make managers less supportive of immediate and future projects. If the projects' weaknesses are identified and adjustments quickly made, not only can more effective projects be developed, but the credibility of and respect for project implementation will be enhanced.

## Teaching the Team

The project team and project evaluator usually have inadequate skills in measurement and evaluation, and will need to develop some expertise. Measurement and evaluation are not always a formal part of the team's or evaluator's job preparation. Consequently, the project team leader must learn ROI methodology and its systematic steps, and the evaluator must learn to develop an evaluation strategy and specific plan, to collect and analyze data from the evaluation, and to interpret results from data analysis. A one- to two-day workshop can help build the skills and knowledge needed to understand the process and appreciate what it can do for project success and for the client organization. Such a teach-the-team workshop can be a valuable tool in ensuring successful implementation of ROI methodology.

# Initiating ROI Studies

The first tangible evidence of the value of using the ROI methodology may be seen at the initiation of the first project for which an ROI calculation is planned. The next sections discuss aspects of identifying appropriate projects and keeping them on track.

## Selecting the Initial Project

It is critical that appropriate projects be selected for ROI analysis. Only certain types of projects qualify for comprehensive, detailed analysis.

Characteristic of projects that are suitable for analysis are those that: (1) are important to strategic objectives; (2) involve large groups of participants; (3) will be linked to major operational problems and opportunities upon completion; (4) are expensive; (5) are time-consuming; (6) have high visibility; and (7) have the interest of management in performing their evaluation. Using these or similar criteria, the project leader must select the appropriate projects to consider for ROI evaluation. Ideally, sponsors should agree with or approve the criteria.

## Developing the Planning Documents

Perhaps the two most useful ROI documents are the data collection plan and the ROI analysis plan. The data collection plan shows what data will be collected, the methods used, the sources, the timing, and the assignment of responsibilities. The ROI analysis plan shows how specific analyses will be conducted, including how to isolate the effects of the project and how to convert data to monetary values. Each evaluator should know how to develop these plans. These documents were discussed in detail in Chapter 2.

## Reporting Progress

As the projects are developed and the ROI implementation gets under way, status meetings should be conducted to report progress and discuss critical issues with appropriate team members. These meetings keep the project team focused on the critical issues, generate the best ideas for addressing problems and barriers, and build a knowledge base for better implementation evaluation of future projects. Sometimes, these meetings are facilitated by an external consultant, perhaps an expert in the ROI process. In other cases, the project leader may facilitate. In essence, the meetings serve three major purposes: reporting progress, learning, and planning.

## Establishing Discussion Groups

Because the ROI methodology is considered difficult to understand and apply, establishing discussion groups to teach the process may be helpful. These groups can supplement formal workshops and other learning activities and are often very flexible in format. Groups are usually facilitated by an external ROI consultant or the project leader. In each session, a new topic is presented for a thorough discussion that should extend to how the topic applies to the organization. The process can be adjusted for different topics as new group needs arise, driving the issues. Ideally, participants in group discussions will have an opportunity to apply, explore, or research the topics between sessions. Group assignments such as reviewing a case study or reading an article are appropriate between sessions to further the development of knowledge and skills associated with the process.

## Preparing the Sponsors and Management Team

Perhaps no group is more important to the use of the ROI methodology than the management team that must allocate resources for the project and support its implementation. In addition, the management team often provides input to and assistance for the ROI methodology. Preparing, training, and developing the management team should be carefully planned and executed.

One effective approach for preparing executives and managers for ROI is to conduct a briefing. Varying in duration from one hour to half a day, a practical briefing such as this can provide critical information and enhance support for ROI use. Managers leave these briefings with greater appreciation of the use of ROI and its potential impact on projects, and with a clearer understanding of their role in the ROI process. More important, they often renew their commitment to react to and use the data collected by the ROI methodology.

A strong, dynamic relationship between the project team and key managers is essential for successful implementation of the ROI methodology. A productive partnership is needed that requires each party to understand the concerns, problems, and opportunities of the other. The development of such a beneficial relationship is a long-term process that must be deliberately planned for and initiated by key project team members. The decision to commit resources and support to a project may be based on the effectiveness of this relationship.

## Removing Obstacles

As the ROI methodology is implemented, there will inevitably be obstacles to its progress. The obstacles are based on concerns discussed in this chapter, some of which may be valid, others of which may be based on unrealistic fears or misunderstandings.

## Dispelling Myths

As part of the implementation, attempts should be made to dispel the myths and remove or minimize the barriers or obstacles. Much of the controversy regarding ROI stems from misunderstandings about what the process can and cannot do and how it can or should be implemented in an organization. After years of experience with ROI, and having noted reactions during hundreds of projects and workshops, we have recognized many misunderstandings about ROI. These misunderstandings are listed below as myths about the ROI methodology:

- ROI is too complex for most users.
- ROI is expensive and consumes too many critical resources.
- If senior management does not require ROI, there is no need to pursue it.
- ROI is a passing fad.
- ROI is only one type of data.
- ROI is not future-oriented; it only reflects past performance.
- ROI is rarely used by organizations.
- The ROI methodology cannot be easily replicated.
- ROI is not a credible process; it is too subjective.
- ROI cannot be used with soft projects.
- Isolating the influence of other factors is not always possible.
- ROI is appropriate only for large organizations.
- No standards exist for the ROI methodology.

For more information on these myths see www.showmethemoney.biz.

## Delivering Bad News

One of the obstacles perhaps most difficult to overcome is receiving inadequate, insufficient, or disappointing news. Addressing a bad-news situation is an issue for most project leaders and other stakeholders involved in a project. Table 14-3 presents the guidelines to follow when addressing bad news. As the table makes clear, the time to think about bad news is early in the process, but without ever losing sight of the value of the bad news. In essence, bad news means that things can change and need to change and that the situation can improve. The team and others need to be convinced that good news can be found in a bad-news situation.

#### Table 14-3  How to Address Bad News

##### Delivering Bad News

- Never fail to recognize the power to learn from and improve with a negative study.
- Look for red flags along the way.
- Lower outcome expectations with key stakeholders along the way.
- Look for data everywhere.
- Never alter the standards.
- Remain objective throughout the process.
- Prepare the team for the bad news.
- Consider different scenarios.
- Find out what went wrong.
- Adjust the story line to "Now we have data that show how to make this program more successful." In an odd way, this puts a positive spin on data that are less than positive.
- Drive improvement.

## Using the Data

It is unfortunately too often the case that projects are evaluated and significant data are collected, but nothing is done with the data. Failure to use data is a tremendous obstacle because once the project has concluded, the team has a tendency to move on to the next project or issue and get on with other priorities. Table 14-4 shows how the different levels of data can be used to

#### Table 14-4  How Data Should Be Used

| Use of Evaluation Data | Appropriate Level of Data | | | | |
|---|---|---|---|---|---|
|  | 1 | 2 | 3 | 4 | 5 |
| Adjust project or program design | ✓ | ✓ |  |  |  |
| Improve implementation |  |  | ✓ | ✓ |  |
| Influence application and impact |  |  | ✓ | ✓ |  |
| Improve management support for the project |  |  | ✓ | ✓ |  |
| Improve stakeholder satisfaction |  |  | ✓ | ✓ | ✓ |
| Recognize and reward participants |  | ✓ | ✓ | ✓ |  |
| Justify or enhance budget |  |  |  | ✓ | ✓ |
| Reduce costs |  | ✓ | ✓ | ✓ | ✓ |
| Market projects or programs in the future | ✓ |  | ✓ | ✓ | ✓ |

improve projects. It is critical that the data be used—the data were essentially the justification for undertaking the project evaluation in the first place. Failure to use the data may mean that the entire evaluation was a waste. As the table illustrates, many reasons exist for collecting the data and using them after collection. These can become action items for the team to ensure that changes and adjustments are made. Also, the client or sponsor must act to ensure that the uses of data are appropriately addressed.

## Monitoring Progress

A final element of the implementation process is monitoring the overall progress made and communicating that progress. Although often overlooked, an effective progress report can help keep the implementation on target and can let others know what the ROI methodology is accomplishing for project leaders and the client.

The initial schedule for implementation of ROI is based on key events or milestones. Routine progress reports should be developed to communicate the status of these events or milestones. Reports are usually developed at six-month intervals but may be more frequent for short-term projects. Two target audiences—the project team and senior managers—are critical for progress reporting. All project team members should be kept informed of the progress, and senior managers should know the extent to which ROI is being implemented and how it is working within the organization.

## Final Thoughts

Even the best model or process will die if it is not used and sustained. This chapter explored the implementation of the ROI process and ways to sustain its use. If not approached in a systematic, logical, and planned way, the ROI process will not be an integral part of project evaluation, and project accountability will consequently suffer. This chapter presented the different elements that must be considered and issues that must be addressed to ensure that implementation is smooth and uneventful. Smooth implementation is the most effective means of overcoming resistance to ROI. The result provides a complete integration of ROI as a mainstream component of major projects.

# Notes

## Chapter 1

1. Nickson, David, and Suzy Siddons, *Project Disasters and How to Survive Them* (London: Kogan Page, 2005).
2. Colvin, Geoffrey, "The FedEx Edge," *Fortune* (April 3, 2006), 49.
3. Pfeffer, Jeffrey, and Robert I. Sutton, *Hard Facts, Dangerous Half-Truths and Total Nonsense: Profiting from Evidence-Based Management* (Boston: Harvard Business School, 2006).
4. Ibid.

## Chapter 2

1. Phillips, Jack J., and Patricia Pulliam Phillips, "Return on Investment Measures Success," *Industrial Management* (March/April 2006), 18–23.

## Chapter 3

1. Langdon, Danny, and Kathleen Whiteside and Monica McKenna, eds., *Intervention Resource Guide: 50 Performance Improvement Tools* (San Francisco: Jossey-Bass Pfeiffer, 1999).

## Chapter 5

1. Miller, W., "Building the Ultimate Resource: Today's Competitive Edge Comes from Intellectual Capital," *Management Review* (January 1999), 42–45.
2. Senge, P., *The Fifth Discipline: The Art and Practice of the Learning Organization* (New York: Random House, 1990).
3. Watkins, Karen E., and Victoria J. Marsick, eds., *Creating the Learning Organization* (Jack J. Phillips, series editor) (Alexandria, VA: American Society for Training and Development, 1996).
4. Lucia, Anntoinette D., and Richard Lepsinger, *The Art and Science of Competency Models: Pinpointing Critical Success Factors in Organizations* (San Francisco: Jossey-Bass/Pfeiffer, 1999).
5. Phillips, Jack J., and Patricia P. Phillips, *Handbook of Training Evaluation and Measurement Methods*, 4th ed. (Woburn, MA: Butterworth Heinemann, 2007).

## Chapter 6

1. Phillips, Jack J., and Patricia Pulliam Phillips, *Handbook of Training Evaluation and Measurement Methods,* 4th ed. (Woburn, MA: Butterworth Heinemann, 2007).

## Chapter 7

1. Nalbantian, Haig R., and Richard A. Guzzo, Dave Kieffer, and Jay Doherty. *Play to Your Strengths: Managing Your Internal Labor Markets for Lasting Competitive Advantage* (New York: McGraw-Hill, 2004).
2. Kaplan, Robert S., and David P. Norton. *The Balanced Scorecard: Translating Strategy into Action* (Boston: Harvard Business School Press, 1996).

## Chapter 8

1. Levitt, Steven D., and Stephen J. Dubner, *Freakonomics: A Rogue Economist Explores the Hidden Side of Everything* (New York: William Morrow, 2005).
2. Surowicki, James, *The Wisdom of Crowds: Why the Many Are Smarter Than the Few and How Collective Wisdom Shapes Business, Economics, Societies and Nations* (New York: Doubleday, 2004).

## Chapter 9

1. Cokins, Gary, *Activity-Based Cost Management: Making it Work—A Manager's Guide to Implementing and Sustaining an Effective ABC System* (New York: McGraw-Hill, 1996).
2. Fishman, Charles, *The Wal-Mart Effect: How the World's Most Powerful Company Really Works—and How It's Transforming the American Economy* ( New York: Penguin, 2006).
3. Farris, Paul W., Neil T. Bendle, Phillip E. Pfeifer, and David J. Ribstein, *Marketing Metrics: 50+ Metrics Every Executive Should Master* (Upper Saddle River, NJ: Wharton School Publishing, 2006).
4. Campanella, Jack, ed., *Principles of Quality Costs*, 3rd ed. (Milwaukee: American Society for Quality, 1999).
5. Rust, Roland T., Anthony J. Zahorik, and Timothy L. Keiningham, *Return on Quality: Measuring the Financial Impact of Your Company's Quest for Quality* (Chicago: Probus, 1994).
6. Hurd, Mark, and Lars Nyberg, *The Value Factor: How Global Leaders Use Information for Growth and Competitive Advantage* (New York: Bloomberg Press, 2004).
7. Ulrich, Dave, ed., *Delivering Results* (Boston: Harvard Business School Press, 1998).
8. Graham, Morris, Ken Bishop, and Ron Birdsong, "Self-Directed Work Teams," in *Action: Measuring Return on Investment*, vol. 1, Jack J. Phillips, ed. (Alexandria, VA.: American Society for Training and Development, 1994), pp. 105–122.

## Chapter 10

1. Boulton, Richard E. S., and Barry D. Libert, and Steve M. Samek. *Cracking the Value Code* (New York: HarperBusiness, 2000).
2. Frangos, Cassandra A. "Aligning Learning with Strategy," *Chief Learning Officer*, March 2004, p. 26.
3. Alden, Jay. "Measuring the 'Unmeasurable,'" *Performance Improvement*, May/June 2006, p. 7.
4. Brown, Stuart F. "Scientific Americans," *Fortune*, September 20, 2004, p. 175.
5. Kandybihn, Alexander and Martin Kihn. "Raising Your Return on Innovation Investment," *Strategy + Business*, Issue 35, 2004.

6. Santos, José, Yves Doz, and Peter Williamson, "Is Your Innovation Process Global?" *MIT Sloan Management Review*, Summer 2004, p. 31.
7. Schwartz, Evan I. *Juice: The Creative Fuel that Drives World-Class Inventors* (Boston, MA: Harvard Business School Press, 2004).
8. McGregor, Jena. "The World's Most Innovative Companies," *Business Week*, April 24, 2006, p. 63.
9. Bates, Stephen, "Linking People Measures to Strategy," *Research Report R-1342-03-RR* (New York: The Conference Board, 2003).
10. Phillips, Jack J., and Lynn Schmidt. *The Leadership Scorecard* (Woburn, MA: Butterworth-Heinemann, 2004).
11. Stobbe, Mike. "Vaccinate Girls against Cancer, Says Panel," *The Birmingham News*, July 3, 2006, p. 3A.
12. Ackerman, Frank, and Lisa Heinzerling. *Priceless: On Knowing the Price of Everything and the Value of Nothing* (New York: The New Press, 2004).

## Chapter 11
1. "Annual Employee Benefits Report," *Nation's Business* (January 2006).

## Chapter 12
1. Armstrong, Scott J., *Principles of Forecasting: A Handbook for Researchers and Practitioners* (Boston, MA: Kluwer Academic Publishers, 2001).
2. Phillips, Jack J., *The Consultant's Scorecard* (New York: McGraw-Hill, 2000).
3. Phillips, Jack J., *ROI in Training and Performance Improvement Programs* (Woburn, MA: Butterworth-Heinemann, 2003).
4. David A. Bowers, *Forecasting for Control and Profit* (Menlo Park, CA: Crisp Publications, 1997).

## Chapter 13
1. Block, Peter, *Flawless Consulting* (San Diego: Pfeiffer, 1981).

# Index

Page number followed by *f* or *t* indicates figure and table respectively.

# Jack J. Phillips, PhD

A a world-renowned expert on accountability, measurement, and evaluation, Dr. Jack J. Phillips provides consulting services for Fortune 500 companies and major global organizations. The author or editor of more than 50 books, Phillips conducts workshops and makes conference presentations throughout the world.

His expertise in measurement and evaluation is based on more than 27 years of corporate experience in the aerospace, textile, metals, construction materials, and banking industries. Phillips has served as training and development manager at two Fortune 500 firms, as senior human resource officer at two firms, as president of a regional bank, and as management professor at a major state university.

This background led Phillips to develop the ROI methodology (a revolutionary process that provides bottom-line figures and accountability for all types of learning, performance improvement, human resource, technology, and public policy programs.

Phillips regularly consults with clients in manufacturing, service, and government organizations in 44 countries in North and South America, Europe, Africa, Australia, and Asia.

Books most recently authored by Phillips include *Building a Successful Consulting Practice* (McGraw-Hill, 2006); *Investing in Your Company's Human Capital: Strategies to Avoid Spending Too Much or Too Little* (Amacom, 2005); *Proving the Value of HR: How and Why to Measure ROI* (SHRM, 2005); *The Leadership Scorecard* (Elsevier Butterworth-Heinemann, 2004); *Managing Employee Retention* (Elsevier Butterworth-Heinemann, 2003); *Return on Investment in Training and Performance Improvement Projects,* 2nd ed. (Elsevier Butterworth-Heinemann, 2003); *The Project Management Scorecard* (Elsevier Butterworth-Heinemann, 2002); *How to Measure Training Results* (McGraw-Hill, 2002); *The Human Resources Scorecard: Measuring the Return on Investment* (Elsevier Butterworth-Heinemann, 2001); *The Consultant's Scorecard* (McGraw-Hill, 2000); and *Performance Analysis and Consulting* (ASTD, 2000). Phillips served as series editor for ASTD's In Action casebook series, an ambitious publishing project featuring 30 titles. He currently serves as series editor for Elsevier Butterworth-Heinemann's Improving Human Performance series, and for Pfeiffer's new series on Measurement and Evaluation.

Phillips has received several awards for his books and work. The Society for Human Resource Management presented him an award for one of his books and honored a Phillips ROI study with its highest award for creativity. The American Society for Training and Development gave him its highest award, Distinguished Contribution to Workplace Learning and Development. *Meeting News* named Phillips one of the 25 most influential people in the Meetings and Events industry, based on his work on ROI for the industry.

Phillips has undergraduate degrees in electrical engineering, physics, and mathematics; a master's degree in Decision Sciences from Georgia State University; and a PhD in Human Resource Management from the University of Alabama.

Jack Phillips has served on the boards of several private businesses—including two NASDAQ companies—and several nonprofits and associations, including the American Society for Training and Development. He is chairman of the ROI Institute, Inc., and can be reached at (205) 678-8101, or by e-mail at jack@roiinstitute.net.

## Patti P. Phillips, PhD

Dr. Patti P. Phillips is president of the ROI Institute, Inc., the leading source of ROI competency building, implementation support, networking, and research. She is also chair and CEO of The Chelsea Group, Inc., an international consulting organization supporting organizations and their efforts to build accountability into their training, human resources, and performance improvement programs with a primary focus on building accountability in public sector organizations. She helps organizations implement the ROI methodology in countries around the world—including South Africa, Singapore, Japan, New Zealand, Australia, Italy, Turkey, France, Germany, Canada, and the United States.

After a 13-year career in the electrical utility industry, Phillips took advantage of the opportunity to pursue a career in a growing consulting business where she was introduced to training, human resources, and performance improvement from a new perspective—a perspective that directly reflected her values of accountability, ROI evaluation. Since 1997, she has embraced the ROI methodology by committing herself to ongoing research and practice. To this end Phillips has implemented ROI in private sector and public sector organizations. She has conducted ROI impact studies on programs such as leadership development, sales, new-hire orientation, human performance improvement, K-12 educator development, educators' National Board Certification mentoring, and faculty fellowship. Phillips is currently expanding her interest in public sector accountability through application of the ROI methodology in community- and faith-based initiatives, including Citizen Corps, AmeriCorps, and the Compassion Capital Fund.

Phillips teaches others to implement the ROI methodology through the ROI certification process, as a facilitator for ASTD's ROI and Measuring and Evaluating Learning Workshops, and as adjunct professor for graduate-level evaluation courses. She speaks on the topic of ROI at conferences such as ASTD's International Conference and Exposition and ISPI's International Conference.

Phillips' academic accomplishments include a Ph.D. in International Development and a master's degree in Public and Private Management. She is certified in ROI evaluation and has earned the designation of Certified Performance Technologist. She has authored a number of publications on the subject of accountability and ROI, including *Return on Investment Basics* (ASTD, 2005); *Proving the Value of HR: How and Why to Measure ROI* (SHRM, 2005); *Make Evaluation Work* (ASTD, 2004); *The Bottom Line on ROI* (Center for Effective Performance, 2002), which won the 2003 ISPI Award of Excellence; *ROI at Work* (ASTD, 2005); the ASTD In Action casebooks *Measuring Return on Investment* Vol. III (2001), *Measuring ROI in the Public Sector* (2002), and *Retaining Your Best Employees* (2002); the ASTD Infoline series, including *Planning and Using Evaluation Data* (2003), *Mastering ROI* (1998), and *Managing Evaluation Shortcuts* (2001); and *The Human Resources Scorecard: Measuring Return on Investment* (Butterworth-Heinemann, 2001). Phillips' work is published in a variety of journals, and she can be reached at patti@roiinstitute.net.

# ABOUT BERRETT-KOEHLER PUBLISHERS

Berrett-Koehler is an independent publisher dedicated to an ambitious mission: Creating a World that Works for All.

We believe that to truly create a better world, action is needed at all levels—individual, organizational, and societal. At the individual level, our publications help people align their lives with their values and with their aspirations for a better world. At the organizational level, our publications promote progressive leadership and management practices, socially responsible approaches to business, and humane and effective organizations. At the societal level, our publications advance social and economic justice, shared prosperity, sustainability, and new solutions to national and global issues.

A major theme of our publications is "Opening Up New Space." They challenge conventional thinking, introduce new ideas, and foster positive change. Their common quest is changing the underlying beliefs, mindsets, institutions, and structures that keep generating the same cycles of problems, no matter who our leaders are or what improvement programs we adopt.

We strive to practice what we preach—to operate our publishing company in line with the ideas in our books. At the core of our approach is *stewardship*, which we define as a deep sense of responsibility to administer the company for the benefit of all of our "stakeholder" groups: authors, customers, employees, investors, service providers, and the communities and environment around us.

We are grateful to the thousands of readers, authors, and other friends of the company who consider themselves to be part of the "BK Community." We hope that you, too, will join us in our mission.

# BE CONNECTED

## Visit Our Website

Go to www.bkconnection.com to read exclusive previews and excerpts of new books, find detailed information on all Berrett-Koehler titles and authors, browse subject-area libraries of books, and get special discounts.

## Subscribe to Our Free E-Newsletter

Be the first to hear about new publications, special discount offers, exclusive articles, news about bestsellers, and more! Get on the list for our free e-newsletter by going to www.bkconnection.com.

## Get Quantity Discounts

Berrett-Koehler books are available at quantity discounts for orders of ten or more copies. Please call us toll-free at (800) 929-2929 or email us at bkp.orders@aidcvt.com.

## Host a Reading Group

For tips on how to form and carry on a book reading group in your workplace or community, see our website at www.bkconnection.com.

## Join the BK Community

Thousands of readers of our books have become part of the "BK Community" by participating in events featuring our authors, reviewing draft manuscripts of forthcoming books, spreading the word about their favorite books, and supporting our publishing program in other ways. If you would like to join the BK Community, please contact us at bkcommunity@bkpub.com.

# Special Offer from The ROI Institute

Send for your own ROI Process Model, an indispensable tool for implementing and presenting ROI in your organization. The ROI Institute is offering an exclusive gift to readers of *Show Me the Money*. This 11" × 25" multicolor foldout shows the ROI Methodology flow model and the key issues surrounding the implementation of the ROI Methodology. This easy to understand overview of the ROI Methodology has proven invaluable to countless professionals when implementing the ROI Methodology. Please return this page or email your information to the address below to receive your free foldout (a $6.00 value). Please check your area(s) of interest in ROI.

Please send me the ROI Process Model described in the book. I am interested in learning more about the following ROI materials and services:

☐ Workshops and briefing on ROI      ☐ Books and support materials on ROI
☐ Certification in the ROI Methodology      ☐ ROI software
☐ ROI consulting services      ☐ ROI Network information
☐ ROI benchmarking      ☐ ROI research

Name _____      Phone _____
Title _____      E-mail Address _____
Organization _____
Address _____

**Functional area of interest:**

☐ Human Resources/    ☐ Learning and    ☐ Public Relations/Community
     Human Capital      Development/Performance      Affairs/Government
       Improvement      Relations

☐ Meetings and    ☐ Sales/Marketing    ☐ Technology/IT Systems
     Events

☐ Project Management    ☐ Quality/Six Sigma    ☐ Operations/Methods/
     Solutions      Engineering

☐ Research and    ☐ Finance/Compliance    ☐ Logistics/Distribution/
     Development/      Supply Chain
     Innovations

☐ Public Policy    ☐ Social Programs    ☐ Other (Please Specify)
     Initiatives      _____

**Organizational Level**

☐ executive    ☐ management    ☐ consultant    ☐ specialist
☐ student    ☐ evaluator    ☐ researcher

Return this form or contact

The ROI Institute
P.O. Box 380637
Birmingham,
AL 35238-0637

or

e-mail information to info@roiinstitute.net
Please allow four to six weeks for delivery.